FREEDOM TO LEARN

STUDIES OF THE PERSON

edited by

Carl R. Rogers
William R. Coulson

*A View of What
Education Might Become*

FREEDOM TO LEARN

Carl R. Rogers

*Resident Fellow
Center for Studies of the Person
La Jolla, California*

CHARLES E. MERRILL PUBLISHING COMPANY
Columbus, Ohio   *A Bell & Howell Company*

... It is in fact nothing short of a miracle that the modern methods of instruction have not yet entirely strangled the holy curiosity of inquiry; for this delicate little plant, aside from stimulation, stands mainly in need of freedom; without this it goes to wrack and ruin without fail.

Albert Einstein

Standard Book Number: 675-09519-0
Library of Congress Catalog Card Number: 72-75629

ISBN   0-675-09519-0 (cloth)
ISBN   0-675-09579-4 (paper)

8 9 10—74 73 72 71

PRINTED IN THE UNITED STATES OF AMERICA

FOREWORD

"Why is there no book of yours on our reading list?" the teacher-in-training asked me. "My instructors quote you and your ideas and methods and theories in education, but nothing of yours is provided for us to read!" This question and comment, repeated many times in various forms over the past decade, constitute one of the personal motivations for this book.

For more than thirty-five years I have been experimenting and innovating in my own approach to students in my classes. For years I have been writing for educators, drawing on many years of experience and research in psychotherapy as well as classroom experience. Most of these writings, however, have been in books whose major focus is on the interpersonal learning relationship we call therapy, or have appeared in journals not widely known to educators. So I could easily understand why no book of mine would be on a reading list for teachers, yet this troubled me too.

Consequently, my first approach to this book was simply to gather together the various papers I had written for teachers and educators and put them inside two covers. But as I began this task I grew increasingly dissatisfied. There was more that I wanted to say. Also the conceptions I wanted to present broadened into the theoretical and philosophical realms. So, the volume as it came into being contains much that is new, much that is developed from previous writings, and several chapters containing broad basic themes which to me are definitely relevant to educators even though they deal more with one's total personal orientation rather than having narrowly to do with education.

As I have worked on this book, I have been genuinely surprised by the inner sense of urgency I have felt. This has been evident in the fact that I have stolen precious time from every one of my current undertakings to complete this manuscript. It has been very evident to my efficient secretary, Mrs. Wetlaufer, who has come to recognize that the completion date for typing each chapter is "day before yesterday"! I have been puzzled by this urgency myself. Do I have some sense of mission, some notion that I can "save" education? I think not, though it will be for the reader to judge. My own conclusion is that the sense of urgency derives from my desire to contribute whatever I can to teachers and educators in a time of literally fearful crisis.

Education today is faced with incredible challenges, different from, more serious than, it has ever met in its long history. To my mind, the question of whether it can meet these challenges will be one of the major factors in determining whether mankind moves forward, or whether man destroys himself on this planet, leaving this earth to those few living things which can withstand atomic destruction and radioactivity. Let me state briefly some of the questions which concern me.

> Can education prepare individuals and groups to live comfortably in a world in which ever-accelerating change is the dominant theme? Or is this an impossible accommodation for the human being to make? Or is it impossible for education to achieve a goal so foreign to its past? I do not know.

> Can education fulfill its central role in dealing effectively with the explosive racial tensions which are steadily increasing? Or will we fail, with resultant civil war? I do not know.

> Can education prepare us to live responsibly, communicatively, in a world of increasing international tensions, increasingly irrational nationalism? Or will it make us more smug and defensive, less open to true communication and interaction between peoples, ending in the inevitable holocaust? I do not know.

> Can educators meet the growing student revolt at the second-

ary and higher education level—revolt against the whole social value system, revolt against the impersonality of our institutions of learning, revolt against imposed curricula? Or will learning move outside of the "halls of learning," leaving them only for the conformists? I do not know.

Can the educational system as a whole, the most traditional, conservative, rigid, bureaucratic institution of our time (and I use those words descriptively rather than critically), come to grips with the real problems of modern life? Or will it continue to be shackled by the tremendous social pressures for conformity and retrogression, added to its own traditionalism? I do not know.

Will education be taken over by profit-making corporations, who can be more innovative, more responsive to social need and demand, and who will also be more governed by the desire to produce the profitable "hardware" of learning? I do not know.

It will be clear that I see our whole educational system at a crisis point—a point of desperately important choice. And it is for this reason that I would like to make available to educators whatever may be useful from my own experience.

The first two sections of the book are, I hope, highly practical, giving many teachers specific channels through which they may risk themselves in experimentation with their classes. The third section provides some of the conceptual basis for such experimentation. The fourth part launches out into the personal and philosophical underpinnings and ramifications of the whole approach. The final section and an epilogue bring the reader sharply back to earth with a program for bringing about self-directed change in an educational system, and the beginnings of the implementation of such a program.

Throughout the book, I believe it will be evident that I rely on the potentiality and wisdom of the human being—if this potential can be released—to bring about the desperately needed changes in education, before it is too late.

This volume began while I was a member of the Western Behavioral Sciences Institute. In 1968 a number of the staff and others not formerly staff members formed the Center for Studies of the Person in order to better achieve our goals. Hence the WBSI staff members referred to in Chapter 3 now are associated with CSP, to which reference is made in Part V.

For their part in the presentation of this material, I gratefully acknowledge the assistance of Phyllis K. Wetlaufer for her research and typing of the manuscript, Alice Elliott for her contribution of the Bibliography selections and annotations, and Andre Auw for his preparation of the Index.

I am deeply pleased that this volume is a part of the series, *Studies of the Person*, being initiated by Charles E. Merrill Publishing Company. Perhaps it can "play a part in validating a concern for man" which is one of the purposes of this series. I hope that it can throw light on the person as learner, a light which has clear social implications.

Carl R. Rogers

La Jolla, California
February, 1969

CONTENTS

ix

part III
Some Assumptions

part IV
The Philosophical and Value Ramifications

part V
A Model for Revolution

Epilogue

Prologue

Learning: What Kind?

I am writing this book because I want to speak to teachers, professors, educators, administrators of schools, colleges, and educational institutions. But what is it I want to say to them? I sit here in my study puzzling over this question. Such a flood of thoughts and feelings flows over me that I have no idea where to begin. Then the thought begins to emerge—I want to speak to them about *learning*. But *not* the lifeless, sterile, futile, quickly forgotten stuff which is crammed into the mind of the poor helpless individual tied into his seat by ironclad bonds of conformity! I am talking about LEARNING—the insatiable curiosity which drives the adolescent boy to absorb everything he can see or hear or read about gasoline engines in order to improve the efficiency and speed of his "hotrod." I am talking about the student who says, "I am discovering, drawing in from the outside, and making that which is drawn in a real part of *me*." I am talking about any learning in which the experience of the learner progresses along this line: "No, no, that's not what I want"; "Wait! This is closer to what I'm interested in, what I need"; "Ah, here it is! Now I'm grasping and comprehending what I *need* and what I want to know!" This is the theme, the topic, of this book.

TWO KINDS OF LEARNING

Learning, I believe, can be divided into two general types, along a continuum of meaning. At one end of the scale is the kind of task psychologists sometimes set for their subjects—the learning of nonsense syllables. To memorize such items as *baz, ent, nep, arl, lud*, and the like, is a difficult task. Because there is no meaning involved, these syllables are not easy to learn and are likely to be forgotten quickly.

We frequently fail to recognize that much of the material presented to students in the classroom has, for the student, the same

3

perplexing, meaningless quality that the list of nonsense syllables has for us. This is especially true for the underprivileged child whose background provides no context for the material with which he is confronted. But nearly every student finds that large portions of his curriculum are for him, meaningless. Thus education becomes the futile attempt to learn material which has no personal meaning.

Such learning involves the mind only. It is learning which takes place "from the neck up." It does not involve feelings or personal meanings; it has no relevance for the whole person.

In contrast, there is such a thing as significant, meaningful, experiential learning. When the toddler touches the warm radiator he learns for himself the meaning of a word, "hot"; he has learned a future caution in regard to all similar radiators; and he has taken in these learnings in a significant, involved way which will *not* soon be forgotten. Likewise the child who has memorized "two plus two equal four" may one day in his play with blocks or marbles suddenly realize, "Two and two *do* make four!" He has discovered something significant for himself, in a way which involves both his thoughts and his feelings. Or the child who has laboriously acquired "reading skills" is caught up one day in a printed story, whether a comic book or an adventure tale, and realizes that words can have a magic power which lifts him out of himself into another world. He has now "really" learned to read.

Another example is given by Marshall McLuhan. He points out that if a five-year-old child is moved to a foreign country, and allowed to play freely for hours with his new companions, with no language instruction at all, he will learn the new language in a few months, and will acquire the proper accent too. He is learning in a way which has significance and meaning for him, and such learning proceeds at an exceedingly rapid rate. But let someone try to *instruct* him in the new language, basing the instruction on the elements which have meaning for the *teacher*, and learning is tremendously slowed, or even stopped.

This illustration, a common one, is worth pondering. Why is it that left to his own devices the child learns rapidly, in ways he will not soon forget, and in a manner which has highly practical meaning for him, when all of this can be spoiled if he is "taught" in a way which involves only his intellect? Perhaps a closer look will help.

A DEFINITION

Let me define a bit more precisely the elements which are involved in such significant or experiential learning. *It has a quality of personal involvement*—the whole person in both his feeling and cognitive aspects being *in* the learning event. *It is self-initiated.* Even when the impetus or stimulus comes from the outside, the sense of discovery, of reaching out, of grasping and comprehending, comes from within. *It is pervasive.* It makes a difference in the behavior, the attitudes, perhaps even the personality of the learner. *It is evaluated by the learner.* He knows whether it is meeting his need, whether it leads toward what he *wants* to know, whether it illuminates the dark area of ignorance he is experiencing. The locus of evaluation, we might say, resides definitely in the learner. *Its essence is meaning.* When such learning takes place, the element of meaning to the learner is built into the whole experience.

THE DILEMMA

I believe that all teachers and educators prefer to facilitate this experiential and meaningful type of learning, rather than the nonsense syllable type. Yet in the vast majority of our schools, at all educational levels, we are locked into a traditional and conventional approach which makes significant learning improbable if not impossible. When we put together in one scheme such elements as a *prescribed curriculm, similar assignments for all students, lecturing* as almost the only mode of instruction, *standard tests* by which all students are externally evaluated, and *instructor-chosen grades* as the measure of learning, then we can almost guarantee that meaningful learning will be at an absolute minimum.

DO ALTERNATIVES EXIST?

It is not because of any inner depravity that educators follow such a self-defeating system. It is quite literally because they do not know any feasible alternative. The elements I have just listed have come to be regarded as the only possible definition of "education."

But there *are* alternatives—alternative practical ways to handle a class or a course—alternative assumptions and hypotheses upon which education can be built—alternative goals and values for which educators and students can strive. I hope that these will become clear in the following chapters.

part I

Freedom: Where the Action Is

Introduction to Part I

There are *practical* ways of dealing with students which stimulate
and facilitate significant and self-reliant learning. These ways eliminate every one of the elements of conventional education. They do
not rely on a carefully prescribed curriculum, but rather on one
that is largely self-chosen; instead of standard assignments for all,
each student sets his own assignment; lectures constitute the most
*in*frequent mode of instruction; standardized tests lose their sancti-
fied place; grades are either self-determined or become a relatively
unimportant index of learning.

It is in the hope of letting teachers know that it is not *necessary* to
follow the conventional pattern that I am going to present three
different examples, written by three different teachers, of new
ways in which a class may be permitted to learn. These three examples come from a sixth grade teacher, a college professor, and an
instructor of a graduate course. Each is marked by a different style
of personality, and the actual methods are quite diverse. It is in the
determined effort to facilitate a significant sort of self-initiated
learning that they are similar.

It seems important to show that such significant, self-initiated, experiential learning is *possible*, that it is possible in sharply different
kinds of educational situations, and that it produces self-reliant
learners. This is the purpose of the three chapters which compose
Part I.

1

A Sixth Grade Teacher "Experiments"

I feel that the diary which constitutes the bulk of this chapter speaks directly to the classroom teacher—harassed by pupil apathy, by discipline problems, by complaining parents, by a set curriculum, by the daily difficulties involved in being continuously in contact with a large and varied group of students. It is a deeply human document; it "tells it the way it is," as the current phrase has it. I hope that it will have the meaning for teachers of all levels that it has had for me—a feeling that there is a basis for hope, even in "impossible" classroom groups. I trust that it will release other teachers to be adventuresome and honest—with themselves and their students—and risk themselves by taking steps the consequences of which cannot be guaranteed but which depend upon trust in human beings.

Quite by chance I came into the possession of some informal notes kept by a teacher who, out of despair and frustration, decided to try a drastic experiment in promoting an experiential type of learning in her sixth grade class. I am deeply indebted to Barbara J. Shiel, the author, for her willingness to have this material used. It is of special practical help because it portrays her own uncertainties and confusions, as well as those of her students, as she launches into this new approach. Clearly it takes courage to attempt the new, and many teachers at every level would, very understandably, lack this courage.

Miss Shiel's experience is most certainly not a model for another teacher to follow. Indeed one of the most meaningful elements in this account is that she risked giving freedom to her pupils only so far as she dared, only so far as she felt reasonably comfortable in doing so. Thus it is an account of a changing, risky, approach to a classroom situation by a changing, risk-taking human being, who felt at times defeated and at times very moved and stimulated by the consequences of what she was attempting.

THE "EXPERIMENT"

When I first came across the document which follows, I was curious about the context in which the "experiment" developed. I wrote to Miss Shiel and asked her a number of questions. Her reply gave me a picture of the initial situation:

> This past year was my thirteenth year of teaching elementary school. I have taught all six elementary grades. The class mentioned in the document (originally intended only as a kind of personal diary) was one of the most difficult I had ever worked with, in terms of discipline, lack of interest, and parental problems. There were 36 in the group, with an I.Q. range of 82 to 135. There were many who were "socially maladjusted," "underachievers," or "emotionally disturbed."

> I had exhausted my resources in an attempt to cope with the situation but had made very little progress. The many discipline problems were notorious; they were constantly in the office, or "on the bench" for varied offenses—their attitude and behavior kept them in constant trouble. Several were suspended for short periods. In addition, the parents were uncooperative and/or defensive—most had a history of blaming the teachers or the school for the child's problems.

It was in this frustrating situation, partly as a result of some reading she had been doing about student-centered teaching, that she came to her decision to experiment.

March 5, We Begin:

A week ago I decided to initiate a new program in my sixth grade classroom, based on student-centered teaching—an unstructured or non-directive approach.

I began by telling the class that we were going to try an "experiment." I explained that for one day I would let them do anything they wanted to do—they did not have to do anything if they did not want to.

Many started with art projects; some drew or painted most of the day. Others read or did work in math and other subjects. There was an air of excitement all day; many were so interested in what they were doing that they did not want to go out at recess or noon!

At the end of the day I asked the class to evaluate the experiment. The comments were most interesting. Some were "confused," distressed without the teacher telling them what to do, without specific assignments to complete.

The majority of the class thought the day was "great," but some expressed concern over the noise level and the fact that a few "goofed off" all day. Most felt that they had accomplished as much work as we usually do, and they enjoyed being able to work at a task until it was completed without the pressure of a time limit. They liked doing things without being "forced" to do them and liked deciding what to do.

They begged to continue the "experiment," so it was decided to do so, for two more days. We would then re-evaluate the plan.

The next morning I implemented the idea of a "work contract." I gave them ditto sheets listing all our subjects with suggestions under each. There was a space provided for their "plans" in each area and for checking upon completion.

Each child was to write his or her contract for the day—choosing the areas in which he would work and planning specifically what he would do. Upon completion of any exercise, drill, review, etc., he was to check and correct his own work, using the teacher's manual. The work was to be kept in a folder with the contract.

I met with each child to discuss his plans. Some completed theirs in a very short time; we discussed as a group what this might mean, and what to do about it. It was suggested that the plan might not be challenging enough, that an adjustment should be made—perhaps going on or adding another area to the day's plan.

Resource materials were provided, suggestions made, and drill materials made available to use when needed.

I found I had much more time, so I worked, talked, and spent the time with individuals and groups. At the end of the third day I evaluated the work folder with each child. To solve the problem of grades, I had each child tell me what he thought he had earned.

Also at this time the group wrote a second evaluation of the experiment, adding comments their parents had made. All but four were excited and enthusiastic about the plan and thought school was much fun. The four still felt insecure and wanted specific assignments. I talked with them about giving the experiment time—

sometimes it took time to adjust to new situations. They agreed to try. The rest of the class was thrilled at the prospect of continuing the rest of the year.

The greatest problem I've encountered is discipline. I have many problem individuals in my class, and there was a regression in terms of control when the teacher's external controls were lifted. Part of the difficulty stems from the fact that I let the children sit where and with whom they liked. The "problems" congregated together, spent much of their day fighting (verbally and physically), "bugging" each other, and generally accomplishing very little, which brings to mind another problem for me—internally. I am having a difficult time watching them do nothing and am concerned at times about their progress, achievement, etc. I have to remind myself constantly that these pupils were "failing" under the old program, and never turned in completed assignments under the old regime either. They only *looked* like they were doing something!

I've considered the possibility of moving some of the seats in the problem area, but I realize that I would be defeating an important aspect of the program if I re-established my control. If we can survive this period, perhaps in time they will develop greater *self-control*.

It is interesting to me that it is upsetting to them too. They all sit close to my desk and say it is too difficult this new way. The "temptation" is too great. This would indicate that they are not as recalcitrant as they seemed.

The class has been delighted in general. They even carry their projects and work outside and have the whole school interested and talking about the idea. And I've heard the story that they think I've really changed (since I've stopped trying to make them conform to my standards and rules, trying to make them achieve *my* goals! !).

The atmosphere is a stimulating, relaxed, happy one (discounting the problem area upheaval).

An interesting project has developed. I noticed that some of the boys were drawing and designing automobiles. I put up a big piece of paper for them to use as they wished. They discussed their plans and proceeded to do a mural on the history of cars, incorporating their designs as cars of the future. I was delighted. They used the encyclopedia as a reference, as well as books on cars they brought in. They worked together, and some began models and scrapbooks, boys who had produced very little, if anything, so far this year.

Other ideas began to appear in other areas; the seed of initiative and creativity had germinated and began to grow.

Many children are doing some interesting research in related (and unrelated) areas of interest. Some have completed the year's "required" work in a few areas, such as spelling.

Most important, to me, is the evidence of initiative and self-responsibility manifested.

March 12, Progress Report:

Our "experiment" has, in fact, become our program—with some adjustments.

Some children continued to be frustrated and felt insecure without teacher direction. Discipline also continued to be a problem with some, and I began to realize that although the children involved may need the program more than the others, I was expecting too much from them, too soon—they were not ready to assume self-direction *yet*. Perhaps a gradual weaning from the spoon-fed procedures was necessary.

I regrouped the class—creating two groups. The largest group is the non-directed group. The smallest is teacher directed, made up of children who wanted to return to the former teacher-directed method, and those who, for varied reasons, were unable to function in the self-directed situation.

I would like to have waited longer to see what would have happened, but the situation for some disintegrated a little more each day—penalizing the whole class. The disrupting factor kept everyone upset and limited those who wanted to study and work. So it seemed to me best for the group as a whole as well as the program to modify the plan.

Those who continued the "experiment" have forged ahead. I showed them how to program their work, using their texts as a basic guide. They have learned that they can teach themselves (and each other) and that I am available when a step is not clear or advice is needed.

At the end of the week they evaluate themselves in each area—in terms of work accomplished, accuracy, etc. We have learned that the number of errors is not a criterion of failure or success. Errors can and should be part of the learning process; we learn through our mistakes. We also discussed the fact that consistently perfect scores may mean that the work is not challenging enough and perhaps we should move on.

After self-evaluation, each child brings the evaluation sheet and work folder to discuss them with me.

Some of the members of the group working with me are most anxious to become "independent" students. We will evaluate together each week their progress toward that goal.

I have only experienced one parental objection so far. A parent felt her child was not able to function without direction.

Some students (there were two or three) who originally wanted to return to the teacher-directed program are now anticipating going back into the self-directed program. (I sense that it has been as difficult for them to readjust to the old program as it would be for me to do so.)

March 19, Progress Report:

Today, from my point of view as a teacher, has been the most satisfying since we began our new program.

It began with an individual evaluation with each child in the teacher-directed program. (I had had conferences with the non-directed group the preceding day.) Several of the children in the former group felt that they were ready to go back into the non-directed group. They had decided they liked the freedom after all and thought they understood the responsibilities involved. It was decided that they would try it for one week to see if they really were ready. I would help them at any time they needed help with their work plan or actual work.

At this point I have only six in the teacher group. One wants to be in the other group, but since her mother was the one parent who complained I told her she must discuss it at home first.

We had an oral evaluation, one of the topics discussed being parental reaction. One boy said his mother said it sounded as if I had given up teaching! Another boy said his father told him that he had tried self-responsibility with him before, and he thought I was nuts to try it with so many at once!

We discussed what we could do to help our parents understand the program. It was suggested (by the children) that we could take our weekly work folders home to show what we were actually accomplishing and that since the intangible work was on the work contract it could be discussed as well.

The rest of the day was spent with as little interference as possible by me. Groups and individuals proceeded with their plans; it was a productive, rewarding day.

The days have fluctuated between optimism and concern, hope and fear. My emotional temperature rises and falls with each rung climbed on the ladder of our adventure.

Some days I feel confident, buoyant, sure that we are on the right track—on other days I am assailed by doubts. All the teacher training, authoritarian tradition, curriculum, and report cards threaten and intimidate me.

I must exercise great control when I see a child doing nothing (productive) for most of a day; providing the opportunity to develop self-discipline is an even greater trial at times.

I've come to realize that one must be secure in his own self-concept to undertake such a program. In order to relinquish the accepted role of the teacher in a teacher-directed program, one must understand and accept oneself first. It is important as well to have a clear understanding of the goals one is endeavoring to work toward.

SOME OF THE PROCEDURES

In another statement, written later, Miss Shiel describes the elements of a school day during the "experiment." I insert it here in order to give more of a picture of how the students, as well as Miss Shiel, operated:

Each day began informally; the first task of each individual was to design his or her work plan, or "contract." Sometimes children planned with one or two others. There was constant self-grouping and regrouping, withdrawal from a group for independent work.

As soon as the contract was made, the child began to study or work on his plan. He could work as long as he needed or wanted to work on a task or project. Because I was not free to discard the state-devised curriculum time schedule, I explained the weekly time-subject blocks to the children—this was to be a consideration in their planning. We also discussed sequential learning, especially in math, mastering a skill before proceeding to the next level of learning. They discovered that the text provided an introduction to a skill, demonstrated the skill, and provided exercises to master it and tests to check achievement. When they felt they were ready to go on, they were free to do so. They set their own pace, began at their own level, and went as far as they were able or self-motivated to go.

I have been constantly challenged, "but how did you teach the facts and new concepts?" The individuals inquiring apparently assume that unless the teacher is dictating, directing or explaining, there can be no learning. My answer is that I did not "teach;" the children taught themselves and each other.

When individuals or groups wished to share their projects, learnings or research with the class, or when there were audiovisual materials of general interest to the class, it was announced on the board and incorporated into the individual planning. For example, if we had a film on South America, the entire class viewed it, but what they did with the film was up to the individual —they could outline it, summarize it, draw pictures of it—or ignore it, if they chose.

Whenever the children felt the need to discuss individual, group, or class "problems" we arranged our desks in a seminar circle and had a "general semantics" session. We also functioned as one group in music (singing) and in physical education.

Since evaluation was self-initiated and respected by the teacher, there was no need for cheating to achieve success. We discovered that "failure" is only a word, that there is a difference between "failure" and making a mistake, and that mistakes are a part of the learning process.

In art the children were free to explore with materials: paper, paints, crayons, chalk, clay, etc., as well as with books and ideas. They discovered for themselves, through manipulation and experimentation, new techniques and new uses of media. No two "products" were alike—although in the beginning, there was considerable dependency on the discoveries of others. In time, individuals developed confidence and openness to experimentation. The results were far more exciting than those achieved in teacher-directed lessons (in spite of the fact that I consider art my greatest strength, or talent)!

The children developed a working discipline that respected the individual need for isolation or quiet study, yet allowed pupil interaction. There was no need for passing of notes, or "subversive" activity, no need to pretend you were busy or interested in a task, that, in fact, had no meaning to you. There was respect for meditation and contemplation as well as for overt productivity. There were opportunities to get to *know* one another—the children learned to communicate *by communicating.*

FINAL ENTRY

I would like now to return to the final entry in the diary which Miss Shiel kept of her experience. It summarizes some of her trials and her joys at this point in her venture.

April 9, Progress Report:

I prefer the term "self-directed" to "non-directional" in describing our program. I believe it better describes the goals, as well as the actual implementation, of the program.

It is directed, in the sense that we must work within the structure of the curriculum, the specific units of study. It is self-directed in that each child is responsible for his own planning within this basic structure.

At this point, I have only four pupils who are not in the program. I try to provide a period each day for them when they are able to assume some responsibility, make some decisions. They are children who need much additional help and are insecure and frustrated without my guidance.

As I went through the process of putting grades on report cards, I began to realize that the most valuable aspects of the childrens' growth could not be evaluated in terms of letter grades. For some there is no observable change, or it is intangible—yet one senses growth, a metamorphosis taking place.

Day to day one can sense the growth in communication, in social development. One cannot measure the difference in attitude, the increased interest, the growing pride in self-improvement, but one is aware that they exist. And how does a teacher evaluate self-discipline? What is easy for me, may not be easy for you!

The report cards are only an indication, but I know the children will be as pleased as I am at the improvement in their grades, and the great decrease in citizenship checks.

In evaluating their work I find them to be fairly perceptive, aware of their capacity and how it relates to their accomplishment. I rarely need to change grades. When I do, sometimes I must upgrade!

I mentioned earlier how many "problems" there have been in this class—both disciplinary and emotional. This program in fact developed out of an attempt to meet the challenge that the "problems" presented. At times I felt whipped, defeated, and frustrated. I felt I was making no headway and resented my role as a policeman.

Since our program has been in full swing I've found that I've undergone change, too. Early in the year I could but bide my time until I could send the "gang" onward and upward—at least see them off to seventh grade.

I find now that I see these children with different eyes, and as I've watched them, I've begun to realize that there *is* hope. I have asked to take this class on, in a self-contained situation, to seventh grade. Scheduling may prevent this becoming an actuality, but I feel these children would continue to progress toward self-actualization within the framework and freedom of the self-directed program.

I feel that now that the mechanics of the program are worked out, now that there is greater understanding and rapport between the children and myself (since I have discarded the authoritarian role), there is greater opportunity for self-growth, not only creativity, initiative, imagination, but self-discipline, self-acceptance, and understanding.

At times when I see children who are not doing what I think they ought to be doing, I must remind myself, again, of the ultimate goals and the fact that they did not produce "required" work when it was assigned previously. They may be drawing something that is not esthetically pleasing to me, but they *are* drawing, and it *is* imaginative! They may not be "busy," but they may be *thinking*; they may be talking, but they are cooperating and learning to communicate; they may fight and respond with signal reactions— abuse one another verbally—but it may be the only way they know. They may not do as much math, but they understand and remember what they do do.

Best of all, they are more interested in school, in their progress. I would venture that this program might result in fewer dropouts, "failures" in school.

It is not the panacea, but it is a step forward. Each day is a new adventure, there are moments of stress, concern, pleasure—they are all stepping stones toward our goal of self-actualization.

SOME OUTCOMES

In her correspondence with me, Miss Shiel carries forward the account of her program, indicating some of the changes she noted:

I continued the program until the end of the term, two months past the last report. In that time there was a continuing change in these children. They still argued and fought among themselves but seemed to develop some regard for our social structure: school, adults, teachers, property, etc. And as they began to better understand themselves, their own reactions—the outbursts and quarrels—diminished.

. . . They developed values, attitudes, standards of behavior *on their own*, and lived up to those standards. They did not become "angels" by any means, but there was a definite change. Other teachers and playground supervisors seldom had to discipline them and commented on the change in behavior and attitude. They were rarely in the office for infractions, and there was not one parental complaint the balance of the year! There was a tremendous change in parental attitude as the children evidenced success and growth, both academic and social.

I have neglected to mention the students who were not problems and those who were above average academically. I firmly believe that the gifted children were the ones who benefited most from this program. They developed a keen sense of competition between one another, interest in mutual projects, and they sailed ahead, not being restricted by the slow learners. Their achievement was amazing to me.

I found that the children who had the most difficulty learning also made great progress. Some who had been unable to retain the multiplication tables (which should have been learned in fourth grade) were able to multiply and divide fractions (!) with a minimum number of errors by June.

I cannot explain exactly what happened, but it seems to me, that when their self-concept changed, when they discovered they *can*, they did! These "slow learners" became "fast learners"; success built upon success.

May I interject here that I am well aware of the fact that in many schools or districts I would not have been allowed the freedom I was permitted to have.

Both my principal and superintendent were interested in and gave support to my effort, and the schedule was structured to enable me to continue on to a self-contained seventh grade. Then it was learned that the people who had been hired for the intermediate positions did not have elementary credentials and therefore could not take my place. I had to be put back into a sixth grade position. The children, the parents, and I were very disappointed.

Partly as a result of this disappointment, Miss Shiel accepted another position. She did not, however, lose all contact with her class. The following autumn she writes of the report which has come to her:

I received a letter from my principal this week in which he states: "I must relate to you . . . that your former students are dedicating themselves to building rather than destroying . . . really, you can take honest breaths about your contribution . . . as I have not had any negative dealings with any of your former pupils, even those who unfortunately find themselves in poor environments . . . Your 'impress' method or whatever, seems to have done the job, and their commitment (to you really) is something to behold . . ."

Miss Shiel continues:

If three months of "self-direction" produced such tangible results at this age level—imagine the potential inherent in a program of greater length! It is an exciting thing to contemplate . . . .

COMMENTS ON THE "EXPERIMENT"

Miss Shiel's account speaks for itself, and comments may be regarded as superfluous. Yet I should like to point out some salient features of the way in which she dealt with this "experiment," and some of the learnings which I see as transferable to other educational situations.

COMMITMENT

Miss Shiel was clearly and deeply committed to a philosophy of reliance upon self-direction and freedom as leading to the most significant learning. This commitment was not a rigid one; indeed her personal doubts and waverings are one of the most significant features in her account, because they indicate that such an approach can be carried through by imperfect, uncertain individuals, who are by no means clothed in the robes of self-assurance. But my point is that this was not simply a technique or "gimmick." Though she calls it an experiment, it was an experiment in which she believed, and about which she had convictions.

The importance of this commitment is shown in a brief paragraph in one of her letters to me. She says, ". . . Several other teachers tried my idea—and failed. Primarily, I think, because they did not really believe in it but were moved to action by the enthusiasm and progress of the children, and by my own enthusiastic reports."

To give self-direction and freedom to children can clearly be a complete failure if it is simply a new "method." Commitment and conviction are essential.

INTERNAL LOCUS OF EVALUATION

Though the ideas which Miss Shiel implemented in her approach had undoubtedly been absorbed from various sources, it is very clear from her document that this is *her* experiment. She trusts her own judgment of what to try, and when to retreat. She is not trying out a scheme devised by someone else.

This maintenance of what I term an internal locus of judgment or evaluation is highly important. She decides when her new program is not working as she wished. She decides that two classes, the self-directed and the teacher-directed, are necessary, even though this had not been a part of her initial plan. By being open to the evidence in the situation, including her own feelings and intuitions, and basing her judgments on that evidence, she keeps herself flexible in the situation, and takes appropriate steps. She is not trying to please someone else, or to follow some "correct" model. She is living and acting and deciding in a fluid situation. She is even aware of the elements most threatening to her and faces those frightening aspects of the experience openly, in herself.

AWARE OF THE REALITIES

The way in which she adjusted to the demands of the real situation—a required curriculum, the necessity of report cards— excites my admiration. I do not know where she came upon the idea of student-initiated contracts. I do not suppose it was original with her, but she utilized it most ingeniously.

The way her pupils accepted these outside demands is, I think, not suprising. Children as well as adults can accept reasonable requirements which are placed on them by society or by the institution. The point is that when freedom and self-direction are given to a group, it is also easier for the members to accept the constraints and obligations which surround the psychological area in which they are free. So her students "cover" all of the work which is required of them and go on to undertake more interesting activities. They even work out a mutually satisfying solution to the vexing problem of report cards.

GROUP PROBLEM SOLVING

One of the evidences of Miss Shiel's commitment to the group and its potentiality is the way in which she handles unexpected problems. I doubt if she had clearly foreseen the parental skepticism which would arise in regard to her plan. But here, as in other areas, she put her trust in the capacity of the group to deal with the problem. Free discussion of the situation brings out very constructive ways of helping to resolve the issue.

EXPERIENCE

If this had been Miss Shiel's first year of teaching, could she have carried off her "experiment"? I do not know. Certainly her years of experience in teaching gave her assurance in dealing with everyday classroom situations and gave her, perhaps, the security to launch out in a very new direction.

On the other side of this coin is the fact that it was the kind of relationship she had built up with pupils over the years which was the very element which changed most markedly. The students were the first to note this change, and Miss Shiel mentions their comments with some amusement, as though the change existed only in their own perceptions. Later she recognizes how profoundly her relationship with the members of the class *has* changed. Thus one might argue that a new teacher would have had less to unlearn. I leave it as an open question.

SUPPORT

Miss Shiel was, of course, fortunate to have the interest and support of her principal and superintendent. This gives a backing and security which makes risk-taking easier. Yet it is quite possible to underestimate the probability of such support. I have known of instances in which teachers simply assumed that no support would be forthcoming from a superior, only to find that when they *asked* if they might try something different, wholehearted backing was forthcoming. Administrators are people and often welcome change and experiment. At least they deserve the chance to make a decision as to whether they will support a new venture on the part of a teacher.

COMMUNICABILITY TO OTHERS

After one more year of experimentation with a self-directed curriculum, Miss Shiel was invited to become coordinator of a new program (in another district) to be designed for "educationally disadvantaged" children, and their teachers and administrators. The aim of the program developed in such a way that it not only endeavored to provide an experiential, self-directed curriculum for the children, but the same kind of opportunity for the teachers. Teachers, too, need support and understanding as they face the struggle and pain of trying to change perceptions and behaviors. Miss Shiel writes:

> . . . The participating teachers spent the morning working with the children, then met in the afternoon with a psychologist in a T-group, or encounter group, to explore together the morning experiences and their feelings and attitudes. The purpose of the workshop was not to show "one way," but to illustrate that possibly "other ways" exist. We wanted the teachers to experience self-direction in the same milieu that was provided for the children. Almost every teacher experienced great anxiety and apprehension

in working with these problem children in an atmosphere of freedom. For all concerned, it was an emotionally trying time, painful —as growth can sometimes be. However, various forms of evaluation indicated the workshop was successful in helping teachers change their perceptions and attitudes.

One teacher was unable to cope with the situation and eventually resigned. The general reaction from teachers, students, and parents ranged from favorable to enthusiastic, and more than thirty additional teachers signed up for a new workshop.

We will hear more about this workshop approach (encounter group or T-group are other terms) in Chapters 3 and 15. Suffice it to say here that it is in part an opportunity for exploration of oneself and one's relationship with others. Perhaps this will explain the first of the following two paragraphs, with which Miss Shiel concludes her report:

> Writing in retrospect, one can never capture the actual tears, pain and guts that go into such exploration. Many of us went deep into our inner selves and discovered that our anxieties, hostilities, and needs profoundly affect us as teachers. The structure of the system can be a refuge of sorts, and to deliberately "rock the boat" can be terribly threatening.

> For me, the experience of finding myself an "instant administrator," (lacking preparation or courses) was a new challenge—at first frightening. "Could I do it? What if I 'failed'? Had I gotten in over my head?" I found it difficult to wear so many hats, and I learned that my patience with the "child" in big people is more limited than it is with little people. I learned that to *be truly* facilitating is quite different from articulating about facilitating.

Certainly this whole program is evidence that the approach Miss Shiel used with her own sixth grade class can, in its essential attitudes, be conveyed to others. But it is clear that this new learning on the part of teachers can only be effective when they *experience* greater self-direction, greater freedom to communicate. It is *not* conveyed on an intellectual level.

SUMMARY

Can significant, meaningful, self-initiated learning be achieved or realized in an elementary school class? I have presented the experience of one venturesome sixth grade teacher and her students, almost all of whom give a resounding "yes" to this question. The elements which made this possible are evident in the teacher's account, and are, I hope, further clarified by my comments.

It is of great importance that the same kind of learning can be achieved in a group of teachers as well.

2

A College Professor Gives
Freedom Within Limits

I find it fascinating to perceive the many differing ways in which educators can provide freedom. At one extreme would be A. S. Neill and the outstanding personal freedom in his "Summerhill" school—an approach which has shocked many educators. Professor Volney Faw—whose way of dealing with a class forms the major portion of this chapter—is close to the opposite pole. He is scientific, hardheaded, educationally cautious, acceptant of many of the traditional institutional requirements. Yet for all this he has, for years, created an island of opportunity—of freedom to learn—for his students.[1]

In our modern educational system, it seems to many that it is quite impossible to give students any freedom to learn, because there are so many limits imposed from the outside. This is perhaps particularly true at the college level. How can students be set free if this is a required course, which they did not elect to take? How can the instructor let his students pursue their own goals if he is teaching one section of a large course, in which the same text and curriculum is required, and the same examinations given, in all sections? Would not the instructor be irresponsible if he permitted a wide range of choice to students, when these same students will be making application to graduate schools, and needing solid evidence to support their applications?

These are all entirely reasonable questions. Yet a growing number of bold and innovative teachers at the college level have been demonstrating that even when *all* of these constricting conditions are present at the same time, it is still possible to focus on the facili-

---

[1] I am very much indebted to Dr. Volney Faw for his permission to make use of an unpublished manuscript (entitled "Undergraduate Education in Psychology") describing his unusual approach to a class in introductory psychology. His material constitutes the core of this chapter, and I am grateful for the opportunity to present it.

tation of meaningful learning; it is still possible to give students a
freedom to learn.

From among these innovators I have chosen to present the manner in which Dr. Volney Faw, of Lewis and Clark College, provides freedom for his students, for his collaborating instructors, and
for himself—in a course in introductory psychology which he and
several colleagues have carried on for a number of years. Approximately one-fourth of the students in this course are taking it because it is required (in Education). The others are taking it as an
elective. Some sections are taught by instructors using a conventional lecture system, but Dr. Faw and several colleagues have used
the approach which will be described. I have chosen the procedure
developed by Professor Faw in part because he is cautiously bold,
and conservatively innovative. He provides a clear indication that
one does not have to be a flaming rebel to try out an approach to
education which is completely at variance with conventional principles.

Like a great many college teachers, Faw is deeply concerned with
promoting creative problem solving in his students. His way of
achieving this goal is set forth in his own words in the material
which follows. I believe this may be particularly helpful to those
teachers at the secondary or college levels who work within
definite, or even rigid, educational limits.

A PROGRAM IN PSYCHOLOGY

Creative problem solving [Dr. Faw writes] has been proposed
as a legitimate and worthwhile objective in education. . . . [Yet]
the problem anticipated by many college faculty as they read
papers on creativity is the possible jettisoning of academic standards
and scholarly rigor for some "will-o'-the-wisp" creative venture.
A disparity between academic rigor and creativity need not exist.
The following material describes how a marriage between academic
rigor and creativity has been performed and maintained over a
six year period. . . .

To gain a first-hand knowledge of this program, the reader might
first imagine himself to be a freshman in college. He has enrolled
in an introductory psychology class and has appeared for the
first meeting. A very ordinary person who appears to be the

instructor walks to the front of the class and states: "I'm going to hand out this description of the course and then you will be dismissed. Take it home and read it. If you are still interested in taking the course, come back tomorrow and we shall proceed with it."

The class is dismissed. At his first opportunity the student reads the following description of the methodology of the course.

Statement of Methodology
Fundamentals of Psychology, Psych. 101

This statement describes the general methodology which underlies the course in Fundamentals of Psychology. To discover what is going on it is suggested that you read this paper thoughtfully and, in addition, read certain other papers placed on reserve in the library (Rogers, 1961, 1963a, 1963b); (Faw, 1949, 1957). Read the references creatively, keeping in mind that this course is a joint enterprise of students and professors attempting to discover ways of relating to each other as real persons in a creative setting.

Where Shall We Begin?

This course begins with YOU, the student! There are other alternatives. We might begin with the subject matter of psychology and give you a floor plan consisting of the structure of propositions and facts which are identified as psychology. We could begin with the scientific method, with the history of psychology, etc. These facts certainly are important, but the basic datum in a course, particularly psychology, is people, their existence and their being. Therefore, it is defensible to begin with YOU as the subject matter.

There are many different facets of YOU, the student. There are your vocational goals and ambitions, there are your feelings—your fears, angers, joys, tears. All of these are descriptive aspects of you. But the central datum is that you exist: you are a being; you are here; your presence is felt.

In recognition of this basic datum you are invited to sign up for an appointment with your instructor. The main purpose of this appointment is to declare your existence. To be! You need not try to impress anyone or be something you are not. Your instructor hasn't prepared anything to tell you and neither do you need to think about what you are to say. Just being, existing, and getting acquainted is intended. Of course accepting this invitation is optional.

What Methods Will Be Used to Teach This Course?

A course has five basic elements or aspects: (1.) Persons, (2.) Interactions, (3.) Procedures, (4.) Content, (5.) Institutional Press. The so-called "method" of a course involves the different arrangements of the above and emphasis on these various elements. This course places the emphasis somewhat more on Persons and Interactions in comparison with Content and Institutional Press than many other courses, for it is believed that in the long run such an emphasis results in a more creative way of dealing with Content and a more realistic way of dealing with Institutional Press.

Persons: The fundamental characteristic encouraged about persons in this course is that persons be free to explore their goals, their needs, their feelings, and ideas. Two kinds of freedom are assumed: "academic freedom" and "inner freedom." Academic freedom permits students and professors to express their ideas and convictions without undue pressure from the outside. "Inner freedom" minimizes inner pressures. The descriptive phrase used by those experiencing "inner freedom" is often: "I feel I can just be myself." This feeling is more completely described in the reference material.

We encourage the development and expression of this inner freedom in teachers and students. To instrument this development, some periods will be teacher-centered. The professor will present his ideas and seek that spontaneity of feeling which has been identified above as, "I can just be myself." Other periods will be devoted to discussion groups in which time will be set aside for student-centered discussions. Students may learn to be free.

Interactions: Interactions refer to the relationship between persons. To instrument the development of the kind of freedom mentioned above, Rogers has described a number of conditions or interactions which facilitate "inner freedom." He describes these as: (a.) confronting a real problem, (b.) a trust in the human organism, (c.) realness in the teacher, (d.) acceptance, (e.) empathy, (f.) providing resources. Rather than repeat the description of these conditions, we refer the student to "Learning to be Free" (Rogers,

1963b). The above processes are applied in the following three arrangements of the class.

1.) In the initial interview with the instructor, the dynamics of interaction between student and teacher (realness, trust in one's feelings, empathy, etc.) are experienced. This may be continued between students by using the H.D.I. [Human Development Institute, Atlanta, Ga.] program, a programmed set of ten lessons in interpersonal relations (Berlin, 1964).

2.) About half of the class time will be spent on student-centered sessions. The role of the instructor during these sessions will be to help maintain students' academic freedom and inner freedom by listening respectfully and acceptingly. He will attempt to understand the students' productions and express a genuine interest in them. These sessions may be of two general kinds: first, those in which student-centered discussions are prominent and second, those in which students present their research, demonstrations, reviews of journal articles, etc.

3.) The remaining time will be spent in instructor-centered sessions. Here the student will play the role of therapist and the instructor will be the client, for it will be the instructor who will voice his ideas and thoughts. The role of the student during these sessions will be in helping to maintain the instructor's academic freedom and inner freedom by listening and responding in an understanding manner.

To instrument the above arrangement between student- and instructor-centered sessions, a sign-up sheet has been posted on the bulletin board outside the classroom. Dates on which the class may convene are listed with five-minute blocks of time under each date. Students and instructor may sign up in advance for the class time they wish to take for their presentation and discussion. For example, let us say that the instructor wishes to present a lecture on Personality Theories on Wednesday, February 15, so he signs up for the time he wishes to take with the title of his presentation. A student who wishes to present the results of an experiment on the following Friday signs up for a 20-minute block of time, or whatever time is required for it, indicating the title of his study. If there is nothing on the agenda, then the class may not convene. In this manner instructor and student become colleagues in their responsibility for class time. The division of class time between teacher- and student-centeredness is informal and in proportion to the need felt for either. It varies with different instructors and different groups of students.

Procedures: Procedures refer to the way in which we relate "content" to "persons" within the limits imposed by "Institutional Press," in a manner which fosters "freedom."

Setting Goals: Since the course begins with *you*, the student, and not with subject content, it is important that you sense your interests, your problems, and your goals and think how the subject matter might instrument these. After the initial interview, you may wish to explore your goals and think of ways in which the course might be helpful to you in pursuing these goals. To give you some idea of the variety of points of view students have when they come into the course, here are a few of the many reasons given for taking the course:

1.) I don't want to be psychoanalyzed. I am a science major, and I want to learn about the content of psychology as it relates to science.

2.) I'm terribly confused. Half the time I'm upset. Can I work on this?

3.) I'm an education major. The only reason I'm taking this course is that it is required by the education department. I doubt it, but if it should help me in becoming a better teacher, then I would like to discover how.

4.) I'm looking forward to becoming a psychologist. I want to learn as much as I can about psychology, but then I guess it is really important to become the kind of person who can relate to people.

5.) I want to know the psychological significance of color.

6.) I hear you people in the Psychology Department are a "bunch of nuts," and I think I would feel right at home.

7.) I noticed an article in the school paper which presented figures based on a report of the National Research Council that 57 per cent of all students graduating from Lewis and Clark who went on to receive their Ph.D. degree majored in psychology. This interests me.

Responses Available to the Student: B. F. Skinner has provided a learning model which differentiates between "emitted responses" and "elicited responses." Without adopting his whole learning model, we would like to use the differentiation which he makes between "emitted responses" and "elicited responses" to describe one aspect of our procedure. Skinner places a hungry pigeon in a Skinner Box. The pigeon is confronted with a problem: to get food in this limited environment. He pecks here and there, perhaps tries to fly out, turns around, and finally, after many varied responses, hits a lever which gives him a pellet of food. These variable responses are "emitted" responses because they arise in the pigeon. Skinner calls them "operants" because they are efforts on the part of the pigeon to solve his problem—to operate, so to speak, in his environment. There is a freedom enjoyed by the pigeon in making any response he wishes (that is, within the confines of the Skinner Box, which is mainly a device to simplify behavior for study, rather than to restrict it).

An "elicited" response, in contrast to an "emitted" one, is one in which priority is given the stimulus which is seen to act upon a fairly passive organism to trigger a response. For example, the experimenter might elicit a response in the pigeon by making a loud sound, flashing a bright light, or even trying to coax the bird to press the lever. Instead of having their origin in the pigeon the stimulus and control originate in the experimenter. The responses which are elicited in this manner are called "respondents." Instead of the bird operating on the environment in a relatively free manner, he responds to a controlling stimuli in a fairly restricted manner.

Most traditionally-taught courses attempt to "elicit" responses from students by stimulating them, coaxing them, lecturing to them, etc. Courses structured along these lines are analogous to the "mug and jug" pedagogical procedure "where the teacher represents the fount of knowledge (the Jug) and the student represents the yawning receptacle." Achievement by conformity often is at a premium in this setting. The student who can pour out the same venerable vintage poured into him excels. The responses available to the student are limited. They are limited by the instructor to responses on a test, a term paper, correctly answering questions in class recitation, etc. Hereafter we shall refer to groups taught in this manner as respondent groups.

We are attempting a procedure in this class which permits great variability in responses. Like operant responses in the pigeon, students have available a wide repertory of responses, which we encourage them to try. A course structured along these lines tends to pose problems, and the student acts independently toward his environment. He may be imaginative, inventive, creative in seeking answers to his own questions and discovering solutions to problems. The uniqueness and imaginativeness of the student's responses are encouraged.

Let us suggest some typical operant responses which might be used by the student in dealing with his major problem in this course. The student is not restricted to the following. These are offered as suggestions. All of them are optional.

Optional Responses Instrumental in Achieving Goals

1.) *Initial interview with the instructor.*

2.) *Statement of goals.* The student may wish to consider his overall occupational goals, the relevancy of this course to them, perhaps the relation of the course to his major, just what he wants to get out of the course, and something about the strategy to be pursued in achieving the stated goals. (Note that goals and purpose come from the student and not the instructor.)

3.) *Review of journal articles and presentation in writing.* Models of good report writing are placed on reserve in the library. A summary may be presented to the class. The instructor is more greatly impressed with articles drawn from professional psychological journals and with the extent that they implement the student's goals than if they are drawn from sources that are more remotely related.

4.) *Research proposals.* The student may have an idea for an experiment. He may write up the idea in the form of an experiment. He may wish to present the idea to the class to get feedback. Three levels of proposals are acceptable. Level 1: the mere idea of "I wonder what would happen if we did this?" Level 2: the idea plus a survey of what has been done on the problem by other researchers. Level 3: the idea with a survey of literature plus the experimental design to be used in testing the hypothesis.

5.) *Individual experiments.* A hypothesis is proposed and tested and results are reported in the form of good report writing (see models placed on reserve). Added credit is allowed where the student seeks the services of a consultant who is an advanced psychology major taking the Experimental Design course. (The consultant also receives credit in his course for serving as a consultant, so do not feel that you are imposing on him.) A list of names of such students who are available as consultants will be posted.

6.) *Group projects.* A group of two or more students may work on some project and present the results as a group to the class. Participants need not be members of this class.

7.) *Demonstrations*. Students may demonstrate some psychological phenomenon or principle to the class.

8.) *Reading of assignments and taking examinations over readings*. This is optional. Students may choose not to take examinations; however, these examinations constitute one of the greatest single sources of credit at a minimal amount of effort in comparison with expenditure of time on some of the other activities, so many elect to take examinations.

9.) *Attendance*. Credit will be given for each class period attended. Daily attendance will be taken at all class periods. No penalty will be attached to missing some or all of the classes. As a matter of fact, students are encouraged to miss a class when they feel that the activity in which they are engaged is of greater psychological significance than attending a class session.

10). *Library-type study*. A student may be interested in the existing research on some subject and choose to write a term paper. The usual criteria of evaluating a term paper will be used. Proper form, bibliography, footnotes, originality, comprehensiveness, organization, relevance to the student's goals, etc., will be factors considered in evaluating the paper.

11.) *Field trips*. Students may take trips to various institutions in the community. These are arranged by students. Please do not over-work certain institutions.

12.) *Battery of tests*. A battery of some eight or ten tests is administered with the purpose of helping the student explore his vocational interests and aptitudes, educational assets and liabilities, and personal emotional factors. (Students will then make an appointment with the instructor for the interpretation of the results.)

13.) *Engage in counseling with some recommended counselor*. Students who are seeking self-improvement might ask the instructor for names of persons who are certified clinical psychologists and who might be of assistance in the particular area of concern. This may be combined with a study and report of various psychotherapeutic approaches, if it should be of significance to the student.

14.) *Human Development Institute Program*. This programmed material has been designed to help people relate to each other in a more satisfying and meaningful way. To receive credit for this activity, students should select some method of making a written report of the experience.

15.) *Other activities may be designed by the student.*

16.) *Self evaluation*. The student may review the work he has done during the course and evaluate it in terms of how meaningful the experience was to him in relation to the goals he set for himself.

The preceding paragraphs illustrate the optional nature of many activities which may instrument the attainment of individually defined goals.

You may decide that the reason you are in this class is to accumulate a large number of facts and a great deal of information of a psychological nature. Perhaps you are more interested in a traditional type course. You would rather hear the lectures, take examinations over the material, etc. You probably would then elect to (a.) attend the lectures regularly, (b.) take all of the examinations which are regularly scheduled, (c.) do a library-type research project, (d.) review and report on various articles contained in the journals.

Perhaps your primary goal is to find yourself. You feel that you have no direction in life. You do not know what your capabilities are. You feel upset much of the time. You may elect to (a.) participate actively in student-centered discussions, (b.) take a battery of tests as a means of exploring yourself and your potentialities, (c.) work through the H. D. I. program, (d.) cover the literature relevant to your problem, (e.) ask your discussion leader to suggest someone you can go to for counseling, (f.) see how you function under stress situations by taking unit tests or give a report or test yourself out in some area which is particularly difficult for you.

A third pattern might be formulated about scientific interests. Suppose you are interested in psychology as a science, particularly in some specific phase such as perception. (a.) you may choose to read all of the journal articles you can on this subject, (b.) cover books which summarize the field, (c.) design an experiment in the field, (d.) carry out the experiment, (e.) consult with students in statistics and experimental courses in regard to your design and statistical processing of data.

Following the above procedure has resulted in a tremendous release of productivity and creativity in students. Past productions of students are placed on file. These can be referred to by students interested in the great variety of activity pursued.

Responsibility: Responsibility for making the course interesting is an individual matter. Students are responsible for their own interests. Instructors are responsible for maintaining their own interests. The instructor is engaged in research, talking about the things that interest him, reading journal articles and books which concern him. In short, he is not putting on a show in the class.

He is engaged in real activities which are meaningful to him. When he gives a lecture, he does so because the topic is important to him. He doesn't do it to fill the hour or entertain students. For him it is the real thing. In this sense he is a real and genuine person pursuing his own interests. He eschews trying to control the interest of students, for this tends to confuse them by directing their attention toward the instructor's goals rather than their own.

Likewise the student is a genuine person pursuing his interests. He has many optional responses available to achieve real, live, meaningful goals. This course isn't play acting for him. It isn't preparation for life; it *is* life. The student isn't going through a set of rituals to get a grade or please the professor. He selects certain options because they are meaningful to him. He is not obligated to do anything which is unmeaningful. If he has selected meaningful goals, if he is free to choose responses which lead to these goals, it is impossible for him to have a dull time in the course. These journal articles he reviews or those experiments he performs are not dull. He has selected and designed ones which are important to him. They are critical to realizing his goals. If he has not so selected his optional responses and the course becomes boring, he has only himself to blame.

The instructor, therefore, is responsible for maintaining his own interests, providing facilities for students to express and realize their goals through the medium of psychology. He is responsible for facilitating the communication between persons with diverse interests and the enhancement of mutual respect between such persons. He is responsible for fulfilling whatever requirements are demanded of him by the institution. He may deem it proper to define the limits of the course, that is, to accept for credit only optional responses which fit within the defined subject matter of the course. He is responsible for expressing his honest opinion of the quality of student productions.

Students are responsible for clarifying their own goals, the selection of and engaging in responses to achieve these goals, the enhancement of their own interests, the quality of their work, creativity, dropping the course if it seems not to provide the medium through which their goals may be realized.

Content: A separate outline of subject matter and suggested readings will be given the student. Productions of students are evaluated in terms of how they use the content of this course to achieve their own goals. In this sense content is instrumental to the attainment of goals.

Institutional Press: Institutional press refers to the expectations of the college, the community, the professional field of psychology, the parents of students, etc. These are imposed on professors and students and are somewhat beyond the control of either. For example, the instructor must hand in grades at the end of the semester, whether he wants to or not. He works in an institutional setting where some kind of evaluation of the student is required of him. He must meet his classes, publish, carry on research, be civil to college deans—and *sometimes* to students.

"Institutional press" is felt from graduate schools by the under-graduate professor. The instructor anticipates that his students going to graduate schools will need to be able to handle the "press" of those institutions. They will need to pass the Graduate Record Examination. They will need to be in possession of certain facts. They will need to be able to handle the stress situations occasioned by doctorate orals, frequent written examinations, preliminaries, etc. This anticipation of future "press" on one's students consti-tutes a present press on every good and conscientious professor. Students feel institutional press in terms of course requirements, examinations, assignments, etc.

What constitutes freedom from "institutional press?" When is one free? Is it the act of changing institutional press which gives us freedom? Would we be free from it if we tried to eliminate it? Probably not. There would be some succeeding expectancy (ex-ternal or internal) which would press upon us.

Take the example of examinations as institutional press. Is one free from an examination if one withdraws from it, perhaps choosing not to take the examinations as may be done in this course, or perhaps choosing courses with a minimum number of tests, or withdrawing from them by engaging in a half-hearted effort? There is always the internal aspect of institutional press. It is not imposed only from the outside. It comes from within as a personal claim on one. We communicate with others in a social system, taking their role and somehow incorporating a set of social expectancies into our selves so we become our own task-masters.

As a college, we might ban all tests. But then there would be the reality of a graduate school requiring tests or an employer giving tests for hiring purposes, or as president of a corporation one might be examined by the stockholders as to policies. There are test-like situations which occur over and over again throughout life. One really isn't freed from tests by creating a temporary island of freedom in a course or college.

Can one be free from tests by escaping from reality? A schizophrenic escape might enable one to split off his feelings from his thinking so less tension would be felt. An hysterical split might enable one to relegate to his muscles and body the fear and anxiety which tortures one. In a sense one would be free from the test. But this would not be true of the self of experience. One's muscles, one's gut, are tortured by the experience, though the self in awareness may be relatively calm and collected.

Then there is a Philistine type approach to being free. One might answer all of the test items not in terms of what one believes or reasons to be true, but in terms of what one thinks is desired by the professor. There are many different shades of this response ranging from a "snow job" to cribbing. One isn't free here; one is deeply controlled. Equally controlled is one who completely rebels, for he lacks the freedom of choosing. He is driven by his needs.

When is one free from tests or other types of institutional press? One is free from them when one has not withdrawn from them or gone down before them. He is free when he first submits himself to the test, when he understands the test items, perhaps when he dares to break with the so-called "correct answer." He does this with fear and trembling because he knows about all the research and thought which went into the formulating of the then-accepted truth. He knows that he is a good student. He accepts his own fears, his own angers and frustrations. He accepts the emotions and feelings in others which may follow from his break with their perceived truth. He rises above the accepted answers. One is free from tests and other forms of institutional press only when one submits oneself to them and rises above them. One's freedom from tests rests in one's oneness, to include within one's perceived self one's feelings, thoughts, choices, sensitivities to others, his viscera, his muscle tension, and all types of responses. To accept all of these experiences as one's own and then to conform to or break with an accepted answer to a test item is the only known way of being free from tests.

Our position on freedom from "institutional press" is not without empirical observations. In 1957 I accentuated the threat of institutional press in an experimental situation by giving a surprise examination to each of three classes: two which had been taught by instructor-centered procedures and one which had incorporated student-centered procedures (Faw, 1957).

Evaluations of stress during the surprise examination indicated a superiority of the student-centered group in dealing with threat. An analysis of variance brings out the most interesting evaluation of the statistical procedures used, in that the two significant variables are learning conditions and the *interaction* between learning conditions and stress. The stress situation (institutional press) by itself does not remain a significant variable. It is only when it interacts with authoritarian learning conditions that stress produces significant pre-test and post-test differences. Thus, the disturbance which is occasioned by the surprise examination can be neutralized if the students have experienced a particular kind of learning situation which makes them free in the sense that they rise above the stress experience.

Perhaps more indicative to some than the statistical tests of significance are the responses of students during the tests. Those having experienced the Rogerian approach to teaching seemed to accept the test but to respect their own responses and feelings. There were descriptive statements from them such as follows:

> At first I felt angry that the prof. would be so low as to pull something like this, and, I recall mentioning, or was about to mention something like this as we were getting ready for the test. Then I felt, oh, hell. I know what I know. I don't have to apologize for what I don't know. I'll put it down and let the chips fall where they may. And then the feeling came over me, and surprisingly enough it was a good feeling, a free feeling, a feeling that I am myself. A little test, even an "F" cannot destroy me. And then I felt sort of an objective curiosity about how I would perform under these conditions and straightway became involved with the test items.

Comments from the instructor-centered groups indicated more splitting of affect from self.

> I felt calm but desperate . . . I had such a terrific headache I could hardly see to read.

There was more cognitive disassociation.

> I felt so confused that I spent the whole time rereading the first question without knowing what it said.

There was more misplaced aggression.

> I suddenly took a dislike for one of the proctors and could hardly control the impulse to go up and sock him on the nose.

When we talk to students and offer them one of two alternatives—(1.) freedom from tests in the sense that they may learn to rise above the tests (but that the test may be difficult, the grade curve rigorous, etc.) or (2.) freedom in the sense that they can avoid the test—our impression has been that most often students have chosen the first type of freedom.

The general setting in which evaluation takes place in this course is the following:

> 1.) Evaluation reflects as accurately as possible the instructor's honest opinion. It does not indicate the absolute worth of the student's work.
>
> 2.) An evaluation is made of the *work*, not the student as a person. A negative evaluation of work does not indicate that the student is bad, lazy, incompetent, stupid. It does not indicate the instructor's like or dislike of the student.
>
> 3.) A student is not free from evaluation to the extent that the instructor withholds evaluation. He is free from it to the extent that he can accept himself as a person. He can listen to the evaluation. He can reject or accept its worth and rise above it.
>
> 4.) The student does not need evaluation to be motivated. That is, he does not work for grades. He works toward the best realization of himself.
>
> 5.) The instructor does not feel a mission to grade everyone. His main function is to create an atmosphere in which students and instructors are free to make new discoveries about self and human behavior. On the other hand, he respects the student's maturity and ability to be free from and not unduly influenced by his evaluation so, therefore, he is not constrained to withhold evaluation. He doesn't need to "pussyfoot" about it.

Methods of Evaluation: Details of each evaluation system will be worked out by each instructor of the sections. The main principle agreed upon by all instructors is that evaluation will be in terms of the quality and quantity of what has been produced during the course in pursuit of self-defined goals. To instrument this principle, a cumulative file of each student's productions during the course will be kept. When the instructor is ready to make a final evaluation for the course he will sit down with the student's file. Before him will be the statement of the student's goals for the course, the products of the operant responses the student has made, (test papers, reports, experiments, etc.), and the final self-evaluation which the student has made of his own work. Different instructors have preferred one of three methods in arriving at an overall evaluation: (1.) a cumulative point system, (2.) a global evaluation, (3.) a combination of (1.) and (2.). The point system involves the instructor indicating beforehand the number of points available for the various responses. For example, he may say there is one point available for each test item answered correctly during the course, 50 points available as a maximum for each experiment, 50 points maximum for abstracts of each journal article, 100 points maximum for self-evaluations, 2 points for each class attended.

The advantage of this system is that (a.) it indicates more clearly to the student the instructor's value system, (b.) it facilitates inter and intra group comparisons in that points may be summed and placed on a curve, (c.) evaluations are continually going on during the course, thus providing feedback to the student. For example, the instructor may allow 20 points on a poor experiment but 30 or 40 on one which is of higher quality. One of the problems of the point system is to weight properly quality with quantity.

Some professors have preferred the global method. They find it rewarding to sit down with the student's file, peruse his goals, read the reports and productions in support of these goals, read the student's self-evaluation and arrive at a global picture of his work.

Regardless of whether a point system or global system is used, all instructors using either with the cumulative file have hypothesized that the evaluation is more valid in respect to predicting future creativity and productivity than the results of objective type examinations which are heavily weighted with a memory factor for information type knowledge. The instructor has before him the products of the student's creative efforts.

RESULTS

Dr. Faw has made a careful study of the outcomes of his approach to this course, and quotations from his findings are in order.

Teachers of psychology reading this statement may be interested in the results of this program. Since the program is an ongoing one and was not set up as an experiment, the observations presented below are largely ex post facto.

Two phases will be of concern: (1.) the possible negative effects of such a free environment, (2.) the possible gains in creativity and productivity.

Possible Negative Effects: One might be concerned about the effect on attendance, achievement on examinations of an objective nature, quality of the productions, focus on material relevant to the core of the course.

Differences in attendance in sections taught in a conventional manner and those in which students were given the freedom to come or not show insignificant differences. The percentage attendance of four sections of 35 students in each of which attendance was required resulted in 87.2 per cent attendance during the semester. Four sections in which attendance was optional resulted in 86.8 per cent attendance. The differences were statistically insignificant. The eight sections were each chosen at random.

Achievement on objective type examinations given during the courses show insignificant differences. Based on four sections, each representative of operant and respondent methods, the mean percentage of items passed was 67.18 and 69.55. In all four of the operant sections, 100 per cent of the students took all of the examinations, as did those in the respondent sections.

Less than one per cent of the student productions were judged by the instructors to be irrelevant to the course subject. Since one of the criteria of evaluating the productions was known to the students as relevancy to the course subject matter, a very high per cent of the productions were basic to the subject matter covered.

The risk on the negative side in respect to poor attendance, poor examination results, poor quality of work, irrelevant productions, appears to be minimal.

Possible Gains in Creativity and Productivity Effected by Program:

It is difficult to assess creativity. Nonetheless a simple tabulation by Faw of the products of two class groups chosen at random from sections taught conventionally and those taught by his "operant" approach is striking indeed.

TABLE   1

NUMBER AND KIND OF PRODUCTIONS IN OPERANT AND RESPONDENT GROUPS

	Respondent Group N 38	Operant Group N 38
Statement of goals	0	26
Journal articles reported	0	165
Research proposals	0	25
Experiments (original)	0	18
Group projects	0	3
Demonstrations	0	2
Library studies (term papers)	38	8
Field trips	0	23
Vocational test batteries	5	7
Counseling	0	1
HDI program	0	19
Interview with instructor	0	32
Other activities	0	4
Course examinations	190	190
Total productions	233	523
Mean number	6.1	13.7

Faw points out that not only is there this difference in number and variety of productions, but that there was a sharp difference in the degree to which the products were stereotyped or original.

Respondent groups tended to be stereotyped in respect to what was assigned students. One professor might ask all students to write a term paper on some topic of the student's choice as was done in the section reported in Table 1. Another professor might concentrate on the reading and reporting of journal articles; so all thirty-eight students would be "grinding out" journal articles in place of thirty-eight term papers. All students typically were expected to do the same thing in respondent groups. In operant groups no two students did the same thing. There were as many different patterns of productivity as there were students.

Not only were the kinds of production more stereotyped in the respondent groups but also the content of such productions tended to be more stereotyped. For example, if experiments were assigned in a respondent section the whole group usually went through a "cookbook" type experiment, perhaps plotting a learning curve in mirror drawing, performing a standard experiment in psychophysics, etc. Variation between students was minimal. In the operant group reported in Table 1, all 18 experiments performed were different. For example, one student tested the hypothesis that freezing does not interfere with learning. He conditioned worms to follow a maze, then froze the worms in a manner which he learned by consulting an intern at the University of Oregon Medical School, and then retested the worms and determined if the learning was retained after they had been thawed out. He compared experimental with control groups. A second student tested whether a noxious sound can become a positive reinforcer. A third student attempted to determine whether hostile behavior toward minority groups might be present on the basis of perceived physiological differences. He proposed to hatch a baby chick along with four ducklings and to reverse the minority with a second group of one duckling and four chicks. Behavior against the minority group was proposed to be compared with behavior toward other members of the majority by making a sociogram of responses.

The above experiments are typical of a large number of experiments which came from the operant groups. All of them were different. They seemed to generate a great deal of excitement among the students in and out of class and frequently became the foci of conversation in small groups. Insofar as upperclassmen often are serving as consultants to freshmen on matters of design and statistics, current experiments become the topic of conversations throughout the department.

HOW DO STUDENTS EXPERIENCE THE COURSE?

These are some of the course outcomes as observed by the instructor. But what meaning did the class have for the students who were involved? Out of hundreds of student evaluations over the years, Dr. Faw has sent me five. Though most students react favorably to the approach, two of the five he has chosen are negative, and indicate the kind of students who tend not to profit from such a course. The other three represent a range of positive reaction, perhaps somewhat more sophisticated than the reports turned in by the average student in the course.

Let us start with the students who have experienced the course negatively. The first is a reasonable response from a student who prefers to be stimulated and led by another, rather than initiating his own learning.

I would rate this course below par for my needs. There was too much class time devoted to listening to students express their ideas, describing journal articles which they only partly understood, and trying to plan experiments. I pay high tuition to listen to an expert who is well trained in his field, not a lot of students who know even less than I do about psychology.

A course which appealed to me much more was a course I took in the history department. The lecturer was dynamic, inspirational, and made his subject live. There were a number of questions from students which he answered in an authoritative way, but students never dominated the class.

As far as making my own goals the dominant feature of the course, I feel that the instructor should set the goals. He knows the material and what should be learned by the student. When I tried to analyze my goals I was completely frustrated.

The second negative reaction proves, if nothing else, that students are not fearful, in courses taught in this fashion, of being completely honest in expressing their feelings to the instructor. The attitude expressed is undoubtedly very common in the great mechanical contraption which we mistakenly label "education."

This course was filled with too much busy work. Everyone was running around taking field trips, doing experiments, reading journal articles, etc.—and all for brownie points. I got scared finally, that I was falling behind, so got busy on several projects. I couldn't afford to pick up a bad grade in this course because I'm pretty close to the border as it is.

Frankly, the course involved too much work and I much prefer a nice easy course where you do the assignments and get graded on what you do in the tests. I can usually bluff my way through these when there has not been sufficient time to study.

This course began to cut into my social life terribly, and I would prefer not to get involved in another one like it.

My goal is to get out of college as soon as possible, but to enjoy it while I'm here! This course just didn't have the ingredients to instrument this goal.

For a quite different reaction we turn to another student whose goal is highly personal.

This has been the most exciting course I have ever taken. School has always meant doing assignments, following instructions, memorizing material and then giving it back to the teacher. If it were approved by the teacher then I received a good grade. I have always received good grades but it never seemed that I got myself into the act. It was always to please someone else and not for me.

I had taken another course in which the instructor met with us and then said, "What would the class like to do?" Well, we spent the main part of the course spinning our wheels. It was pretty disorganized. But in *this* course there was a well defined organization which gave me a feeling that the instructor knew what he was doing but still permitted me the maximum of freedom . . . to work on something I wanted to work on.

I decided what I wanted more than anything else was to feel more organized within myself; to be a better adjusted person. I entered the preliminiary interview with some skepticism, thinking that this goal of mine would somehow turn out to be unacceptable. But I came away from the interview feeling that this was a very worthwhile endeavor and that I was worthwhile for thinking of it.

The course to me was an exciting adventure exploring "me." These are some of the things I did. (1) I kept a diary of my own reactions to various situations. But I sensed that this diary was a very superficial account of my feelings, so, (2) I read Freud and some other authors who seemed to be working at a deeper level and I wound up keeping a diary of my dreams. (3) I went through the H. D. I. program twice, once with a male and once with a female. I was interested in the differences of my reactions; (4) I joined a group in group therapy; (5) I took a field trip to Morningside hospital and concluded that it wouldn't be so bad if I did crack up; (6) I read the textbook thoroughly because I felt it was presenting something to me; (7) in addition I covered several journal articles which were relevant to my problem. I felt they gave some empirical evidence on some important issues.

The final outcome is the feeling that I have a knowledge about psychology which is internalized and which is part of me. It isn't just for passing exams, although I took all of the examinations and did very well there too.

It is a particularly rewarding thing to discover how such a course appears to a student who comes to it from a thorough background in a "hard" science.

I'm a senior and a physics major. I took this course just to fill in a few hours where no others seemed to fit. Also, since this is a rather popular subject, I felt that I should know something about it. My most dominant attitude at first was a strong feeling of skepticism that psychology could ever become a science. Probably a primary goal for me was to show up the psychologists as pseudo-scientists and to question the whole field as a legitimate science.

The instructor, to my surprise, was quite understanding of this goal. (I expected him to be rather defensive.) He commented that this was a feeling shared by a number of individuals and suggested a number of journal articles which might be helpful to me in pursuing this goal. I read with considerable interest articles by Skinner, Hull, Stevens, Dewey, to mention but a few. This finally led to parts of Marx' *Theories in Contemporary Psychology*, Stevens' *Handbook of Experimental Psychology*, and Osgood's *Method and Theory in Experimental Psychology*.

My next step was to take several psychological experiments reported in the journals and attempt to evaluate them from the point of view of their scientific validity. This was also the orientation I adopted in reading the text.

Finally I attempted to set up an experiment of my own to experience the methodological problems involved in studying behavior.

The whole experience was extremely rewarding and I must admit that the procedures followed in the teaching of this course were first rate. Physics and chemistry laboratory work could benefit by incorporating the feeling of discovery which pervades this class.

I regard myself as much more mature than most of the freshmen and sophomores taking the course; but I honestly believe either a freshman or a graduate student could take this course and get a great deal out of it.

I came out of the course with considerable respect for what psychologists are doing in a scientific way. As a matter of fact, psychologists seem to be doing some of the most fundamental thinking in respect to scientific methodology.

Finally, a report from a student who made his own personal survey of student reactions to the course.

I'm an education major and took this course because it was required. Since my major interest is in educational procedures, the methods followed by the instructor were of considerable interest to me. I decided to make a study of the reactions of students to this approach so talked to quite a number of students in this section as well as other sections.

My conclusions are these:

1.) It is a good course for most students but is less appealing to the fairly rigid type student who wants direction or who wants to please the teacher. It does not appeal to the lazy student or to one who does not know what he is after, although among these latter some seemed to be able to make their indecision a problem to work on and came out of the course with some good results.

2.) The course emphasizes the importance of the active learner as opposed to the passive learner. Passive learners who had achieved some success in the past had a more difficult time adjusting to this course. Those who were productive on their own seemed to adjust very rapidly.

3.) The course placed a premium on creativity rather than mere memorization, on planning instead of conforming to the plans of others, on problem solving rather than recall.

4.) Aggressive students tended to respond better than withdrawn students.

5.) The course recognized individual differences and permitted a great variety in types of productivity.

6.) It seemed to me that students either liked the course very much or disliked it. There were fewer students falling in between than in most classes.

7.) Some students produced great quantities of work to get a grade rather than in pursuit of their goals.

8.) Some students overloaded themselves with field trips and neglected important reading. They would have benefited from having an idea of what to look for before they took the field trip.

9.) The teacher's role in the class was different than in a traditional class. He didn't seem to play the part of an authority but tried to stimulate students to discover things for themselves. He occupied the center of the stage less than the usual course.

10.) Students would do better in a course like this if they had previous experience with self direction in courses at lower levels.

11.) The course motivated students more than the average course and more closely met the needs of most students. However, it misfired on some.

SOME COMMENTS

I should like to add a few comments in order to make clear why, to me, Professor Faw's approach in his class may be particularly useful to educators.

EASILY TRANSLATABLE

In the first place this is an approach which could be used in any field of knowledge, in any kind of institution. It could be adapted with relative ease to the teaching of physics in a college with highly rigid standards, or to a course in literature in a college with "liberal" leanings. It could, with a little more effort, be adapted to the teaching of high school courses. Thus it constitutes a realistic alternative to any teacher who is dissatisfied with conventional methods but who hesitates, whether because of confining circumstances or a fear of failure, to attempt something drastically different.

NON-THREATENING CHARACTER

Related to this is the fact that Faw's method appears suitably academic and scholarly, that it gives very adequate training in research, has a place for such standard elements as examinations, term papers, book reviews, and the like. Consequently, it is unlikely to frighten a college administrator or fellow faculty members. In spite of all these familiar externals, however, the course is built upon assumptions which are the exact opposite of the assumptions in a conventional course.

STRESS UPON CHOICE AND INITIATIVE

One of the most basic of these assumptions is that the course belongs, fundamentally, to the *student*, and that there will be no learning of any kind if he simply behaves in the passive manner expected of him in other courses. It is up to him to choose his goals, and to continue making choices at every step, from a very wide range of alternatives. Nor are these simply abstract choices. He chooses, acts upon his choice, and lives with the consequences. There is ample encouragement given and many personal and material resources easily available, but this does not alter the fact that the student learns by making independent choices of goals and means, making these choices in terms of what will be valuable to him, and taking the initiative in implementing these choices.

A PLACE FOR THE INSTRUCTOR

When the central focus is upon learning rather than teaching, there is no doubt that some teachers fear they will be left out, that they no longer have a place on the stage. Faw has handled this, in my estimation, realistically and well. The instructor in no way denies his own interests. He recognizes his desire to instruct, to teach. Like the student, he chooses those things he wants to present, and takes the initiative in making his place in the life of the class. But he does avoid the hum-drum and the routine of lecturing, and has a ready measure of the interest of the class in himself and his work, since students are free to come or stay away from his presentations.

A RATIONALE FOR EVALUATION AND GRADES

Another striking element in Faw's approach is his clearly worked out views in the realm of evaluation. Not everyone would agree with these views (which may account for his somewhat lengthy presentation of them). Nonetheless, he has come to terms with the issue in an open, thoughtful way which is in accord with his convictions and his personality. To me the greatest value of his approach to grading is that it shows that new ways of adapting to this perplexing problem can be worked out—ways which are both creative and realistic. He has found a way which suits him, and which helps to put grades in a perspective for the student which maintains the student's self-respect.

DESIRABLE OUTCOMES

Simply to look at Faw's listing of student productions is evidence of outcomes very different from those of the conventional course. For two-thirds of the students to work out definite goals for themselves, for a similar number to draw up research proposals on their own initiative, and for more than half of the class to initiate field trips—clearly these are unusual outcomes. Half of the group used programmed learning to try to improve their inter-personal relationships, and an equal number undertook original laboratory experiments. Any resemblance to the usual sterile "introductory course" is certainly coincidental. Small wonder that a surprising proportion of those who have been exposed to this kind of learning experience tend to go on for advanced degrees.

SUMMARY

A college professor, keeping himself quite strictly within a conventional educational framework, has fashioned a freshman course of a most unusual sort. While it maintains many of the external trappings of the customary course, these have been transformed by turning them over to the students to use in those ways which have meaning and significance for them. Thus the student's curiosity, his desire to learn, his ability to select and follow his own path of learning, are the basis of the course. Yet this revolutionary basis is softened and made relatively non-threatening to fellow educators, by virtue of its use of such commonplace elements as occasional lectures, scholarly term papers, examinations, and grades, all of which exist in a context built of *student* purposes.

References

Berlin, J. I. *H. D. I. General relationship improvement program.* Atlanta: Human Development Institute, Inc., 1964.

Faw, V. E. A psychotherapeutic method of teaching psychology. *American Psychologist,* 1949, *4* (4), 104-109.

Faw, V. E. Learning to deal with stress situations. *Journal of Educational Psychology,* 1957, *48* (3), 135-144.

Rogers, C. R. Significant learning: In therapy and in education. In C. R. Rogers, *On becoming a person.* Boston: Houghton Mifflin, 1961. Pp. 279-295.

Rogers, C. R. Learning to be free. In S. M. Farber & R. H. Wilson (Ed.), *Conflict and creativity: Control of the mind.* (Part 2) New York: McGraw-Hill, 1963. Pp. 268-288. (a)

Rogers, C. R. Graduate education in psychology: A passionate statement. Western Behavioral Sciences Institute, 1963. (In slightly revised form, this is presented as Chapter 8 in this book.) (b)

3

My Way of Facilitating a Class

I wanted to include in this book a description of my own way of dealing with students. I took as my example a course which had been completed just prior to writing this volume, because I felt that its recency would permit me to present it with more vividness. I have tried to build the chapter around quotations from the students, to give the real flavor of the experience as it occurred in them. It had been a course which seemed to me and to the students to have been very successful. I would certainly like to emphasize that I have had courses which were less satisfying to me and to the students.

Although this happened to be a graduate course, I am sure I would have followed the same principles, and many of the same procedures, whether it had been an elementary, high school, or college course, though I might not have been able to follow such an unorthodox schedule.

Every effective educator has his own style of facilitating the learning of his students. There is certainly no one way of achieving this. Yet, unfortunately, there are very few specific accounts of the way in which a given educator operates. I believe newcomers to the field could profit from such records. This is why I have presented two such accounts in the preceding chapters. For the same reason, in the pages which follow, I am going to try to set down, as accurately as I can, the manner in which I conducted a recent graduate course, the reactions of the students to the experience, and the observations of three individuals who assisted me.

The way in which learning was facilitated in this course is by no means presented as a model. If I had conducted the course ten years ago I would have done it quite differently. Perhaps five years from now I will do it in still newer and (I hope) more creative ways. It is simply presented for its stimulus value. It would be unfortunate if anyone tried to deal with a course for which he is responsible in exactly the same way.

BACKGROUND CONTEXT

This course was taught in a very favorable context. California Western University, with some consultation from the members of the staff of the Western Behavioral Sciences Institute (WBSI), had just recently inaugurated a doctoral program in educational leadership and human behavior. From the very first it was planned that this would be an innovative and unconventional type of program. Students would be encouraged rather than continually threatened with examinations. The emphasis would be upon releasing professional potential and encouraging professional growth, rather than upon meeting requirements set by some "wise" faculty committee. Put in other terms, the emphasis would be upon trusting the student rather than upon evaluative or punitive action .There would be a good deal of opportunity for independent study. The curriculum would be tailored so far as possible to meet the needs of the individual rather than pushing him into some set pattern. It was hoped that it would have very little resemblance to the conventional, often dull, doctoral programs in education. The catalog described the purposes as being to "assist the student in achieving the following:

A better understanding and knowledge of human behavior;

Knowledge and understanding of the philosophies and principles of leadership;

Ability to translate this knowledge and understanding into patterns of effective leadership in education."

Because the program seemed to be exciting and creative, I agreed to teach a course on "Values in Human Behavior (Including Sensitivity Training)." The account which follows is a description of this course.

All of the candidates for this doctoral degree have at least a master's degree from an accredited institution and a minimum grade point average of 3.5 for graduate work completed. There were other requirements for admission which need not concern us here.

At the time that students signed up for the course, they were told that there would be one meeting on a Saturday from 9:00 a.m. to noon, and then two weekend workshops, spaced three weeks apart running from Friday evening through Sunday noon, and a final Saturday morning meeting at the end of the course. Students were requested not to sign up for the course unless they could be free during these periods of time, and desired to participate in the workshops.

It was intended to limit registration to 22 but due to the usual pressures the actual registration was 25. In addition, two post-doctoral fellows at WBSI participated as group leaders on the weekends and in all of the meetings of the group, and a visiting Japanese scholar also joined the group on an informal basis. Thus the total number, including myself, was 29.

FIRST MEETING OF THE COURSE

As students came in to this first meeting they were asked to help arrange the chairs in a circle. Then they were handed the memo which follows.

Memo to: Students in HB 624, Cal. Western University

From: Carl R. Rogers

Values in Human Behavior (Including Sensitivity Training)! Wow! What a title for a course. To me it seems to be an opportunity to do anything that we wish which will add significantly to our own learning. It gives an opportunity for each of us to read about and think about such things as these: personal values as they relate to the meaning that one perceives in life; the values one regards as significant in one's personal behavior; values as related to sexual and family behavior; values in interpersonal relationships; values as they relate to the philosophy and practice of the behavioral sciences; special value problems such as prejudice, ethnic attitudes, and the like. I am sure this is only a partial list but a least it gives some notion of the broad range in which each can develop his own personal curriculum.

Here are some of my thoughts for the course thus far. I have had relatively little time to think about the matter and all of these plans are subject to change if you wish, within the limits of my own schedule and yours.

The First Meeting Saturday, 9:00 a.m. - 12:00 noon,
Cal. Western University

This should be a long enough session to enable us to get acquainted, to consider plans for the remainder of the course, and to go over the reading list.

I would also like to use this as a time to draw out your own notions of other value issues which may be of even greater concern to you than those previously mentioned. For example, I have said nothing about values in education nor the value system by which a teacher guides his or her behavior in dealing with the community, the administration, and students. I hope this will be a free-for-all discussion.

Reading List

I was encouraged by the coordinator of the program to prepare a broad gauge reading list and I have tried to do this. I hope that a copy of the reading list was given to you when you registered for the course. [It had been.] It includes a wide range of writings from different philosophical and religious orientations—Protestant, Catholic, Jewish, agnostic, and a delightful little book on Zen Buddhism.

The reading list also includes everything from very substantial and sophisticated books on the philosophy of science to the Playboy philosophy, taken from *Playboy Magazine*. Because of my own interests I am sure the list is slanted somewhat in an existential direction but I would be happy to have suggestions which would give it wider range.

There is no intention at all that the reading list constitutes anything required. It represents instead a rich storehouse from which you may draw the kinds of things that have the most meaning to you. You may also want to go well beyond this list into other areas that have special interest for you.

I regret that I did not have time to annotate the book list when I drew it up. I will comment in our first course meeting on each of the books on the list about which I have personal knowledge. This should help you to choose the points where you want to start.

First Workshop

My suggestion is that we hold this at WBSI and plan to meet from 7:30 to 10:30 Friday evening, 9:00 a.m. to 6:00 p.m. on

Saturday (with a sandwich lunch); and Sunday from 9:00 to 12:00 noon. We can discuss more specific plans for this but I would hope that it would include some sessions of the whole group together and that most of the time would be spent in smaller basic encounter groups led by members of the WBSI staff. Just how I will distribute my time among the groups is something that both you and I will need to settle together. In general, the topic of this weekend, insofar as it has a cognitive topic, might be: "What are the sources of my values?"

Second Workshop

The framework for this second weekend will be similar to the previous one, and will run from Friday evening through Sunday noon. If it needs a theme or topic, this might well be "What human values do I stand for?"

Requirements

There are several aspects of the course which will be required. These are as follows: I wish to have a list of the readings you have done for the course turned in before the end of the course, with an indication of the way you have read the book. For example, you might list a book and state "Chapters 3 and 6 were read thoroughly." You might list another book and state "Skimmed the book and found it was over my head." You might list another book and say, "I got so much out of this book that I read it twice and made careful notes on Chapters 5 through 12." You might state, "I was repelled by the whole point of view and only read enough to become convinced that I was disgusted with the author." In other words, what is wanted is an honest account of what you have read and the depth to which you have read the material you covered. The books do not necessarily have to be on this reading list.

The second requirement is that you write a paper which may be as brief or as lengthy as you wish about your own most significant personal values and the ways they have changed or not changed as a result of this course.

A third requirement is that you turn in to me a statement of your own evaluation of your work and the grade that you think is appropriate. This statement should include a) the criteria by which you are judging your work; b) a description of the ways in which you have met or failed to meet those criteria; and c) the

grade which you think appropriate to the way you have met or
failed to meet your own criteria. If I find that my own estimate
of your work is quite at variance with yours I will have a personal
talk with you and we will see if we can arrive at some mutually
satisfactory grade which I can in good conscience sign and turn in.

The final requirement is to be your personal reaction to the course
as a whole. I would like this turned in to me in a sealed envelope
with your name on the outside. You are at liberty, however, to
mark on it, "please do not open until the final grades have been
turned in." If you mark the envelope in this fashion, I assure you
I will honor your request.

In this reaction I would like you to state very honestly what the
course has meant to you, both positively and negatively. I would
like any criticisms you have to make of the course and suggestions
of ways in which it might be improved. This in short is your
opportunity to evaluate the course, the instructor, and the manner
in which the course has been carried out. It will in no case have
any influence on your final grade but if you are fearful that it
might have such an influence please mark your envelope as suggested, and I will not open it until all grades have been turned in.

A final grade in the course will not be turned in until all of these
requirements have been fulfilled.

I opened the session by suggesting that we might tell what our
interests were, why the individual was in this doctoral program,
and why he had selected this course. I led off by telling something
of my current interests, including my interest in the use of the
basic encounter group as a tool for change in educational systems.
Each person in turn spoke of himself in his own way.

The interests and occupations of the members of the group were
varied. They were all people of some experience. To give a sampling of the positions held, there was a faculty member of Cal.
Western who had formerly been a school superintendent; a sixth
grade teacher; several principals and vice-principals; a science
coordinator; a high school counselor; a mother who was working
as a substitute teacher; a head resident of a dormitory; a clinical
psychologist in a school for delinquents; a counselor-teacher dealing
with delinquents in a continuation school; a minister who was
interested in broadening his ways of working in his church; the

director of a remedial reading clinic; and individuals from big city and small town school systems.

As members spoke of their interest in the doctoral program and in this particular course, there were great variations from some who were quite personal and talked rather freely about their interests and some who were rather formal and simply gave their positions and little more. A high school teacher who is also trained as a psychologist told how she was working part time with a physician in a counseling position because she could not stand to be a full-time teacher in the constricting atmosphere of a high school. One former superintendent of schools told how he was "going to try to be lazy this year, simply being a full-time graduate student." The minister told how he was trying to find new directions for himself in his work.

Since I took few notes at this first meeting of the class, I later gathered the three individuals who had served as co-leaders of the small groups and asked them for their memories of that Saturday morning meeting. They spoke about going around the group, and one of these leaders said that the thing that interested him was that I had "validated each person." The others enthusiastically agreed. I was somewhat puzzled by this and asked what they meant. I learned that it was not anything I had consciously done but perhaps had accomplished on an intuitive basis. Their joint description was that I nearly always responded with some question or comment to each person who spoke up indicating that I had really received his message and respected it or had some understanding of the kind of situation he was facing. If this is what I achieved, I can see why it would help to set a climate for free expression which certainly is one of my goals.

Following this I made some comments on the book list so that they would have some basis for knowing which books they were interested in and where they might wish to start reading. I feel that I spent too much time on this and that an annotated book list carefully prepared in advance would have served the same purpose and would not have taken the group's time.

In going over the book list, which I had prepared too hastily, a number of errors were discovered and one member of the group offered to make it her responsibility to carefully check each book, its author, publisher, date, and library number, and get out a new and improved list and mail it to each of the members. I feel that this completely voluntary action on her part was not only helpful but again was an important step in setting up the climate of the course, indicating that this was a group where people could volunteer to take responsibility if they so desired. Out of the discussion of the reading list, eleven new books were added to the thirty-three which had been listed and later the member who had volunteered prepared a beautifully accurate and complete book list for everyone in the course.

In order to make possible her mailing and also other mailings, we passed around a sheet on which everyone wrote down his name, address, and phone number so intercommunication would be easy. Another member of the group volunteered to have this list duplicated and mailed to every member of the seminar.

There followed free-for-all discussion about some of the value issues in which they were interested and which they hoped would be dealt with in the course. Toward the very end of the time I suggested that they take a few moments to write an anonymous answer to this question: "What is the single, most important, unsettled value issue for you right now?" These responses were gathered together, and the session was over.

Later when I examined these brief, anonymous statements, there were three that were concerned with identifying personal problems. The others, however, seemed in no way really identifying and I decided that it might be thought provoking to the group if they were distributed. Consequently, all of these were mailed out to each member of the group. Most of the responses are those that might be found anywhere in any group of professional or pre-professional individuals. Here is a sampling of the statements that were turned in.

VALUE ISSUES

Anonymous answers to the question, "What is the single most important unsettled value issue for you right now?"

> I find *my* value system to be changing—I find the value system of my immediate family (*spouse*) to be remaining static. My problem: I find myself being drawn to associates with similar values. This is not necessarily a problem of sex, etc.

*   *   *

What is really my place right now? Who am I? What do I want to be? The professional, competitive administrator or the woman —wife. Is it more important for me to spend more time at home with my children, or to continue in the tremendously exciting search for the way for myself in terms of study and "life work?" How much of both can I do well?

*   *   *

Should I talk about what's really bothering me?

*   *   *

At the moment it appears that the single most important unsettled value issue for me is: "To what extent—if any—should I argue against or point out what appears to be flaws in the reasoning of my profession?"

*   *   *

Whether or not to accept the literal interpretation of the life of Christ as presented in the New Testament. I have no factual basis for refuting it.

*   *   *

What is *my* purpose? Where is *my* place in the scheme of things? Have I lived before? Will I live again . . . i.e., . . . what is *my* value? . . . Who am "*I*" in the cosmic "schema" of things?

*   *   *

How can we or should we be influenced in our modern day thinking and actions from the standpoint of moral and religious values, when the basis of Christian religion is set down in the Bible?

*   *   *

The lack of spiritual emphasis in our public school systems!

*   *   *

I have tried to follow a policy of "fair, firm, and friendly" in my dealings with students, but in disciplinary matters I am accused of inconsistency and "playing favorites" as a result of attempting to treat students as individuals with individual problems.

*   *   *

Nothing is currently keeping me awake nights. But liberalism vs. conservatism is a continual confrontation.

*   *   *

Counseling people with respect to adultery or fornication.

*   *   *

On what should my values of good or bad be based and how
can I judge the rightness or wrongness of the values?

*   *   *

What are my rock bottom values? What *are* rock bottom values?
People, feelings, acts, freedom, family, wife, children?

*   *   *

To what extent may an individual subordinate what he "should"
do in his relationships with others to what he "wants" to do?
Is it morally wrong to assume that one can sometimes express
his own life aims, even when these are in conflict with the well-
being of others?

THE WEEKEND ENCOUNTER GROUPS

We met on Friday evening in a room at Western Behavioral
Sciences Institute which was too small to accommodate the whole
group comfortably, which made it necessary for some to sit on
the carpeted floor. I mention this, because it added to the informality of the group.

A list was handed out showing the distribution of the class
into three groups of 9 or 10 each. It was explained that this was
a random selection, except that the women were distributed as
evenly as possible among the groups. (Of the total group of 29,
there were 5 women and 24 men.) The two post-doctoral fellows,
and one class member who had worked with me previously, were
listed as facilitators.

I opened the session by saying that I was going to show a film
of an interview of mine with Gloria, a young woman who posed
many ethical, moral, and value issues during my half-hour encounter with her.[1]

In the discussion which followed, Al (all names are fictitious)
took what appeared to be a rather hard and moralistic stand, and
was attacked—somewhat intolerantly—by various members of the
group. As the discussion continued, I could not help but recognize
that Al's "hardness" was mostly a façade, and I said that my own

---

[1] This is the first film in "Three Approaches to Psychotherapy," produced and
distributed by Dr. Everett Shostrom, 205 W. 20th Street, Santa Ana, California.

guess was that he was "a real softy inside." He looked embarrassed, as though he had been "found out," and his eyes were moist with tears. It had been a lively interaction, with many members participating. We then cut off the discussion in the total group, and broke into the three small groups, which met in separate rooms.

It is quite impossible to convey the quality of the experience in the two weekend encounter groups, spaced three weeks apart. I myself distributed my time about evenly among the three groups. I endeavored, so far as possible, to be a real participant in each group during the time I was there, as well as to act facilitatively, usually with an empathic response when this seemed appropriate. In one group I shared with the members some of the frustrations and humiliation which I had recently been experiencing.

We decided that the members of the class would be reshuffled into new combinations for the second weekend. The class was evenly divided as to whether they wished the same, or reshuffled grouping, and we tried the latter arrangement. This was, I think, a mistake. There were several indications that it would have been more profitable if the same groupings had been continued through both weekends.

At the end of two weekends, I came to the conclusion that I would never again distribute myself among three groups. It means being in on some of the significant happenings in each group but leaves me somewhat fragmented at the conclusion. Also, by the time of the second weekend, when the group coherence was stronger, I was somewhat of an intruder. One of the group facilitators describes this as follows: "Carl came back to the group for the last session. With one exception the group stayed at a completely intellectual level and seemed almost to refuse to allow Carl to become involved in the group. One of the people in the group said to Carl that the group was better when I was here alone with them. This took quite a bit of courage on his part. Carl accepted this as being probably but regretfully true."

VIGNETTES FROM THE ENCOUNTER GROUPS

I requested brief accounts from the three facilitators because I felt their observations could be more complete than my own. I was a part of several of these events, but because I shifted from group to group, I rarely saw the beginning and the end of any individual's experience. Here, with as much identifying data removed as possible, are descriptions of what appeared to happen to several individuals. It will be clear from reading the student reactions later, that the facilitators have given low-keyed, modest, and objective accounts of these personal events.

DESCRIPTIONS BY THE FACILITATORS

Jim, an ex-administrator, who had lost his job in a way he perceived as most humiliating, was faced in the group with two staff members from his own school district. He had heard that one of them was actively preventing his ever being rehired in this district. With great hesitancy he brought up the personal misgivings he had about being in the same group with these two people. Both of them were able to reassure him that they never held any animosity toward him, and that especially when they heard him tell his very moving story they felt close to him. This was very meaningful to Jim in that he was able to take a big step toward changing his view that most of the school people in the district belittled him behind his back.

*   *   *

John, a very tight-lipped former Marine, made his position clear at the beginning of the group that he strongly believed that "good fences make good neighbors." He understood that part of what goes on in a basic encounter group is "confession of sins," and he let the group know that he wanted no part of it. If that was what we were about, he would just as soon have stayed home, as he had an awful lot of work he should be doing. In spite of this stand, which he repeated periodically, John proved to be one of the most empathic group members. When Jim was telling of the humiliation he felt as a result of losing his job, John said with great feeling that he could understand just how he felt and perhaps could offer some hope to him. He had been court martialed several years before on a charge for which he did not personally feel directly responsible. For a long while afterward, he lived with the same humiliation Jim described.

Later I [the facilitator] remarked that it must have been a little difficult for John to tell us about the court martial. John replied that it was; in fact he hadn't mentioned it to anyone in a very long time.

In other incidents John was sensitive and understanding of the feelings of other group members as well as being able to talk about very meaningful private matters, in spite of his repeated warnings to the group that he would stand off.

Al and Bill were consistently hostile and picking at John's "good fences" stand. In spite of it being pointed out frequently how sensitively involved and helpful John was, Al and Bill remained his adversaries to the end of this first weekend.

During the second weekend John was in a different group with another facilitator whose reaction was somewhat different:

John seemed to be completely unreachable. Problems were things that seemed to happen to other people and he talked incessantly about how lucky he had been, how wonderful his life had been, how good his marriage was. He seemed about as completely uninvolved an individual as I have ever seen. When Joanne tried to offer him a compliment he didn't even want to hear it, and it later came out that one of the reasons for this was that she was so attractive and this might be letting her get too close.

I found myself getting quite angry with him and I remarked that I was going to tell him something that I didn't like to say. I said that I was saying it to provoke him but that this was the way I felt. I told him that if I had the power to select who should be in or out of the doctoral program, that I would wash him out of the program, since I couldn't possibly imagine what he would ever do with a Ph.D. I got no reaction from him at all.

* * *

Joanne was a very attractive divorcee and an experienced teacher. She seemed quite open and emotional as she talked about her relationship with her ex-husband and her father. Her father had always wanted a boy so she had never been a satisfactory child for him. When she got married, her father didn't like her husband. When she got divorced, her father became good friends with her former husband and *even* her former husband's new wife. Her father was still critical of Joanne even after the divorce. The oppressively high standards held by her father had a detrimental effect not only on Joanne but on her two sons. Joanne had never been able to sit down with her father and tell him how she felt because she was too intimidated by him.

In discussing her situation and how she might handle it, Carl suggested that he would role-play Joanne, and asked her to role-play her father. Carl simply expressed the frightened but resentful and disappointed feelings she had been expressing in the group, and

Joanne, as her father, gradually became more understanding. She (as herself) resolved to do something about approaching her father, since she now realized that an expression of her feelings was possible.

In the second weekend Joanne was again in my group. She seemed to show much more sensitivity than she had before and seemed much more accurate in her comments than I had remembered her being in the previous group. She said that she had not as yet spoken to her father but that when the time was right she would, and I feel quite confident that this will take place.

*   *   *

The next person in the group I want to mention is Joe. Joe was a quiet, serious-minded teacher, with a tense, quivering voice. He was not very active in the group and seemed to be fearful and careful. In fact one of the main things he talked about was the fact that he played the horses and was afraid of winning heavily because he might receive notoriety for this. He received very little prodding and remained rather inactive for the entire weekend.

During the second encounter group with the same leader, the picture changed somewhat for Joe:

Joe seemed to start out in much the same manner as he had before. I remember telling him that to me he seemed half dead. The change that followed seemed rather remarkable. He got color in his cheeks, his voice lost much of its quiver and he became quite active in the group and also quite personal. He was able to talk about himself and some of the problems that he had with his wife who seemed frustrated at not having a more active role in his life. He showed compassion for other people in the group and was able to ask the group for advice. The group responded by offering a number of alternate suggestions, although no outright advice was ever given. In the last session he was the only one who was really quite personal, even with Carl being there. He told me after the group was over that he had voted for a change in group facilitators but now he was glad that it had turned out he was in the same group with me again. The feeling was mutual.

*   *   *

Al was in my group. Al was a retired Army man and now a teacher. In the early hours of the group he was extremely talkative on a superficial level and Carl got exasperated. Al finally said, "I feel I'm talking too much, but I don't know what to do." Carl said, "You could button your lip." It took about twenty minutes for Al to react with hurt to this, and Carl ended up apologizing (although I wished he hadn't).

It seemed as though Al went through the whole experience of the two weekends relatively untouched and somewhat puzzled by what it was all about.

*   *   *

Steve, an energetic teacher with administrative experience, spoke with great difficulty and tenseness about a problem he did not feel free to explain fully. He said he lived with the greatest anxiety all the time because his wife had indicated recently that she knew what he had been doing. He had connected her knowing with a statement she had made a year earlier in which she had said, concerning friends of theirs, that she knew exactly what she would do were she in the position of the wife. She would publicly expose the husband. Now Steve lived in the greatest fear that his wife was going to expose him and ruin his career. I suggested that more often than not, a greater degree of openness in a case like this would be beneficial.

Steve returned to the group the following morning visibly relieved. The change in his attitude was very marked. He had spoken to his wife the night before, albeit in a very guarded manner. She had replied that she didn't want to talk about their problem for at least a year. Steve took this to mean that she was granting him this time to "take care of" the problem, which is exactly what he wanted. He was able at this session to talk very freely about the nature of the problem and how he envisioned solving it.

*   *   *

Paul began the second weekend group almost in tears over a problem with his school board in the district he served as superintendent. He said he could hardly wait to get to the meeting, and that he had been saving this problem to talk about in the group. He spoke very freely of it and was able to get much sympathy, understanding, and insight from the group.

As he revealed later, he had come to the first group with great misgivings and even fear. He had believed that the people in the group would do a lot of digging into a person's private affairs and a lot of attacking of individuals. After he realized that this was not going to happen, he was able to benefit from the first group and could "hardly wait" to get to the second.

*   *   *

Albert, a tense, talkative person with specialized educational training, took up considerable time in the first encounter group with highly intellectual, well thought-out, generalized statements. He seemed to feel somewhat superior to the group, and appeared to be giving them nuggets of his wisdom. When he was challenged for giving "lectures" to the group, he seemed genuinely astonished. He said "But that's what my wife is always telling me," as though he had disbelieved her, but now could not disbelieve the group. Gradually his "lecturing" approach changed to more personal reactions, with much more use of "I" and "me" in his conversations.

Albert was assigned to a different facilitator for the second weekend. He missed the first evening session. In the morning session he revealed that he had not come because of severe chest pains he experienced the evening before, a symptom he once had in the past. He was sufficiently worried to go to a doctor and had been reassured that his heart was normal. He said that he still felt *very* tense in the group, and that he guessed the chest pains were a result of his not wanting to come the night before.

Albert then talked at length of his need to be perfect. He has terrific standards and feels tremendous pressure to achieve. He said he felt great fear and anxiety about revealing in the group any aspects of himself which he considered less than perfect. He had the feeling that if the group members really knew him, they would not like him.

Several group members remarked how different he seemed in this group as compared with the last one, and how much they did like him, especially now that they knew more of him as a real person. In fact, the more he revealed himself, the more they felt close to him.

Later in the group, Albert said in his typical jesting way that he hoped the group would not be offended if he went to sleep. He felt completely relaxed, as though he had had a huge dose of tranquilizers, and that his sleeping would be a compliment to the group for helping him, and not an insult!

MY ROLE IN THE COURSE AND IN THE GROUPS

I find it very easy to give freedom to a group. I believe this is because, over a period of nearly forty years, I have discovered it to be very rewarding to give freedom to clients, to discussion groups, to classes, to staff groups, and to encounter groups. I recognize that for others this can be a risky and dangerous thing to do, and that consequently they cannot, genuinely, give this degree of freedom. To these I would suggest: experiment by giving that degree of freedom which you genuinely and comfortably can, and observe the results.

Actually, ten or fifteen years ago, I probably would have given the group even more freedom, presenting them with the opportunity (and the task) of constructing the whole course. I have learned that this arouses a great deal of anxiety, and a great deal of frustration and anger directed toward me. ("We came to learn from you!" "You're *paid* to be our teacher!" "We can't plan the course. We don't know the field.") I am not sure that this resentment is necessary. Consequently, whether out of cowardice or wisdom, I have come to provide enough limits and requirements, which can be *perceived* as structure, so that students can comfortably start to work. It is only as the course progresses that they realize that each "requirement" separately, and all of them together, are simply different ways of saying, "Do exactly what you wish to do in this course, and say and write exactly what *you* think and feel." But freedom seems less frustrating and anxiety-laden when it is presented in somewhat conventional sounding terms as a series of "requirements." On the other hand, if I were to have this same group of individuals in another course, I am sure none would be frightened if I simply started out by saying, "Now we're here. What is it that we would like to do which would enrich our personal and intellectual learning?"

In an encounter group I love to give, both to the participants and to myself, the maximum freedom of expression. This attitude usually gets across fairly quickly because it is real. I do *trust* the group, and find it often wiser than I in its reactions to particular situations. Thus it was a new experience for me to find that by participating for only a portion of the time in each of the three groups (six groups considering the fact that they were reshuffled for the second weekend) I was not always able to have this impact. In some groups I was perceived as an inhibiting threat, even though in others I was seen as a freeing participant. For me this is an argument for keeping the group and the facilitator constant.

THE FAVORABLE CONTEXT

I can hear some of my readers saying, "In a permissive and unconventional context, and with three congenial co-workers, of course you can grant freedom in this way. But I'd like to see you do it in *my* situation." I grant that this was an unusually favorable context for such a course. But I challenge the conclusion.

I—and others whom I know—have carried on very similar courses in much less favorable settings. For example, I have taught one section of a large course, in which the curriculum and text were specified, and in which all sections of the course were to be evaluated by the same examination, which I had had no part in formulating. There were, in that course, just as many excitedly learning individuals, just as many individual projects, as in the course described in these pages. Judging by my own experience and that of others, the *amount* of freedom which can be given to the group is not particularly important. The class and the instructor may have to accept the constrictions of a rigid examination, of a pre-set curriculum and text, and other limitations. What is important is that within these limits the freedom that is given is *real*, is not hesitantly or guardedly given by the leader, and is perceived as real by the students. Then—even in a seemingly narrow sector of their work—they can experience freedom of choice, freedom of expression, freedom to be.

To turn to another aspect, I was undoubtedly fortunate in having two post-doctoral fellows who were eager to assist, and a student in the course who had worked with me previously. But if I had not had this good fortune I could have achieved much the same goals in several alternative ways. I could have divided the group in two, with one group each weekend meeting as a leaderless group while I met with the other. I could have chosen two members of the class and given them a half-day of training in group facilitation, and then used myself, first with one group and then with the other. With such a small amount of training such facilitators would not undertake the kind of strongly interventive procedures which are dangerous, but would simply provide a minimum feeling of structure in the group.

TRUST

For me, trust is *the* important ingredient which the facilitator provides. He may also be sensitively empathic. He will, I hope, participate with his own feelings (owned as *his* feelings, not projected on the other person). He may risk himself in expressing his problems and his weaknesses. He may suggest to the group procedures he believes might be helpful. But underlying all of these behaviors is the trust he feels in the capacity of the group to develop the human potential which exists in that group and its separate members. This trust is something which cannot be faked. It is not a technique. The facilitator can only be as trusting as he in fact is. Thus he may be able to trust, and give freedom, in a very restricted area in which he is not risking much. But if it is real and complete, even in a narrow area, it will have a facilitating effect upon the process of the group.

MY OVERALL IMPRESSIONS FROM
THE WEEKEND ENCOUNTER GROUPS

With the exception of two men who seemed relatively untouched by the group experiences, I believe every member of the course found them helpful, in varying degrees. To let down your guard somewhat, to let others know you in ways you do not ordinarily reveal, was a very meaningful experience for many individuals. They found they were liked even better when their weaknesses, as well as their strengths, were openly known. It was an awesome thing for some people to discover that individuals who appeared competent, confident, and without conflicts, actually carried a heavy burden of both personal and circumstantial problems. This made them more human and likeable. It also put one's own problems in a different perspective. Another noteworthy element was the degree of interpersonal involvement and communication which developed. A number had "known" each other in several previous courses, but this kind of acquaintance bore no resemblance to the closeness which was formed in the groups. Finally there was much risk-taking by the individual, both in expressing himself in a less guarded way, and in trying out new modes of interpersonal behavior, not only in the group but outside.

These are my own impressions of the effects of the weekends.

The course members voice their own views in the section which follows.

STUDENT REACTIONS

I wish to let the students speak for themselves about the course. There are available to me hundreds of pages of the papers they wrote, the comments on their readings, personal notes to me, and general reactions to the course. Out of this wealth of material I have tried to select many reactions which would meet the following criteria:

1.) None should be specifically identifying.

2.) They should include a wide range of reactions—cognitive, subjective, and behavioral.

3.) Although only a sampling of positive reactions can be given, my professional conscience demands (perhaps unreasonably) that any negative reactions should be included almost in toto.

It seemed best to cluster these reactions under a number of headings, partly to give coherence to the presentation, partly to avoid identification. Thus a given student may provide statements under several of the headings, and rarely are there more than two or three paragraphs in sequence from one student. While this sacrifices something of the unique pattern of reaction in each student, it helps to avoid identification, and gives perhaps a better picture of the overall group response to the experience of this course.

My reason for including such a large number of student statements was to impress upon the reader the fact that these are not a few handpicked, biased quotations but the nearest approximation I can achieve to a cross section of the total reaction, the only bias being that the very few negative statements are quoted almost 100%, while the positive statements are only a selection from a larger number.

REACTIONS TO THE READING

Class members made good use of the reading list, some confining their reading to the list; others using it simply as a springboard. One of the latter said to me at one of the weekends, "I've gotten interested in Erich Fromm. I read the book of his which was listed, and now I've been reading almost everything he has written. I feel quite guilty about this." (This is what "education" does to students!) I replied, "Do you really feel guilty about following a vital interest of your own?" "Well, I think we are supposed to acquire breadth." My reply was, "I'll take a chance on that."

How much did class members read? Since they read portions of some books, skimmed others, and read some books three times, an accurate answer is impossible. From going over the reading lists I would say that a modest estimate is that the students averaged eight to ten books apiece in a twelve-week quarter, and some read *much more* than that.

Here, then, are some of the written reactions to the experience of reading freely, in terms of one's own purposes, in the general field of the course.

> I love to read but I read slowly and rather erratically. Some books I like to read from cover to cover. With some I like to skip around. Others I read over and over. Generally speaking most courses, for me at least, do not lend themselves well to this kind of reading and I often end up feeling quite pressured, "I *must* get that book read. I haven't read chapter 10." In this course I felt no pressure at all. I really enjoyed what I read, got far more out of it than usual and found that I was not at a disadvantage because of my reading habits.

One student read most of 27 books for the course plus a number of papers. In regard to one of the books, William Barrett, *Irrational Man*, he says:

> I read this book three times at least, some parts on Kierkgaard maybe more. I have used this book as my bible, so to speak. Much of my other reading has stemmed from Barrett's suggestions— Camus, Buber, Tillich, and so forth. He even forced me to go back and read Durant's *The Story of Philosophy*, to review Plato, Aristotle, and others.

In regard to one of the papers he says:

> Read mimeographed copy available at the library. Also circulated among the faculty at my school. A very good response in spite of some of the unorthodox suggestions in the paper. Most teach-

ers agreed with the idea of teaching as being overrated in comparison with learning.

Here are comments from other students:

I sincerely would like to read every book on the list and probably will. My one criticism would be that I have never had an opportunity to discuss these books with anyone.

*   *   *

I did not read, during the course, with the intention of keeping a record of the pages covered, pleasing the instructor, or to fulfill the "requirements" of this course. For the first time I read for my own enjoyment. I read to "put things together" for myself. I read to clarify some of my own concepts. For instance, May's *Existential Psychology* was a very didactic exposition. I needed that. Bronowski's *Science and Human Values* is to me a classic! A valuable, deep, unique experience. I have had fun trying to relate the existential inner self, monitor, or mediating structure to Wooldridge's thoroughly behaviorist description of the reticular activating system (a monitor). I am still reading . . .

*   *   *

My horizons have expanded. I had thought about values before— rather deeply at times as a result of involvement in a close church community—but I have now begun to look into specific approaches new to me: existentialism and ideas of individual writers, most of whom I hadn't read before. This intellectual growth was greatly satisfying and encouraging to me in continuing explorations.

*   *   *

I would like to have read even more but actually read more than ever before for a course and more eagerly *by far*. It was really too much fun to feel as though I expended great amounts of energy. Grading isn't relevant somehow. The *experience* is.

*   *   *

I like an article I once read of yours in which you say that "knowledge" is to "have sport with ideas." I have long loved to read someone's thesis on a subject and then look for the antithesis of that person's thinking. The resultant playing or having sport with the two and coming to my own synthesis has always been exciting. I have been challenged by this class to take this bibliography and have sport with it. This I have done.

PERSONAL REACTIONS TO THE WEEKEND ENCOUNTER GROUPS

Nearly everyone had definite, though often different, reactions to the two weekend sessions. For most it was a new and unusual experience, as is indicated in the quotations which follow.

I had always wanted to be loved, accepted, and esteemed and felt that this could only be brought about by certain values which came from others, that *I* could not rock the boat, and how *I* really felt didn't matter. In our first encounter group I felt mixed up but good when I related some of my deep personal problems, when the feedback was pleasant, when I tried to truly see myself. But I found that maybe this wasn't really me after all. Maybe there was another me who had something to say, but did he have the "right to speak up?" [He tells how he began to express his feelings and] . . . here I was truly relating to others how I was *really* feeling, actually being aware of what I was experiencing. As I write this I am becoming emotional and have very wet eyes at this moment.

I feel that I am definitely moving away from "oughts" and meeting expectations, that I don't always have to please others, that I can become myself and actually become aware of what I am experiencing, and that this isn't any crime and I do have some rights. Truly a significant change in some of my personal values. I find that I am moving more toward trusting myself though this is going to take time.

*   *   *

Originally I must admit I doubted the value of the encounter group but I honestly tried to approach it with an open mind. Now while I am still somewhat uncertain I begin to see some of the worthwhile things that can come from such encounters. On the other hand, I still question whether such a group artificially contrived is really necessary. My basic negative reaction centers on the pressure to divulge one's very personal experiences and feelings.

*   *   *

The weekend workshops were terrific. I wish there was some way to make this a continuous part of the doctoral program. I don't think it should be a requirement but available periodically to the candidate so that as problems and pressures come up we could have the opportunity to discuss and work them out in our own terms.

After telling about some of the questions raised by his reading, one student says:

It was at this point that we had our first sensitivity session for a weekend. My values withstood the session except that I became aware of how little concern I had really been feeling for others. Since that time I believe I *see* people and *hear* people more clearly.

*   *   *

For the first time in the sensitivity training group last weekend I felt safe enough to really reveal myself to the group. This was a meaningful experience for me.

*   *   *

Shall I say what really *happened*? I wonder if I want Dr. Rogers to know that I haven't resolved my questions yet. I am not certain what happened to me during this course. Would I want him to know that I am confused? . . . it goes back a few weeks to that *damned T group*. Why? Why did they get on me like that? Now don't think that I am defensive. Who's defensive? If they just understood what I meant to say . . . why did he say I was trying to teach the group? I was only . . . Hell, I'm not really like that. Am I really like that? Hey, that guy is real. I've felt that way. He seems to understand me too. I wonder if I should tell them how I *really* feel? I wonder what they'd think of me if I told them about . . . Man, I need to say it. You know it kinda hurts. (I didn't know it bothered me that much. Can I trust them? Can I trust people?) Why did I say that? It felt good. I needed to say that. Boy, they understood. He has felt that way too. Say, *I like this group*—I feel close to these people. Are all people like this? Why can't I be open all the time? Why am I so fearful? Why do I need acceptance? I would like to trust more.

*   *   *

Since the last workshop encounter I have been turned on and have been experiencing myself, my wife and children, and my work, in a clearer, more involved, more meaningful way. Ideas, thoughts, emotional insights keep bubbling up and influencing me toward freer, more open behavior in these areas. I attribute these changes to my workshop experiences.

*   *   *

I became tellingly aware of the fact that I have been trying to *prove* myself. I don't have to prove myself. All I really have to do, that is, my only responsibility, is to *be* myself. I value myself more as a person—my dependency needs, my anxieties, my proving needs, my inadequacies, and limitations, as well as my warm feelings for others, my knowledge, my competencies, my worthiness, my potential.

* * *

I have always hoped that people in groups would give me feedback on how they react to me. I have had the feeling for so long that they never do because they are afraid I couldn't take it. I haven't had the courage to ask for it but in our last session I did and the group responded. They said so many positive things! They liked me! And I believed them! What a great feeling! So, not only do I have more confidence in possibilities for myself in the professional world but I *personally* feel liked and likeable!

* * *

As I reflect on the experiences afforded me in the small groups I realize that I had developed a kind of channelled perception; that is, I was filtering out those things that didn't fit my idea of the way the thing "ought to be."

Small group members helped me to see my irrational behavior, not only by pointing it out to me, but by being open and interacting with each other. . . . As the group sessions drew to a close I began to experience a good feeling. I had developed a desire to face my problem in a positive way and in so doing I have since learned that what I had feared for five years really wasn't so important.

Since the basic encounter group experiences I believe that I can learn to accept myself. I am well aware that this will take time but I feel certain that as I learn to be less critical of myself I will be happier. I am sure that this course has helped me in this regard.

* * *

One area I [it is a man speaking] have come to appreciate this quarter and one in which I did some reading, and a point dealt with in small group discussion, is sex and sexual behavior. Frankly, I am amazed at my general ignorance in this area.

One indication that I achieved something, at least from my point of view, is that I finally have been able to come to grips with a problem that has hurt and haunted me for many years. Regardless of the grade, I shall remain happy in the thought that a solution seems to be near.

* * *

I have changed a number of my values and as a result I feel a number of my attitudes have also undergone a change. I know that I have become a better person through my participation in our sensitivity group. The experience has been a moving one for me. At this point I can't keep from being enthusiastic about the tremendous possibilities that sensitivity holds for the field of education. The changes that I have experienced were not brought about through external means. They came from within me and something caused me to become intrinsically motivated to learn more about myself.

Before our first meeting as a group I was apprehensive. I was not accustomed to an unstructured environment when participating as a member of a group. The central-most thought in my mind was concerned with what I should discuss. As I became involved in the first session I can remember that I felt self-conscious. The others began talking on an intellectual level. I listened and participated at the same level. Our facilitator did not push us or pry. At this point I became more comfortable. Someone in the group then said something that I sensed he wouldn't say to another person. I can't remember what the topic was, but I do remember that I felt close to that person at that point.

We *listened*, and here was that thing that I had been reading about —*empathy*. (I realized this when I began to think about the session while on the way home.) During the sessions we shared ideas, feelings, and ourselves. No one received an answer to his problem or conflict but from my association it seems easier to reach satisfaction within myself . . . When I revealed a feeling, the group did not react in such a way as to cause me to rationalize or resort to any other form of defense. They accepted me just as I was. I simply had a feeling of well being and that I was among friends that could be trusted.

Speaking of his dependence on others in making decisions one student says:

I discussed this with the group and as a result I don't seem to worry about approval now. This does not mean that I no longer care what others think. I am able to act with a greater inner freedom. I know that if I have done my best and considered all facets of the problem that confronts me I can make the decision with less wear and tear on myself.

Speaking of the problem he has had about long-term goals, the same person says:

I couldn't develop long term goals for my life. I felt that I must be different than most of the individuals I know. . . . I have discovered that others have the same problem that I have had. Through the process of discussion I no longer feel that long term goals are necessary. I realize that I have always had short term goals . . . Short term goals are the most suitable for me as they seem to fit my needs.

A NEGATIVE REACTION

The quotation which follows is probably the most deeply negative statement received:

My negative reaction to the course is that for me personally it is a depressing experience to see how many truly deeply troubled people we have in our group, some with personal troubles so deep and complicated that I fear they will never overcome them. Of course, on the other hand, I can be thankful that I am not in their shoes but somehow this feeling doesn't seem to overcome the concern that these weekends generated in me, for the many troubled people we have drifting around as associates in this life. . . . I myself personally received no help from these group encounters . . . but I accept the fact that they are of immense value to my troubled associates.

I realized that many of these persons had grave personal problems and had really no one to turn to but this assemblage of practically complete strangers. They tended to reject the help a God would offer them and seemed incapable of developing any rapport with immediate members of their families. The result is that many of them are living now in a hell of their own creating. For these unfortunate persons I can now see a benefit offered by these basic encounter groups. . . . however, I still believe it is only a temporary assist and that permanent cure will come only after they develop an intimate rapport with their God.

PERSONAL VALUES AND THEIR CHANGING QUALITY

For many individuals in the course, personal values underwent a reappraisal. This is not surprising, considering the course title, "Values in Human Behavior." In some instances old values were retained with a fresh understanding of them. For others, there was a significant shift in the value stance. It is quite clear from the quotations which follow, taken largely from their papers, that many changes were experiential—including feelings, cognition, and behavior—not simply intellect.

For me, the first statement which follows is a peculiarly poignant and meaningful one. The writer, a man, is an experienced school principal with many years of education (or was it training?) behind him, as well as years of heavy practical responsibility. Yet it is clear that this is the first time he has ever spoken from *within* himself, *for* himself. How many people have been thus starved and deprived, for decades on end?

The opening paragraphs give the spirit which pervades his entire paper:

> As I sit at my desk to begin this paper, I have a real feeling of inner excitement. This is an experience that I have never had. For as I write I have no format to follow and I will put my thoughts down as they occur. It's almost a feeling of floating for to me it doesn't seem to really matter how you, or anyone for that matter, will react to my thoughts. Nevertheless, at the same time, I feel that you will accept them as mine regardless of the lack of style, format, or academic expression. . . . My real concern is to try to communicate with myself so that I might better understand myself.

> I guess what I am really saying is that I am writing not for you, nor for a grade, nor for a class, but for *me*. And I feel especially good about that, for this is something that I wouldn't have *dared* to do or even *consider* in the past.

> You know I guess it bothers me if others don't think well of me. . . . But I now realize that I really want people to like me *now* for what I *am*, for what I *really* am, not just for what I pretend to be.

A woman mentions that she has been embarrassed because she has regarded herself as idealistic:

> But there has been a change. Foolish, impossible, idealistic, no matter what. My beliefs and values are *mine*. With this feeling they no longer seem outlandish but very real. In turn, because they have taken on a new dimension of reality, I find I am happier keeping some, changing others.

> It occurred to me that there are many times when I do enjoy thinking only of myself and behaving accordingly as anything but idealistic. It's downright fun. This in itself is not a change for I have known this for a long time. But what is a change is that my

idealistic values are far more compatible and not really in conflict with this feeling of delight I have in being my "off beat" self.

*   *   *

To value learning more than a position, persons more than prestige, and honesty with self more than approval of others is what I want as a value system. I honestly cannot evaluate my development toward this goal.

*   *   *

One value that really did seem to "pop out" has been the manner in which I regard death, or maybe my life span. . . . All of a sudden there it was, a feeling of foreverness. I actually said it out loud on my way home—I am going to live forever! This is not a feeling of immortality but more like "always." My life is *always* going to *be* for me.

Before it seemed to me that having positive direction, knowing where I was going, what I believed in, who I am, was maybe not so much *a* value but valuable to me. Now about the only thing I am *sure* of is that I don't know the answers to these questions. I can look, though, and find answers for what *is* right now, but if I regard these answers as positive final ones it seems to me I shut the door. How perfectly horrible! That to me would be an end and I can see no end to living.

*   *   *

As a result of this course I do not feel that my basic values have changed, yet I do feel a greater sense of awareness of others and a greater insight into myself and the effect of my actions on them. I have found that frequently the things I say are not interpreted as I meant them to be, and my feelings as expressed, rather than resulting in acceptance, are met with resistance or even antagonism by others. Perhaps this is a result of lack of awareness of the feelings of others in my attempts to be true to myself.

Additionally, I am more aware that I have used my wife and family as a sounding board, becoming so engrossed in my own problems that I have not been aware of them and their needs. This awareness has resulted in my efforts to meet and accept them as a greater part of myself and my living rather than to view them as something outside my basic concerns or my job and its future. Frequently I have said, "I am doing it for you. On my success lies our future." Yet in so doing I have cut them out to a certain extent from my present living.

Thus my value "to thine own self be true" still holds but this course has resulted in my realization that I must be aware of others and their feelings. I feel that I am more aware and am behaving accordingly. I still have far to go even though the first steps have been taken.

*   *   *

Values are a state of being, a way of saying who I am. Of the many shades which define myself, the two strongest which continually recur are these: I am a mother and I am a turned-on, swinging, lover of life.

The mother part of me expresses itself positively in a powerful appreciation and love of my own as well as other children. . . . The turned-on life lover part of me is a very beautiful, free, creatively expressive, inquisitive being, seldom fully let out but often present in the impetus for many fantasies.

During the course two important value surges took place in me. The first was after the first weekend group. At that time I lived in a strong sense of peace and contentment with myself as mother of my own children and guardian of others. This was such a powerful certainty that I said at one point, "so this is what it means to be yourself."

The strength of the feeling had subsided somewhat by the time of the second weekend meeting, and I was again bursting inside with the urge to release the free, life-loving spirit. This did happen for me in the group and by Saturday night I was exhausted but feeling blithely in love with being alive. What seems to have occurred is not only a pulling of the stopper on my urges to embrace life as it comes and is, but also a synthesis of these two equally important existential values in me. I could feel good about being a turned-on, swinging, life-loving mother.

One participant tells how by the time of the second sensitivity group he was going through a second level of change:

I . . . was wondering why I was still so uneasy, settled down inside in some ways that I had never felt before, but still emotionally off balance and full of undefined doubts.

He began to realize that part of his trouble was that he had been working for some years on the development of a theory of a basic integrating role for the individual and that the instructor seemed to assume there should be no roles. This was deeply disturbing both intellectually and emotionally. He says:

> It struck me with full intensity in the group as I sat there half listening, watching you, going back over what I had read and understood, that you really did mean a *rolelessness* and that this could be a deeper or final growth for a person. That the basic integrating role could be an intermediate step before reaching this roleless state where the individual could finally emerge and *be* the same to everyone and that this would truly be a wonderful condition for man. . . . There is still much for me to work out, but I have never felt better about my research and at the other level have achieved some real insight on my own aggravating hostilities.

Speaking about values in the area of sex, a wife says:

> When it comes to questions on the sex life of married people I get down to me. The problem which we discussed too briefly in our group remains for me: How friendly can I be with other men? I enjoy men's company, but it is sometimes too easy to sort of slip from friendliness to flirting. I want to be admired by men, but I don't want to hurt my husband or my marriage. How to act? I guess our groups tended to increase the problem because of the close relationships that developed. I suspect that situation ethics *can* be used as an excuse for some actions, though hopefully an attitude of love would minimize such possibilities. Though this area has never been a severe problem for me, it has been helpful to focus on it in some of my reading and thinking and to have become more aware of the problems that do exist and need more understanding.

*   *   *

This brings me to the concept of "glimpsing" which has a lot of meaning for me. In a state of powerful love of self such as I experienced after the second weekend group, I glimpsed what it would be like in this sort of state all the time. I imagined what it would mean in my day-to-day relationships to be as open and loving, peaceful and whole, as I did feel for a while. In the readings that I did for the course, for example, I caught a meaningful glimpse in Polanyi and Koch of the idea of personal knowledge and for a moment I was able to live, myself, in the world with that concept of knowledge mine. These personal experiences, these glimpses, however brief, become a memory which I value in the sense that I hold them as goals.

BEHAVIOR CHANGES OUTSIDE THE CLASS

It would not be unreasonable to assume that any changes in behavior would scarcely be discernible until *after* the course was over. Surprisingly, however, a considerable portion of the group reportedly immediate and current changes in their behavior. A number of these are in family relationships, but behavior in the educational situation also appears to be undergoing change.

A psychologist states:

> At work, insights continue to bubble up and first I became acutely aware of the intense anxiety that a person experiences while discussing problems with an untrusting person. Also, I became aware from this what my role as psychologist or therapist did to the relationship. (I have since moved my desk up against a wall in order to eliminate it as a barrier between me and the client.) I now find myself better able to get through to the person, better able to reach his own feelings, his self, since I have a better awareness of my own.

As a result of her reading, a teacher and mother says:

> I am looking at my relationship to my children in a newish thoughtful way. I really am seeing some things differently and acting differently. I have a greater *awareness* of individuality in my children (in spite of the fact that I have always believed in this) and desire at least some freedom to allow them to be more themselves instead of what I want or think others want. I am able more often, somehow, to put myself inside my children's skins momentarily. I expect to have ups and downs here but I know I won't quite go back to where I was before.

*   *   *

> I value my wife more as a person. I realize now that in trying to prove what a big man I am I added to her frustrations by cutting her off from being able to fulfill her helping needs, her desires to be helpful to me. I need and want her help, her nourishment, her warmth, sometimes even her anger and frustration (this is hard for her to understand), and her love. The love I experienced in the workshop released in me these feelings toward my wife. I have tried to be more open with her as well as my children, particularly the older girls from whom I had withdrawn. The increased value I have placed on *my* life I have placed upon *theirs*.

*   *   *

My ideas on teaching have changed quite a lot in just this last year and especially this quarter. I fear I am not a free enough person—yet—to allow quite the freedom for students that I would like. But I surely have some ideas and would like a chance to work at them. . . . I know I will try them when I have the chance.

*   *   *

I brought much of the learning in the small groups to bear on the problems facing my wife and myself. While we have a long way to go, at least we have made progress in terms of accepting each other for what we are. Prior to this course both of us had images for each other, and neither one of us could possibly meet or satisfy the requirements imposed by the images.

*   *   *

A good thing just happened to me that I am beginning to like about myself—keeping my mouth shut and ears open. Being quiet I hear a lot more and learn. I learned this in our two group experiences. It has made me much more accepting and understanding of students.

*   *   *

This [expression of feeling] carried on during the next three weeks but I wasn't so sure I liked this "new" guy. I sure wasn't about to lose friends. At first when this happened I tried to say something nice the minute I said what I truly felt, so as not to lose the person or dare let them have bad thoughts about me. But to my surprise nothing really changed. I didn't lose any friends and didn't seem to mind "speaking up" although most of this just came out and wasn't planned. I guess that I heard myself speaking from within for possibly the first time. This was quite a dramatic experience for me. . . .

I know that with my children I am trying to be a better father. I have changed my ideas as to some of the things that I thought were important in the raising of children. I can't give my children my thoughts. I have profited from listening to the mistakes made by others. I have heard these things before but they never made the impression on me that they now have. Why, I can't say unless it is because I was truly emotionally involved with the people in the group.

A school principal states:

My staff meeting Tuesday was truly significant as I was able to relate to the staff how I really felt. Many told me afterwards that they were very surprised and impressed and wanted to applaud, not because I had said anything so different, but it was the way I said it. I have had various teachers in my office daily who have wanted to relate to me and state they now find me more accepting than ever. . . . I feel that life has so much more meaning.

*   *   *

I have already started incorporating some of what I have learned into my teaching methods and relationships with my groups of students in sociology classes. I already have a response from the students that this change in method is for the better.

*   *   *

I like your method of evaluation. It's the best that I ever experienced. I have since used this method in the classes I teach.

*   *   *

Part of the real value of the course for me was the resulting deep friendships made with other doctoral students, some of whose value systems differ from mine. For these experiences and for all the growth that has taken place I am deeply grateful.

One discovery I have made lately is that as I value myself more highly, I also value others more highly. Consequently, I have been more able to put into practice these ideas that I have held for a number of years. What this says as far as this course goes is that my basic ideas have not changed but my ability to put them into practice has been increased.

*   *   *

As a result of this class I believe I have made a start at attempting to match more closely my experiencing, awareness, and communication. I think two examples of my behavior during the past month will serve to illustrate this. [His second illustration is as follows:] In my relationship with my wife there are a few things which she does that arouse a great deal of hostility in me. In the past I have usually set about to roundly condemn her when she exhibits these behaviors with the end result being a lot of ruffled feathers and little or nothing accomplished in the way of reducing my hostility. These ruffled feathers were usually smoothed over by me by an apology from less than sincere motives. Recently she behaved in such a way that I almost became violent with her. Instead of condemning her, I tried to express the way her behavior had made me feel. Although this brought the usual ruffled feathers at the beginning, by the time we retired for the evening we seemed to have reached an understanding which had not existed before. The feathers were no longer ruffled, and our relationship had definitely increased in warmth. During this time I was aware of the clean and satisfied feeling that I had experienced.

A school administrator says:

I worked with a new church group in a radically different way. I tried to be open, empathic, and accepting. I abandoned the role of an impartial moderator or a domineering leader in order to become a facilitator for the group. The results were fantastic. I discovered a new way of being with groups by just being myself. I came to realize the valuable contributions that others make when I give them the opportunity to tell me how they feel. I have continued this work with the church. It has been a deeply satisfying experience. I think I will be a different kind of principal next year because of this experience.

THE CRITERIA FOR SELF-EVALUATION AND THE GRADE

For me, and for most of the members of the class, grades in a course of this type are absurd. But the members worked honestly at the task, though one student simply refused, saying, "A grade for such a course as this cheapens it for me." I gave him an "A" on the basis of his work.

The majority of the group gave themselves an "A" grade, which in almost every instance I felt was thoroughly justified by the reading and thinking done, or the personal insights gained, or the behavioral changes made, or a combination of these. Some assigned themselves a "B." One student asked me to choose between an "A" and a "B" for him. I chose the latter, because I felt he had not made full use of his potentiality in the course. In another instance I felt uncomfortable about the "A" a student had given himself. I told him of my questions and doubts, but said that if he would contact me after thinking it over, I would give him whatever grade he thought he deserved, because he knew the situation better than I. He phoned after a couple of days to say that he, too, had vacillated, but decided that "B" was a more accurate evaluation.

The following quotations suggest some of the criteria and some of the thinking which entered into this matter of self-evaluation:

I enjoyed doing the papers but I must say that I had some qualms about naming the grade I think is appropriate. I feel it should be optional. I can't always tell how much I grow in a course. I'm too close to it to be objective. I have often thought that it would be a good idea to hold grades for two or three months and then do the evaluating when the student and maybe even the professor can be more objective. I think I would be able to tell you more accurately what I think my grade should be six months from now.

*   *   *

Criteria. It seems necessary to give two sets of criteria:

A. criteria that are personally most meaningful:

1.) amount of satisfaction I found in the work, what I got from it;
2.) whether or not I grew, intellectually and personally;
3.) how much of myself I put into the course;
4.) am I inspired to pursue some things that came from the course?

B. criteria imposed from outside, or taken on in the past:

1.) amount and depth of reading;
2.) effort put into all phases, meetings, reading, papers;
3.) effort relative to my effort in other courses for a particular grade;
4.) effort relative to others in the class.

One man had nine criteria by which he judged himself. The first had to do with his readings. He had thought he would try to read fifteen books or papers. He says:

I absolutely astounded myself when I counted twenty-six as having been completed. This in numbers is quite significant but even more so are the various learnings which are quite pertinent to my own situation.

*   *   *

The one criterion on which I wish to base the grade that I am to receive in this course is the degree to which I have become congruent . . . congruence has provided me with feelings which I like and which enable me to like myself. These feelings I have come to value as most precious to me.

*   *   *

Criteria for judging my work in this class are as follows: a) my basic foundation in the field upon beginning the course and the position in which I find myself at its close; b) participation in class sessions and basic changes in my thinking as a result thereof; c) reading done for the course and new understandings gained; d) ability to adapt and use concepts gained from the course in my daily living.

[In regard to d) he says:]

My ability to adapt and use the concepts gained has been for me truly remarkable. There has never been a course in which I did not gain and use something, but it has been a long time since I have found and used so much from one course as I have from this one.

*   *   *

I have exceeded my expectations for the course. I have increased my knowledge to a far greater degree in the area of behavioral science than I would have done merely to meet the requirements of the course if they were developed by the instructor alone.

I have increased my self-confidence, my trust in people, and my desire to learn more.

Viewing myself in retrospect where I was eight weeks ago and where I am now, I have grown and I have changed. I feel that others can sense that something has occurred in me.

Our group has already met once outside of the scheduled sessions. We plan to meet again. What better success can any course achieve?

OVERALL REACTION TO THE COURSE

These came in response to the request for overall evaluation of the course and the instructor, and suggestions for future improvement. Some quotations from these evaluations have been given in preceding sections, but here are some additional varied responses:

My personal reaction to this course is without doubt a very positive one. In all fairness, however, I must tell you that my reaction to every course is a positive one. I feel I am a rather poor judge because I am like a sponge about my education. I can't get enough.

*   *   *

I have been more involved in terms of thought, emotion, and reading than I have experienced in any other class.

*   *   *

Most of my college work has been largely required courses with a required curriculum to follow (and to some extent memorize). I have never before had the opportunity to learn about a field of study in such a way that it had real personal meaning for me. This course offered me this chance. I took it. I roamed the field reading those books that had meaning for me. I explored, not with the pressure of reports and examinations, but with an inner pressure to find out and learn more. The really interesting outcome for me is that now that the course is ending, I am just beginning. . . . Most important to me is that I have gained an inner desire and commitment to continue growing. . . . Perhaps I didn't cover as much material as I would have under pressure but that which I did cover had much more impact upon my behavior. I felt that I was able to take some time to think about what I had read and see how the various ideas related to my life. I suppose my only criticism for the course is sincere regret that it is now ended. But to that I can honestly add that for me it has just begun.

*   *   *

Reaction to the course: Why aren't others as exciting?

*   *   *

I have enjoyed the course and feel grateful for the opportunities to have been free to work at the rate and go in the direction that I wanted to go without pressure from an authority figure (who felt that he could better test and evaluate what I had done than I could). I have felt the only person I could fail was myself. I have appreciated the trust involved in the assignment of my own grade. This class has been a welcome relief as well as a challenge; in fact, I have never been more challenged. The motivation to study came from within and was not imposed. I *felt* the *need* to reciprocate that trust in some way.

*   *   *

Of all the courses I have ever taken I can think of none even closely approximating the value of this one. I have changed and *I know* I have changed! What I have read and what I have experienced is *an integral part of me*, and I will build upon it. In terms of my own way of looking at things this course has just begun for me. I will be taking it for many years to come! On the basis of my own criteria, judged in the light of my own conscience, I would have to give myself the strongest "A" I have ever received.

*   *   *

I was at first disconcerted to find that although the topic of the course related to values, there was very little discussion of what values actually are. However, upon completing the course and experiencing the changes which had occurred in my own behavior, I came to realize that defining values was not the intent of the course. I was then aware of the fact that the important thing to me was not so much what values were but that the valued aspects of my life had changed in definite ways.

*   *   *

I have never I think gotten such joy and satisfaction from a course. I simply gobbled up *everything*, the class sessions, the reading, the relationships that developed.

*   *   *

The course was a rich and valuable experience for me. I feel that I am a better educator, a better student, a better parent, but most of all a better person because of this class.

WHAT WAS LEARNED?

It is obviously quite impossible to summarize in any adequate way the total impact of the course upon the students. Yet from reading all that they turned in—reports, reactions, personal letters (which I have tried fairly to sample in the foregoing section) I do have certain impressions.

In the first place it seems clear that when students perceive that they are free to follow their own goals, most of them invest more of themselves in their effort, work harder, and retain and use more of what they have learned, than in conventional courses.

One deficiency in this course (being corrected in plans for the future) is that students did not have sufficient opportunity to discuss the cognitive-personal learnings which they had gained from their readings. The gains from independent study are impressive, but they wished to *discuss* these ideas also. They valued the weekend groups so much as a personal experience that they did not wish to use that time for exchanging views about what they had personally gained from the reading. Clearly some intermediate type of experience—a dialogue, a seminar interchange—is needed in addition.

From the encounter groups, one of the themes which emerges again and again in different contexts is that the individual gains not only a better understanding of, but a deeper *acceptance* of, himself. The faults and deficiencies and weaknesses which he has hidden so carefully from others are not only no longer concealed, but prove to be a basis for a greater responsiveness and warmth from others. Most surprising of all to the person is the learning that when he accepts these imperfections, they often become either assets to his functioning or springboards for future development, or both.

Another learning is that when the person accepts *himself*, he is much more free to hear and understand and come close to the other. So we find more understanding and closer relationships to spouses, children, co-workers, and fellow students, growing out of this self-acceptance.

An element which recurs quite frequently is that in the climate of psychological safety and trust which develops in the group, individuals can accept and use constructively both negative and positive feedback from other participants. They can take in, believe , and utilize such different reports as that they are irrational, intellectualizing, or lovable.

One aspect of the learning which stands out is that it is immediately translated into behavior. One does not learn *about* family adjustments; he begins to behave differently with his spouse and his children. One does not learn *about* innovation in education; he begins to behave differently with his students or his staff. One does not learn *about* the value of expressing feelings and personal meanings; he does just that both in and outside of the group.

Another learning has to do with the sharply different criteria which individuals utilize in evaluating their work and themselves. The usual iron mold of evaluation into which we try to fit everyone oppears even more ridiculous in the light of these facts.

A sad aspect of the learning is that even in these mature professional people, freedom to think, to feel, to express, to behave, to be, has been almost entirely absent from their lives. It is for many a new experience.

These are some of the themes that I have gleaned from a careful study of the student products, and from observations of the encounter groups. To me they all involve examples of *significant* learning.

CONCLUSION

I have tried to present my own conduct of a recent course in sufficient detail that the reader may form his own picture of the methods and the process, and also his own conclusions as to the outcomes, intellectual and personal. To me it constitutes one more bit of evidence, to be added to the preceding chapters, revealing the events which occur when students are *trusted* to *learn*.

part II

Creating a Climate of Freedom

Introduction to Part II

For the educator who finds himself "turned on" by the examples of freedom to learn which formed Part I, there still remain the questions of the qualities which promote such freedom among students, the methods which might be used to facilitate such learning. It is my hope that this second portion of the book will suggest some possible answers.

Chapter 4 could all be summed up in a beautiful statement by Martin Buber, who says the good teacher ". . . must be a really existing man and he must be really present to his pupils; he educates through contact. Contact is the primary word of education." The attitudes which help a facilitator to be really present to his students, really in contact with them, are discussed here.

Chapter 5 is not intended to be more than a brief survey of some of the many methods which a facilitator of freedom in learning may wish to choose. If I had had more direct experience in various levels of education, I might have been able to present a much longer list. But since every educator must choose his own style, develop his own methods, I make no apology for the limited number of methods described.

Part II, then, is for that person who wants to know "How can I move toward becoming more encouraging of a freedom to learn on the part of my students?"

4

The Interpersonal Relationship
in the Facilitation of Learning

Though it may be considered unseemly for me to say so, I like this chapter very much, because it expresses some of the deepest convictions I hold regarding those who work in the educational field. The essence of it was first presented as a lecture at Harvard University, but that essence has been revised and enlarged for this book.[1]

I wish to begin this chapter with a statement which may seem surprising to some and perhaps offensive to others. It is simply this: Teaching, in my estimation, is a vastly over-rated function.

Having made such a statement, I scurry to the dictionary to see if I really mean what I say. Teaching means "to instruct." Personally I am not much interested in instructing another in what he should know or think. "To impart knowledge or skill." My reaction is, why not be more efficient, using a book or programmed learning? "To make to know." Here my hackles rise. I have no wish to *make* anyone know something. "To show, guide, direct." As I see it, too many people have been shown, guided, directed. So I come to the conclusion that I *do* mean what I said. Teaching is, for me, a relatively unimportant and vastly overvalued activity.

But there is more in my attitude than this. I have a negative reaction to teaching. Why? I think it is because it raises all the wrong questions. As soon as we focus on teaching the question arises, what shall we teach? What, from our superior vantage point, does the other person need to know? I wonder if, in this modern world, we are justified in the presumption that we are wise about the future and the young are foolish. Are we *really* sure as to what they should know? Then there is the ridiculous question of coverage. What shall the course cover? This notion of coverage is based

---

1 This chapter is a revised version of a presentation first published in *Humanizing Education*, ed. R. Leeper, ASCD, NEA, 1967. Copyright © by the Association for Supervision and Curriculum Development, NEA.

on the assumption that what is taught is what is learned; what is presented is what is assimilated. I know of no assumption so obviously untrue. One does not need research to provide evidence that this is false. One needs only to talk with a few students.

But I ask myself, "Am I so prejudiced against teaching that I find no situation in which it is worthwhile?" I immediately think of my experiences in Australia, not so long ago. I became much interested in the Australian aborigine. Here is a group which for more than 20,000 years has managed to live and exist in a desolate environment in which modern man would perish within a few days. The secret of the aborigine's survival has been teaching. He has passed on to the young every shred of knowledge about how to find water, about how to track game, about how to kill the kangaroo, about how to find his way through the trackless desert. Such knowledge is conveyed to the young as being *the* way to behave, and any innovation is frowned upon. It is clear that teaching has provided him the way to survive in a hostile and relatively unchanging environment.

Now I am closer to the nub of the question which excites me. Teaching and the imparting of knowledge make sense in an unchanging environment. This is why it has been an unquestioned function for centuries. But if there is one truth about modern man, it is that he lives in an environment which is *continually changing*. The one thing I can be sure of is that the physics which is taught to the present day student will be outdated in a decade. The teaching in psychology will certainly be out of date in 20 years. The so-called "facts of history" depend very largely upon the current mood and temper of the culture. Chemistry, biology, genetics, sociology, are in such flux that a firm statement made today will almost certainly be modified by the time the student gets around to using the knowledge.

We are, in my view, faced with an entirely new situation in education where the goal of education, if we are to survive, is the *facilitation of change and learning*. The only man who is educated is the man who has learned how to learn; the man who has learned how to adapt and change; the man who has realized that no knowledge is secure, that only the process of *seeking* knowledge gives a basis for security. Changingness, a reliance on *process* rather than upon static knowledge, is the only thing that makes any sense as a goal for education in the modern world.

So now with some relief I turn to an activity, a purpose, which really warms me—the facilitation of learning. When I have been able to transform a group—and here I mean all the members of a group, myself included—into a community of *learners*, then the excitement has been almost beyond belief. To free curiosity; to permit individuals to go charging off in new directions dictated by their own interests; to unleash the sense of inquiry; to open everything to questioning and exploration; to recognize that everything is in process of change—here is an experience I can never forget. I cannot always achieve it in groups with which I am associated but when it is partially or largely achieved then it becomes a never-to-be-forgotten group experience. Out of such a context arise true students, real learners, creative scientists and scholars and practitioners, the kind of individuals who can live in a delicate but ever-changing balance between what is presently known and the flowing, moving, altering, problems and facts of the future.

Here then is a goal to which I can give myself wholeheartedly. I see *the facilitation of learning* as the *aim* of education, the way in which we might develop the learning man, the way in which we can learn to live as individuals in process. I see the facilitation of learning as the function which may hold constructive, tentative, changing, *process* answers to some of the deepest perplexities which beset man today.

But do we know how to achieve this new goal in education, or is it a will-o'-the-wisp which sometimes occurs, sometimes fails to occur, and thus offers little real hope? My answer is that we possess a very considerable knowledge of the conditions which encourage self-initiated, significant, experiential, "gut-level" learning by the whole person. We do not frequently see these conditions put into effect because they mean a real revolution in our approach to education and revolutions are not for the timid. But we do, as we have seen in the preceding chapters, find examples of this revolution in action.

We know—and I will briefly describe some of the evidence—that the initiation of such learning rests not upon the teaching skills of the leader, not upon his scholarly knowledge of the field, not upon his curricular planning, not upon his use of audiovisual aids, not upon the programmed learning he utilizes, not upon his lectures and presentations, not upon an abundance of books, though each of these might at one time or another be utilized as an important resource. No, the facilitation of significant learning rests upon certain attitudinal qualities which exist in the personal *relationship* between the facilitator and the learner.

We came upon such findings first in the field of psychotherapy, but increasingly there is evidence which shows that these findings apply in the classroom as well. We find it easier to think that the intensive relationship between therapist and client might possess these qualities, but we are also finding that they *may* exist in the countless interpersonal interactions (as many as 1,000 per day, as Jackson [1966] has shown) between the teacher and her pupils.

QUALITIES WHICH FACILITATE LEARNING

What are these qualities, these attitudes, which facilitate learning? Let me describe them very briefly, drawing illustrations from the teaching field.

REALNESS IN THE FACILITATOR OF LEARNING

Perhaps the most basic of these essential attitudes is realness or genuineness. When the facilitator is a real person, being what he is, entering into a relationship with the learner without presenting a front or a façade, he is much more likely to be effective. This means that the feelings which he is experiencing are available to him, available to his awareness, that he is able to live these feelings, be them, and able to communicate them if appropriate. It means that he comes into a direct personal encounter with the learner, meeting him on a person-to-person basis. It means that he is *being* himself, not denying himself.

Seen from this point of view it is suggested that the teacher can be a real person in his relationship with his students. He can be enthusiastic, he can be bored, he can be interested in students, he can be angry, he can be sensitive and sympathetic. Because he accepts these feelings as his own he has no need to impose them on his students. He can like or dislike a student product without implying that it is objectively good or bad or that the student is good or bad. He is simply expressing a feeling for the product, a feeling which exists within himself. Thus, he is a person to his students, not a faceless embodiment of a curricular requirement nor a sterile tube through which knowledge is passed from one generation to the next.

It is obvious that this attitudinal set, found to be effective in psychotherapy, is sharply in contrast with the tendency of most teachers to show themselves to their pupils simply as roles. It is quite customary for teachers rather consciously to put on the mask, the role, the façade, of being a teacher, and to wear this façade all day removing it only when they have left the school at night.

But not all teachers are like this. Take Sylvia Ashton-Warner, who took resistant, supposedly slow-learning primary school Maori children in New Zealand, and let them develop their own reading vocabulary. Each child could request one word—whatever word he wished—each day, and she would print it on a card and give it to him. "Kiss," "ghost," "bomb," "tiger," "fight," "love," "daddy"— these are samples. Soon they were building sentences, which they could also keep. "He'll get a licking." "Pussy's frightened." The children simply never forgot these self-initiated learnings. But it is not my purpose to tell you of her methods. I want instead to give you a glimpse of her attitude, of the passionate realness which must have been as evident to her tiny pupils as to her readers. An editor asked her some questions and she responded: "A few cool facts you asked me for . . . I don't know that there's a cool fact in me, or anything else cool for that matter, on this particular subject. I've got only hot long facts on the matter of Creative Teaching, scorching both the page and me" (Ashton-Warner, 1963, p. 26).

Here is no sterile façade. Here is a vital *person*, with convictions, with feelings. It is her transparent realness which was, I am sure, one of the elements that made her an exciting facilitator of learning. She doesn't fit into some neat educational formula. She *is*, and students grow by being in contact with someone who really and openly *is*.

Take another very different person, Barbara Shiel, whose exciting work in facilitating learning in sixth graders has been described earlier. She gave her pupils a great deal of responsible freedom, and I will mention some of the reactions of her students later. But here is an example of the way she shared herself with her pupils—not just sharing feelings of sweetness and light, but anger and frustration. She had made art materials freely available, and students often used these in creative ways, but the room frequently looked like a picture of chaos. Here is her report of her feelings and what she did with them.

I find it maddening to live with the mess—with a capital M! No one seems to care except me. Finally, one day I told the children . . . that I am a neat, orderly person by nature and that the mess was driving me to distraction. Did they have a solution? It was suggested there were some volunteers who could clean up . . . I said it didn't seem fair to me to have the same people clean up all the time for others—but it would solve it for me. "Well, some people like to clean," they replied. So that's the way it is (Shiel, 1966).

I hope this example puts some lively meaning into the phrases I used earlier, that the facilitator "is able to live these feelings, be them, and able to communicate them if appropriate." I have chosen an example of negative feelings, because I think it is more difficult for most of us to visualize what this would mean. In this instance, Miss Shiel is taking the risk of being transparent in her angry frustrations about the mess. And what happens? The same thing which, in my experience, nearly always happens. These young people accept and respect her feelings, take them into account, and work out a novel solution which none of us, I believe, would have suggested. Miss Shiel wisely comments, "I used to get upset and feel guilty when I became angry. I finally realized the children could accept *my* feelings too. And it is important for them to know when they've 'pushed me.' I have my limits, too" (Shiel, 1966).

Just to show that positive feelings, when they are real, are equally effective, let me quote briefly a college student's reaction, in a different course:

. . . Your sense of humor in the class was cheering; we all felt relaxed because you showed us your human self, not a mechanical teacher image. I feel as if I have more understanding and faith in my teachers now . . . I feel closer to the students too. . . .

Another says:

. . . You conducted the class on a personal level and therefore in my mind I was able to formulate a picture of you as a person and not as merely a walking textbook.

Another student in the same course:

. . . It wasn't as if there was a teacher in the class, but rather someone whom we could trust and identify as a "sharer." You were so perceptive and sensitive to our thoughts, and this made it all the more "authentic" for me. It was an "authentic" *experience*, not just a class (Bull, 1966).

I trust I am making it clear that to be real is not always easy, nor is it achieved all at once, but it is basic to the person who wants to become that revolutionary individual, a facilitator of learning.

PRIZING, ACCEPTANCE, TRUST

There is another attitude which stands out in those who are successful in facilitating learning. I have observed this attitude. I have experienced it. Yet, it is hard to know what term to put to it so I shall use several. I think of it as prizing the learner, prizing his feelings, his opinions, his person. It is a caring for the learner, but a non-possessive caring. It is an acceptance of this other individual as a separate person, having worth in his own right. It is a basic trust—a belief that this other person is somehow fundamentally trustworthy. Whether we call it prizing, acceptance, trust, or by some other term, it shows up in a variety of observable ways. The facilitator who has a considerable degree of this attitude can be fully acceptant of the fear and hesitation of the student as he approaches a new problem as well as acceptant of the pupil's satisfaction in achievement. Such a teacher can accept the student's occasional apathy, his erratic desires to explore by-roads of knowledge, as well as his disciplined efforts to achieve major goals. He can accept personal feelings which both disturb and promote learning—rivalry with a sibling, hatred of authority, concern about personal adequacy. What we are describing is a prizing of the learner as an imperfect human being with many feelings, many potentialities. The facilitator's prizing or acceptance of the learner is an operational expression of his essential confidence and trust in the capacity of the human organism.

I would like to give some examples of this attitude from the classroom situation. Here any teacher statements would be properly suspect, since many of us would like to feel we hold such attitudes, and might have a biased perception of our qualities. But let me indicate how this attitude of prizing, of accepting, of trusting, appears to the student who is fortunate enough to experience it. Here is a statement from a college student in a class with Dr. Morey Appell:

Your way of being with us is a revelation to me. In your class I feel important, mature, and capable of doing things on my own. I want to think for myself and this need cannot be accomplished through textbooks and lectures alone, but through living. I think you see me as a person with real feelings and needs, an individual. What I say and do are significant expressions from me, and you recognize this (Appell, 1959).

One of Miss Shiel's sixth graders expresses much more briefly her misspelled appreciation of this attitude: "You are a wounderful teacher period!!!"

College students in a class with Dr. Patricia Bull describe not only these prizing, trusting attitudes, but the effect these have had on their other interactions.

. . . I feel that I can say things to you that I can't say to other professors. . . . Never before have I been so aware of the other students or their personalities. I have never had so much interaction in a college classroom with my classmates. The climate of the classroom has had a very profound effect on me . . . the free atmosphere for discussion affected me . . . the general atmosphere of a particular session affected me. There have been many times when I have carried the discussion out of the class with me and thought about it for a long time.

*   *   *

. . . I still feel close to you, as though there were some tacit understanding between us, almost a conspiracy. This adds to the in-class participation on my part because I feel that at least one person in the group will react, even when I am not sure of the others. It does not matter really whether your reaction is positive or negative, it just *IS*. Thank you.

*   *   *

. . . I appreciate the respect and concern you have for others, including myself. . . . As a result of my experience in class, plus the influence of my readings, I sincerely believe that the student-centered teaching method does provide an ideal framework for learning; not just for the accumulation of facts, but more important, for learning about ourselves in relation to others. . . . When I think back to my shallow awareness in September compared to the depth of my insights now, I know that this course has offered me a learning experience of great value which I couldn't have acquired in any other way.

*   *   *

. . . Very few teachers would attempt this method because they would feel that they would lose the students' respect. On the contrary. You gained our respect, through your ability to speak to us on our level, instead of ten miles above us. With the complete lack of communication we see in this school, it was a wonderful experience to see people listening to each other and really communicating on an adult, intelligent level. More classes should afford us this experience (Bull, 1966).

As you might expect, college students are often suspicious that these seeming attitudes are phony. One of Dr. Bull's students writes:

. . . Rather than observe my classmates for the first few weeks, I concentrated my observations on you, Dr. Bull. I tried to figure out your motivations and purposes. I was convinced that you were a hypocrite. . . . I did change my opinion, however. You are not a hypocrite, by any means. . . . I do wish the course could continue. "Let each become all he is capable of being." . . . (Bull, 1966).

I am sure these examples are more than enough to show that the facilitator who cares, who prizes, who trusts the learner, creates a climate for learning so different from the ordinary classroom that any resemblance is "purely coincidental."

EMPATHIC UNDERSTANDING

A further element which establishes a climate for self-initiated, experiential learning is empathic understanding. When the teacher has the ability to understand the student's reactions from the inside, has a sensitive awareness of the way the process of education and learning seems *to the student*, then again the likelihood of significant learning is increased.

This kind of understanding is sharply different from the usual evaluative understanding, which follows the pattern of, "I understand what is wrong with you." When there is a sensitive empathy, however, the reaction in the learner follows something of this pattern, "At last someone understands how it feels and seems to be *me* without wanting to analyze me or judge me. Now I can blossom and grow and learn."

This attitude of standing in the other's shoes, of viewing the world through the student's eyes, is almost unheard of in the classroom. One could listen to thousands of ordinary classroom interactions without coming across one instance of clearly communicated, sensitively accurate, empathic understanding. But it has a tremendously releasing effect when it occurs.

Let me take an illustration from Virginia Axline, dealing with a second grade boy. Jay, age 7, has been aggressive, a trouble maker, slow of speech and learning. Because of his "cussing" he was taken to the principal, who paddled him, unknown to Miss Axline. During a free work period, he fashioned a man of clay, very carefully, down to a hat and a handkerchief in his pocket. "Who is that?" asked Miss Axline. "Dunno," replied Jay. "Maybe it is the principal. He has a handkerchief in his pocket like that." Jay glared at the clay figure. "Yes," he said. Then he began to tear the head off and looked up and smiled. Miss Axline said, "You sometimes feel like twisting his head off, don't you? You get so mad at him." Jay tore off one arm, another, then beat the figure to a pulp with his fists. Another boy, with the perception of the young, explained, "Jay is mad at Mr. X because he licked him this noon." "Then you must feel lots better now," Miss Axline commented. Jay grinned and began to rebuild Mr. X. (Adapted from Axline, 1944.)

The other examples I have cited also indicate how deeply appreciative students feel when they are simply *understood*—not evaluated, not judged, simply understood from their *own* point of view, not the teacher's. If any teacher set himself the task of endeavoring to make one non-evaluative, acceptant, empathic response per day to a student's demonstrated or verbalized feeling, I believe he would discover the potency of this currently almost non-existent kind of understanding.

WHAT ARE THE BASES OF FACILITATIVE ATTITUDES?

A "PUZZLEMENT"

It is natural that we do not always have the attitudes I have been describing. Some teachers raise the question, "But what if

I am *not* feeling empathic, do *not*, at this moment, prize or accept or like my students. What then?" My response is that realness is the most important of the attitudes mentioned, and it is not accidental that this attitude was described first. So if one has little understanding of the student's inner world, and a dislike for his students or their behavior, it is almost certainly more constructive to be *real* than to be pseudo-empathic, or to put on a façade of caring.

But this is not nearly as simple as it sounds. To be genuine, or honest, or congruent, or real, means to be this way about *oneself*. I cannot be real about another, because I do not *know* what is real for him. I can only tell—if I wish to be truly honest—what is going on in me.

Let me take an example. Early in this chapter I reported Miss Shiel's feelings about the "mess" created by the art work. Essentially she said, "I find it maddening to live with the mess! I'm neat and orderly and it is driving me to distraction." But suppose her feelings had come out somewhat differently, in the disguised way which is much more common in classrooms at all levels. She might have said, "You are the messiest children I've ever seen! You don't care about tidiness or cleanliness. You are just terrible!" This is most definitely *not* an example of genuineness or realness, in the sense in which I am using these terms. There is a profound distinction between the two statements which I should like to spell out.

In the second statement she is telling nothing of herself, sharing none of her feelings. Doubtless the children will *sense* that she is angry, but because children are perceptively shrewd they may be uncertain as to whether she is angry at them, or has just come from an argument with the principal. It has none of the honesty of the first statement in which she tells of her *own* upsetness, of her *own* feeling of being driven to distraction.

Another aspect of the second statement is that it is all made up of judgments or evaluations, and like most judgments, they are all arguable. Are these children messy, or are they simply excited and involved in what they are doing? Are they *all* messy, or are some as disturbed by the chaos as she? Do they care nothing about tidiness, or is it simply that they don't care about it every day? If a group of visitors were coming would their attitude be different? Are they terrible, or simply children? I trust it is evident that when we make judgments they are almost never fully accurate, and hence cause resentment and anger as well as guilt and apprehension. Had she used the second statement the response of the class would have been entirely different.

I am going to some lengths to clarify this point because I have found from experience that to stress the value of being real, of *being* one's feelings, is taken by some as a license to pass judgments on others, to project on others all the feelings which one should be "owning." Nothing could be further from my meaning.

Actually the achievement of realness is most difficult, and even when one wishes to be truly genuine, it occurs but rarely. Certainly it is not simply a matter of the *words* used, and if one is feeling judgmental the use of a verbal formula which sounds like the sharing of feelings will not help. It is just another instance of a façade, of a lack of genuineness. Only slowly can we learn to be truly real. For first of all, one must be close to one's feelings, capable of being aware of them. Then one must be willing to take the risk of sharing them as they are, inside, not disguising them as judgments, or attributing them to other people. This is why I so admire Miss Shiel's sharing of her anger and frustration, without in any way disguising it.

A TRUST IN THE HUMAN ORGANISM

It would be most unlikely that one could hold the three attitudes I have described, or could commit himself to being a facilitator of learning, unless he has come to have a profound trust in the human organism and its potentialities. If I distrust the human being then I *must* cram him with information of my own choosing, lest he go his own mistaken way. But if I trust the capacity of the human individual for developing his own potentiality, then I can provide him with many opportunities and permit him to choose his own way and his own direction in his learning.

It is clear, I believe, that the three teachers whose work was described in the preceding chapters rely basically upon the tendency toward fulfilment, toward actualization, in their students. They are basing their work on the hypothesis that students who are in real contact with problems which are relevant to them wish to learn, want to grow, seek to discover, endeavor to master, desire to create, move toward self-discipline. The teacher is attempting to develop a quality of climate in the classroom, and a quality of personal relationship with his students, which will permit these natural tendencies to come to their fruition.

LIVING THE UNCERTAINTY OF DISCOVERY

I believe it should be said that this basically confident view of man, and the attitudes toward students which I have described, do not appear suddenly, in some miraculous manner, in the facilitator of learning. Instead, they come about through taking risks, through *acting* on tentative hypotheses. This is most obvious in the chapter describing Miss Shiel's work, where, acting on hypotheses of which she is unsure, risking herself uncertainly in new ways of relating to her students, she finds these new views confirmed by what happens in her class. I am sure Professor Faw went through the same type of uncertainty. As for me, I can only state that I started my career with the firm view that individuals must be manipulated for their own good; I only came to the attitudes I have described, and the trust in the individual which is implicit in them, because I found that these attitudes were so much more potent in producing learning and constructive change. Hence, I believe that it is only by risking himself in these new ways that the teacher can *discover*, for himself, whether or not they are effective, whether or not they are for him.

I will then draw a conclusion, based on the experiences of the several facilitators and their students which have been included up to this point. When a facilitator creates, even to a modest degree, a classroom climate characterized by all that he can achieve of realness, prizing, and empathy; when he trusts the constructive tendency of the individual and the group; then he discovers that he has inaugurated an educational revolution. Learning of a different quality, proceeding at a different pace, with a greater degree of pervasiveness, occurs. Feelings—positive, negative, confused— become a part of the classroom experience. Learning becomes life, and a very vital life at that. The student is on his way, sometimes excitedly, sometimes reluctantly, to becoming a learning, changing, being.

THE EVIDENCE

Already I can hear mutterings: "A very pretty picture—very touching. But where is the solid evidence? How do you know?"

I would like to turn to this evidence. It is not overwhelming, but it is consistent. It is not perfect, but it is suggestive.

First of all, in the field of psychotherapy, Barrett-Lennard (1962) developed an instrument whereby he could measure these attitudinal qualities: genuineness or congruence, prizing or positive regard, empathy or understanding. This instrument was given to both client and therapist, so that we have the perception of the relationship both by the therapist and by the client whom he is trying to help. To state some of the findings very briefly it may be said that those clients who eventually showed more therapeutic change as measured by various instruments, perceived *more* of these qualities in their relationship with the therapist than did those who eventually showed less change. It is also significant that this difference in perceived relationships was evident as early as the fifth interview, and predicted later change or lack of change in therapy. Furthermore, it was found that the *client's* perception of the relationship, his experience of it, was a better predictor of ultimate outcome than was the perception of the relationship by the therapist. Barrett-Lennard's original study has been amplified and generally confirmed by other studies.

So we may say, cautiously, and with qualifications which would be too cumbersome for the present volume, that if, in therapy, the client perceives his therapist as real and genuine, as one who likes, prizes, and empathically understands him, self-learning and therapeutic change are facilitated.

Now another thread of evidence, this time related more closely to education. Emmerling (1961) found that when high school teachers were asked to identify the problems they regarded as most urgent, they could be divided into two groups. Those who regarded their most serious problems, for example, as "Helping children think for themselves and be independent"; "Getting students to participate"; "Learning new ways of helping students develop their maximum potential"; "Helping students express individual needs and interests" fell into what he called the "open" or "positively oriented" group. When Barrett-Lennard's Relationship Inventory was administered to the students of these teachers, it was found that they were perceived as significantly more real, more acceptant, more empathic than the other group of teachers whom I shall now describe.

The second category of teachers were those who tended to see their most urgent problems in negative terms, and in terms of student deficiencies and inabilities. For them the urgent problems were such as these: "Trying to teach children who don't even have the ability to follow directions"; "Teaching children who lack a desire to learn"; "Students who are not able to do the work required for their grade"; "Getting children to listen." It probably will be no surprise that when the students of these teachers filled out the Relationship Inventory they saw their teachers as exhibiting relatively little genuineness, acceptance, trust, or empathic understanding.

Hence we may say that the teacher whose orientation is toward releasing the student's potential exhibits a high degree of these attitudinal qualities which facilitate learning. The teacher whose orientation is toward shortcomings of his students exhibits much less of these qualities.

A small pilot study by Bills (1961, 1966) extends the significance of these findings. A group of eight teachers were selected, four of them rated as adequate and effective by their superiors, and also showing this more positive orientation to their problems. The other four were rated as inadequate teachers and also had a more negative orientation to their problems, as described above. The students of these teachers were then asked to fill out the Barrett-Lennard Relationship Inventory, giving their perception of their teacher's relationship to them. This made the students very happy. Those who saw their relationship with the teacher as good were happy to describe this relationship. Those who had an unfavorable relationship were pleased to have, for the first time, an opportunity to specify the ways in which the relationship was unsatisfactory.

The more effective teachers were rated higher in every attitude measured by the Inventory: they were seen as more real, as having a higher level of regard for their students, were less conditional or judgmental in their attitudes, showed more empathic understanding. Without going into the details of the study it may be illuminating to mention that the total scores summing up these attitudes vary sharply. For example, the relationships of a group of clients with their therapists, as perceived by the clients, received an average score of 108. The relationship with the four most adequate high school teachers as seen by their students, received a score of

60. The relationship of the four less adequate teachers received a score of 34. The lowest rated teacher received an average score of 2 from her students on the Relationship Inventory.

This small study certainly suggests that the teacher regarded as effective displays in her attitudes those qualities I have described as facilitative of learning, while the inadequate teacher shows little of these qualities.

A more comprehensive study, by Macdonald and Zaret, studied the recorded interactions of nine teachers with their students. They found that both teacher and student behaviors could be reliably categorized. When teacher behaviors tended to be "open"—clarifying, stimulating, accepting, facilitating—the student responses tended to be "productive"—discovering, exploring, experimenting, synthesizing, deriving implications. When teacher behaviors tended to be "closed"—judging, directing, reproving, ignoring, probing, or priming—the student responses tended to be "*re*productive"—parroting, guessing, acquiescing, reproducing facts, reasoning from given or remembered data. The pairing of these two sets of teacher-student behaviors were significantly related (Macdonald & Zaret, 1966). Though they are careful to qualify their findings, it would appear that teachers who are interested in process, and facilitative in their interactions, produce self-initiated and creative responses in their students. Teachers who are interested in evaluation of students produce passive, memorized, "eager to please" responses from their students. This evidence fits in with the thesis I have been presenting.

Approaching the problem from a different angle, Schmuck (1963) has shown that in classrooms where pupils perceive their teachers as understanding them, there is likely to be a more diffuse liking structure among the pupils. This means that where the teacher is empathic, there are not a few students strongly liked and a few strongly disliked, but liking and affection are more evenly diffused throughout the group. In a later study he has shown that among students who are highly involved in their classroom peer group, "significant relationships exist between actual liking status on the one hand and utilization of abilities, attitude toward self, and attitude toward school on the other hand" (1966, pp. 357-358). This seems to lend confirmation to the other evidence by indicating that in an understanding classroom climate where the teacher is more empathic, every student tends to feel liked by all the others, to have a more positive attitude toward himself and toward school. If he is highly involved with his peer group (and this appears probable in such a classroom climate), he also tends to utilize his abilities more fully in his school achievement.

But you may still ask, does the student actually *learn* more where these attitudes are present? Here an interesting study of third graders by Aspy (1965) helps to round out the suggestive evidence. He worked in six third-grade classes. The teachers tape-recorded two full weeks of their interaction with their students in the periods devoted to the teaching of reading. These recordings were done two months apart so as to obtain an adequate sampling of the teacher's interactions with her pupils. Four-minute segments of these recordings were randomly selected for rating. Three raters, working independently and "blind," rated each segment for the degree of congruence or genuineness shown by the teacher, the degree of her prizing or unconditional positive regard, and the degree of her empathic understanding.

The Reading Achievement Tests (Stanford Achievement) were used as the criterion. Again, omitting some of the details of a carefully and rigorously controlled study, it may be said that the children in the three classes with the highest degree of the attitudes described above showed a significantly greater gain in reading achievement than those students in the three classes with a lesser degree of these qualities.

So we may say, with a certain degree of assurance, that the attitudes I have endeavored to describe are not only effective in facilitating a deeper learning and understanding of self in a relationship such as psychotherapy, but that these attitudes characterize teachers who are regarded as effective teachers, and that the students of these teachers learn more, even of a conventional curriculum, than do students of teachers who are lacking in these attitudes.

THE EVIDENCE FROM STUDENTS

I am pleased that such evidence is accumulating. It may help to justify the revolution in education for which I am obviously hoping. But the most striking learnings of students exposed to such a climate are by no means restricted to greater achievement in the three R's. The significant learnings are the more personal ones— independence; self-initiated and responsible learning; release of creativity; a tendency to become more of a person. I can only illustrate this by picking, almost at random, statements from students whose teachers have endeavored to create a climate of trust, of prizing, of realness, of understanding, and above all, of freedom.

Again I must quote from Sylvia Ashton-Warner one of the central effects of such a climate. ". . . The drive is no longer the teacher's, but the childrens' own . . . the teacher is at last with the stream and not against it, the stream of childrens' inexorable creativeness" (Ashton-Warner, p. 93).

If you need verification of this, here is one of a number of statements made by students in a course on poetry lead (not taught) by Dr. Samuel Moon.

> In retrospect, I find that I have actually enjoyed this course, both as a class and as an experiment, although it had me quite unsettled at times. This, in itself, made the course worthwhile since the majority of my courses this semester merely had me bored with them and the whole process of "higher education." Quite aside from anything else, due mostly to this course, I found myself devoting more time to writing poetry than to writing short stories, which temporarily interfered with my writing class.

> . . . I should like to point out one thing very definite which I have gained from the course; this is an increased readiness on my part to listen to and to seriously consider the opinions of my fellow students. In view of my past attitude, this alone makes the course valuable. I suppose the real result of any course can be expressed in answer to the question, "Would you take it over again?" My answer would be an unqualified "Yes" (Moon, 1966, p. 227).

I should like to add to this several comments from Dr. Bull's sophomore students in a class in adolescent psychology. The first two are mid-semester comments.

> This course is proving to be a vital and profound experience for me. . . . This unique learning situation is giving me a whole new conception of just what learning is. . . . I am experiencing a real

growth in this atmosphere of constructive freedom . . . the whole experience is challenging.

*   *   *

I feel that the course had been of great value to me. . . . I'm glad to have had this experience because it has made me think. . . . I've never been so personally involved with a course before, especially *outside* the classroom. It has been frustrating, rewarding, enjoyable, and tiring!

The other comments are from the end of the course:

. . . This course is not ending with the close of the semester for me, but continuing. . . . I don't know of any greater benefit which can be gained from a course than this desire for further knowledge.

*   *   *

. . . I feel as though this type of class situation has stimulated me more in making me realize where my responsibilities lie, especially as far as doing required work on my own. I no longer feel as though a test date is the criterion for reading a book. I feel as though my future work will be done for what *I* will get out of it, not just for a test mark.

*   *   *

I have enjoyed the experience of being in this course. I guess that any dissatisfaction I feel at this point is a disappointment in myself, for not having taken full advantage of the opportunities the course offered.

*   *   *

I think that now I am acutely aware of the breakdown in communications that does exist in our society from seeing what happened in our class. . . . I've grown immensely. I know that I am a different person than I was when I came into that class. . . . It has done a great deal in helping me understand myself better . . . thank you for contributing to my growth.

*   *   *

My idea of education has been to gain information from the teacher by attending lectures. The emphasis and focus were on the teacher. . . . One of the biggest changes that I experienced in this class was my outlook on education. Learning is something more than a grade on a report card. No one can measure what you have learned because it's a personal thing. I was very confused between learning and memorization. I could memorize very well, but I doubt if I ever learned as much as I could have. I believe my attitude toward learning has changed from a grade-centered outlook to a more personal one.

*   *   *

I have learned a lot more about myself and adolescents in general. . . . I also gained more confidence in myself and my study habits by realizing that I could learn by myself without a teacher leading me by the hand. I have also learned a lot by listening to my classmates and evaluating their opinions and thoughts . . . this course has proved to be a most meaningful and worthwhile experience . . . (Bull, 1966).

If you wish to know what this type of course seems like to a sixth grader, let me give you a sampling of the reactions of Miss Shiel's youngsters, misspellings and all.

I feel that I am learning self abilty [sic]. I am learning not only school work but I am learning that you can learn on your own as well as someone can teach you.

*   *   *

I have a little trouble in Socail [sic] Studies finding things to do. I have a hard time working the exact amount of time. Sometimes I talk to [sic] much.

*   *   *

. . . My parents don't understand the program. My mother say's [sic] it will give me a responsibility and it will let me go at my own speed.

*   *   *

I like this plan because there is a lot of freedom. I also learn more this way than the other way you don't have to wate [sic] for others you can go at your own speed rate it also takes a lot of responsibility (Shiel, 1966).

Or let me take two more, from Dr. Appell's graduate class:

. . . I have been thinking about what happened through this experience. The only conclusion I come to is that if I try to measure what is going on, or what I was at the beginning, I have got to know what I was when I started—and I don't . . . so many things I did and feel are just lost . . . scrambled up inside. . . . They don't seem to come out in a nice little pattern or organization I can say or write. . . . There are so many things left unsaid. I know I have only scratched the surface, I guess. I can feel so many things almost ready to come out . . . maybe that's enough. *It seems all kinds of things have so much more meaning now than ever before. . . .* This experience has had meaning, has done things to me and I am not sure how much or how far just yet. I think I am going to be a better me in the fall. *That's one thing I think I am sure of* (Appell, 1963).

*   *   *

. . . You follow no plan, yet I'm learning. Since the term began I seem to feel more alive, more real to myself. I enjoy being alone as well as with other people. My relationships with children and other adults are becoming more emotional and involved. Eating an orange last week, I peeled the skin off each separate orange section and liked it better with the transparent shell off. It was juicier and fresher tasting that way. I began to think, that's how I feel sometimes, without a transparent wall around me, really communicating my feelings. I feel that I'm growing, how much, I don't know. I'm thinking, considering, pondering and learning (Appell, 1959).

I can't read these student statements—sixth grade, college, graduate level—without being deeply moved. Here are teachers, risking themselves, *being* themselves, *trusting* their students, adventuring into the existential unknown, taking the subjective leap. And what happens? Exciting, incredible *human* events. You can sense persons being created, learnings being initiated, future citizens rising to meet the challenge of unknown worlds. If only one teacher out of one hundred dared to risk, dared to be, dared to trust, dared to understand, we would have an infusion of a living spirit into education which would, in my estimation, be priceless.

THE EFFECT UPON THE INSTRUCTOR

Let me turn to another dimension which excites me. I have spoken of the effect upon the *student* of a climate which encourages significant, self-reliant, personal learning. But I have said nothing about the reciprocal effect upon the instructor. When he has been the agent for the release of such self-initiated learning, the faculty member finds *himself* changed as well as his students. One such says:

To say that I am overwhelmed by what happened only faintly reflects my feelings. I have taught for many years but I have never experienced anything remotely resembling what occurred. I, for my part, never found in a classroom so much of the whole person coming forth, so deeply involved, so deeply stirred. Further, I question if in the traditional setup, with its emphasis on subject matter, examinations, grades, there is, or there can be a place for the "becoming" person with his deep and manifold needs as he struggles to fulfill himself. But this is going far afield. I can only report to you what happened and to say that I am grateful and that I am also humbled by the experience. I would like you to know this for it has enriched my life and being (Tenenbaum in Rogers, 1961, p. 313).

Another faculty member reports as follows:

Rogers has said that relationships conducted on these assumptions mean "turning present day education upside down." I have found this to be true as I have tried to implement this way of living with students. The experiences I have had have plunged me into relationships which have been significant and challenging and beyond compare for me. They have inspired me and stimulated me and left me at times shaken and awed with their consequences for both me and the students. They have led me to the fact of what I can only call . . . the tragedy of education in our time—student after student who reports this to be his first experience with total trust, with freedom to be and to move in ways most consistent for the enhancement and maintenance of the core of dignity which somehow has survived humiliation, distortion, and corrosive cynicism (Appell, 1959).

TOO IDEALISTIC?

Some readers may feel that the whole approach of this chapter —the belief that teachers can relate as persons to their students— is hopelessly unrealistic and idealistic. They may see that in essence it is encouraging both teachers and students to be creative in their relationship to each other and in their relationship to subject matter, and feel that such a goal is quite impossible. They are not alone in this. I have heard scientists at leading schools of science and scholars in leading universities, arguing that it is absurd to try to encourage all students to be creative—we need hosts of mediocre technicians and workers and if a few creative scientists and artists and leaders emerge, that will be enough. That may be enough for them. It may be enough to suit you. I want to go on record as saying it is *not* enough to suit me. When I realize the incredible potential in the ordinary student, I want to try to release it. We are working hard to release the incredible energy in the atom and the nucleus of the atom. If we do not devote equal energy—yes, and equal money—to the release of the potential of the individual person then the enormous discrepancy between our level of physical energy resources and human energy resources will doom us to a deserved and universal destruction.

I'm sorry I can't be coolly scientific about this. The issue is too urgent. I can only be passionate in my statement that people count, that interpersonal relationships *are* important, that we know something about releasing human potential, that we could learn much more, and that unless we give strong positive attention to the human interpersonal side of our educational dilemma, our civilization is on its way down the drain. Better courses, better curricula, better coverage, better teaching machines, will never resolve our dilemma in a basic way. Only persons, acting like persons in their relationships with their students can even begin to make a dent on this most urgent problem of modern education.

SUMMARY

Let me try to state, somewhat more calmly and soberly, what I have said with such feeling and passion.

I have said that it is most unfortunate that educators and the public think about, and focus on, *teaching*. It leads them into a host of questions which are either irrelevant or absurd so far as real education is concerned.

I have said that if we focused on the facilitation of *learning*— how, why, and when the student learns, and how learning seems and feels from the inside—we might be on a much more profitable track.

I have said that we have some knowledge, and could gain more, about the conditions which facilitate learning, and that one of the most important of these conditions is the attitudinal quality of the interpersonal relationship between facilitator and learner. (There are other conditions, too, which I will endeavor to spell out later.)

Those attitudes which appear effective in promoting learning can be described. First of all is a transparent realness in the facilitator, a willingness to be a person, to be and live the feelings and thoughts of the moment. When this realness includes a prizing, a caring, a trust and respect for the learner, the climate for learning is enhanced. When it includes a sensitive and accurate empathic listening, then indeed a freeing climate, stimulative of self-initiated learning and growth, exists. The student is *trusted* to develop.

I have tried to make plain that individuals who hold such attitudes, and are bold enough to act on them, do not simply modify classroom methods—they revolutionize them. They perform almost none of the functions of teachers. It is no longer accurate to call them teachers. They are catalyzers, facilitators, giving freedom and life and the opportunity to learn, to students.

I have brought in the cumulating research evidence which suggests that individuals who hold such attitudes are regarded as effective in the classroom; that the problems which concern them have to do with the release of potential, not the deficiencies of their students; that they seem to create classroom situations in which there are not admired children and disliked children, but in which affection and liking are a part of the life of every child; that in classrooms approaching such a psychological climate, children learn more of the conventional subjects.

But I have intentionally gone beyond the empirical findings to try to take you into the inner life of the student—elementary, college, and graduate—who is fortunate enough to live and learn in such an interpersonal relationship with a facilitator, in order to let you see what learning feels like when it is free, self-initiated and spontaneous. I have tried to indicate how it even changes the student-student relationship—making it more aware, more caring, more sensitive, as well as increasing the self-related learning of significant material. I have spoken of the change it brings about in the faculty member.

Throughout, I have tried to indicate that if we are to have citizens who can live constructively in this kaleidoscopically changing world, we can *only* have them if we are willing for them to become self-starting, self-initiating learners. Finally, it has been my purpose to show that this kind of learner develops best, so far as we now know, in a growth-promoting, facilitative, relationship with a *person*.

References

Appell, M. L. Selected student reactions to student-centered courses. Unpublished manuscript, Terre Haute, Indiana: State University of Ind., 1959.

Appell, M. L. Self-understanding for the guidance counselor. *Personnel & Guidance Journal*, October, 1963, 143-148.

Ashton-Warner, Sylvia. *Teacher*. New York: Simon and Schuster, 1963.

Aspy, D. N. A study of three facilitative conditions and their relationship to the achievement of third grade students. Unpublished doctoral dissertation, University of Kentucky, 1965.

Axline, Virginia M. Morale on the school front. *Journal of Educational Research*, 1944, 521-533.

Barrett-Lennard, G. T. Dimensions of therapist response as causal factors in therapeutic change. *Psychological Monographs*, 1962, 76 (Whole No. 562).

Bills, R. E. Personal correspondence. 1961, 1966.

Bull, Patricia. Student reactions, Fall, 1965. Unpublished manuscript, State University College, Cortland, New York, 1966.

Emmerling, F. C. A study of the relationships between personality characteristics of classroom teachers and pupil perceptions. Unpublished doctoral dissertation, Auburn University, Auburn, Alabama, 1961.

Jackson, P. W. The student's world. Unpublished manuscript, University of Chicago, 1966.

Macdonald, J. B. & Zaret, Esther. A study of openness in classroom interactions. Unpublished manuscript, Marquette University, 1966.

Moon, S. F. Teaching the self. *Improving College and University Teaching*, *14*, Autumn, 1966, 213-229.

Rogers, C. R. *On becoming a person*. Boston: Houghton Mifflin, 1961.

Schmuck, R. Some relationships of peer liking patterns in the classroom to pupil attitudes and achievement. *The School Review*, 1963, *71*, 337-359.

Schmuck, R. Some aspects of classroom social climate. *Psychology in the Schools*. 1966, *3*, 59-65.

Shiel, Barbara J. Evaluation: A self-directed curriculum, 1965. Unpublished manuscript, 1966.

5

Methods of Building Freedom

"Could I do this in my classroom?" This question, it seems to me, would be raised at this point by the teacher who has been favorably impressed by the preceding chapter. So in this chapter I have tried to point up some of the specific ways in which teachers have been able to provide opportunities for more self-reliant learning. In so doing, I have drawn upon the work of various educators and research workers, acknowledging their contributions by the references. I have also drawn upon two papers of my own (1966, 1967). I hope the resulting material will give both reassurance and stimulation to the teacher who wishes to step into the chilly waters of classroom innovation.

If a teacher is desirous of giving to his students a freedom to learn, how can this be achieved? The preceding chapter has presented those personal and subjective attitudes which are basic to the creation of such a climate. And there is no doubt that the teacher who is in the process of achieving these attitudes will develop modes of building freedom into his classroom which are suited to his own style, and which grow out of his own free and direct interaction with his students. Thus he will develop a growing methodology of his own—undoubtedly the best procedure.

Yet it is quite natural that the teacher who is taking the risk of being experimental would like to know what others have tried, what ways others have found of implementing these personal attitudes in the classroom in such a way that students can perceive and use the freedom which is being offered them. It is the purpose of this chapter to set forth briefly a few of the approaches, methods, techniques, which have been used by teachers who are trying to be facilitators, who are endeavoring to give a freedom to learn.

BUILDING UPON PROBLEMS PERCEIVED AS REAL

If self-initiated learning is to occur, it seems essential that the individual be in contact with, be faced by, a problem which he perceives as a real problem for him. Success in facilitating such learning often seems directly related to this factor. Professional persons who come together in a workshop because of a concern with problems they are facing constitute a good example. Almost invariably, when given freedom in the context of the attitudes described in the last chapter, they at first resist the notion of being responsible for their own learning and then gradually seize upon this as an opportunity, and use it far beyond their expectations. On the other hand, students in a required course expect to remain passive and may find themselves extremely perplexed and frustrated at being given freedom. "Freedom to do what?" is their quite understandable question.

It seems reasonably clear that for learning of the sort we are discussing it is necessary that the student, of whatever level, be confronted by issues which have meaning and relevance for him. In our culture we try to insulate the student from any and all of the real problems of life, and this constitutes a difficulty. It appears that if we desire to have students learn to be free and responsible individuals, then we must be willing for them to confront life, to face problems. Whether we are speaking of the inability of the small child to make change or the problem of his older brother in constructing a hi-fi set or the problem of the college student in formulating his views on racial problems or the fear of a teacher-in-training conducting her first practice teaching or the adult dealing with his interpersonal relationships or marital problems, some real confrontation by a problem seems a necessary condition for this type of learning.

It thus would seem wise for any teacher to try to draw out from his students those problems or issues which are real for them and which are relevant to the course at hand. The problem may be as simple as "I need these credits in order to graduate," or it may be a genuine interest in some aspect of the field. Whatever it may be the teacher would be well advised to nourish it.

Since in general students are so insulated from problems, it may be necessary to confront them with situations which will become real problems to them. In some of the later sections of this chapter, in describing such things as simulation and the "conduct of inquiry," circumstances are set up which involve the student deeply and confront him with a problem which becomes very real for him.

I become very irritated with the notion that students must be "motivated." The young human being is intrinsically motivated to a high degree. Many elements of his environment constitute challenges for him. He is curious, eager to discover, eager to know, eager to solve problems. A sad part of most education is that by the time the child has spent a number of years in school this intrinsic motivation is pretty well dampened. Yet it is there and it is our task as facilitators of learning to tap that motivation, to discover what challenges are real for the young person, and to provide the opportunity for him to meet those challenges.

PROVIDING RESOURCES

When a teacher is concerned with the facilitation of learning rather than with the function of teaching, he organizes his time and efforts very differently than the conventional teacher. Instead of spending great blocks of time organizing lesson plans and lectures, he concentrates on providing all kinds of resources which will give his students experiential learning relevant to their needs. He also concentrates on making such resources clearly available, by thinking through and simplifying the practical and psychological steps which the student must go through in order to utilize the resources. For example, it is one thing to say that a given book is available in the library. This means that if the student looks it up in the catalog, waits around to find that it is already on loan, returns the next week to ask for it, he may obtain the book. Not every student will have the patience or interest to go through these steps. But I have found that if I can make a shelf of books and reprints available for loan in the classroom, the amount of reading done, and the resulting stimulation to use the library in pursuing individual needs, grows by leaps and bounds.

In speaking of resources, I am thinking not only of the usual academic resources—books, articles, work space, laboratory room and equipment, tools, maps, films, recordings, and the like. I am also thinking of human resources—persons who might contribute to the knowledge of the student. Frequently there are outsiders who might be brought in to illuminate certain problems with which the students are concerned. Most important however in this respect is the teacher himself as a resource. He makes himself and his special knowledge and experience clearly available to the students, but he does not impose himself on them. He outlines the particular ways in which he feels he is most competent, and they can call on him for anything he is able to give. But this is an offer of himself as a resource and the degree to which he is used is up to the students.

Some of the ways in which a teacher may thus make himself available have been indicated in Part I of this book. Miss Shiel makes herself available for individual consultation, for students who are having difficulty with the tasks on which they are working. Professor Faw not only has this kind of consultation but sets up channels so that field trips and other resources and learning experiences can be easily arranged. He also makes his own special interests available through the lectures which he chooses to give. An unusual human resource which he offers, and which could be used much more widely, is making older and more experienced students available as consultants for the beginning students. This is a most valuable experience on both sides.

Professor Richard Dean, of California Institute of Technology, teaching a course in higher mathematics in a very free fashion, made use of himself first by providing "feedback" sheets in which he tried to summarize the major problems discussed or resolved in each session (as well as the problems opened up and not resolved) for the use of the class. A student coming into any class meeting was supplied with a feedback sheet from the previous session which helped to refresh his mind on what the class had done. Later Professor Dean stated that any student could volunteer to provide a feedback sheet also, and in this way both he and some of the students summarized the discussions. In addition, he or the student frequently would add their own analysis of what had gone on, or their own solution to issues and problems which had been raised.

One point I would like to make is that if we spent the same amount of time that is now spent on planning for prescribed curricula, lectures, and examinations, on the imaginative provision of a multitude of resources for learning, we would come up with all kinds of new ways of surrounding the student with a learning environment from which he could choose those elements which best met his needs.

USE OF CONTRACTS

One open-ended device which helps to give both security and responsibility within an atmosphere of freedom is the use of student contracts. There is no doubt that this also helps to assuage the uncertainties and insecurities which the facilitator may be experiencing. We have seen how Miss Shiel quite quickly made use of daily contracts with her pupils. This enables the pupil to set a goal for himself and to plan what he wishes to do. It provides a sort of transitional experience between complete freedom to learn whatever is of interest, and learning which is relatively free but which is within the limits of some institutional demand.

Professor Arthur Combs has used a type of contract for college and graduate students which has some interesting features. He explains at the beginning of the course that a student may obtain any grade he wishes. If all he desires is to take a passing grade in the course and receive the credits for it, he can do so by certifying that he has read a certain amount of assigned textbook material and passing examinations which cover this material. No stigma is attached to this decision. If, however, the student wishes a higher grade then he makes plans for himself which he thinks would justify a "B" or an "A" and Professor Combs consults with each student on the contract he has developed. Often these are too grandiose and need to be cut down to more reasonable size. When instructor and student have come to a mutual agreement on the contract, and that it deserves either a "B" or an "A" grade, then the student can rest assured that he will get that grade providing simply that he completes his contractual obligations before the end of the course. This removes any fear and apprehension from class sessions and makes genuinely free discussion possible. Students can differ with the professor without feeling that they may be endangering their grade. They can express what they really feel and think.

DIVISON OF GROUP

It does not seem reasonable to impose freedom on anyone who does not desire it. Consequently it seems wise, if it is at all possible, that when a group is offered the freedom to learn on their own responsibility, there should also be provision for those who do not wish or desire this freedom and prefer to be instructed and guided. Miss Shiel recognized this problem and divided her sixth graders into two groups—one self-directed and one conventional. The fact that they had freedom to move back and forth between these two approaches made this a very happy solution to the situation. Professor Dean, in teaching higher mathematics, made it possible for students who did not like the freedom he was giving them to transfer into conventional sections of the same course.

Such easy solutions may not always be possible, but it is a problem which the facilitator of learning will always wish to consider. If students are free, they should be free to learn passively as well as to initiate their own learning. Perhaps, as programmed learning develops, this will offer another alternative. Those students who prefer to be guided on a carefully pre-determined path of learning may choose to take the programmed learning. Those who prefer to follow their own directions and initiate their own learning can meet as a group or follow any of the various patterns which have thus far been described.

ORGANIZATION OF FACILITATOR-LEARNING GROUPS

Is it possible to provide any freedom of learning within large classes? This is a question which is often and deservedly raised. Professor Weldon Shofstall (1966), teaching prospective high school teachers, has come up with an interesting way of handling this problem.

In the first place he sets the climate for the class with some general comments:

> I am a facilitator of learning and you are the learner. There is no teacher in the traditional sense. Whether you learn or not is entirely your own personal responsibility. My sole job is to allow you to take this responsibility by using your own initiative. . . . I am always available for personal conferences. You are urged and advised to start these personal conferences during the first week. . . .

In addition, personal conferences are very helpful to me as your facilitator because I wish also to be a learner. I can learn only if you raise questions, objections, and make suggestions to me personally.

He then provides for the formation of relatively autonomous "facilitator-learning" groups.

You will be assigned to an FL group of from 7 to 10 students. Within this group you can either waste your time and the time of others or you can find this one of the most stimulating and worthwhile learning experiences you have ever had. For most of you there will be no middle ground. . . . I will attend your FL group upon the invitation of the group only. Please let me know the day before if you want me to attend your group meeting.

He suggests a considerable amount of structure for these groups.

The FL group should select a chairman. It is suggested that the chairman serve for not more than one week at a time. The chairman is the group moderator and must report to me before every FL group meeting. In addition to selecting a chairman one member of the group should be designated as the group reporter. This person will report to me after each group meeting. It is suggested that the group plan the FL group work and make assignments for not more than two meetings in advance. . . . Failure on the part of individual members to *prepare* for the group meetings is a serious handicap to the effective functioning of the group.

At the end of each of these courses, Professor Shofstall asks that the students write letters to new students who will be taking the course the following year. Here is an excerpt from one of those letters:

To begin with, friend, if you have gone through all of your college career sitting in lectures, taking notes on what the teacher wanted you to get, reading what the teacher wanted you to read, writing or reporting what the teacher wanted you to write or report on, and taking tests over what the teacher wanted you to know at the end of his course—and you *like* this method of education—then drop this course . . . But if you are willing to try honestly and sincerely to become involved with assuming responsibility for your own learning, then welcome!

It is certain that there are many other ways of dividing up large classes into small, functional, self-motivated groups. Members can be clustered in terms of special interests or in terms of particular topics and in other ways. The description of Professor Shofstall's method is simply intended to indicate that if we are willing to give as much attention to planning for the facilitation of learning as we ordinarily do for the preparation of lectures, many of the seemingly insuperable problems can be resolved.

THE CONDUCT OF INQUIRY

A specialized type of participative and experiential learning which has been receiving increasing emphasis in the last few years has been developing in the field of the sciences. Various individuals and national groups have been working toward a goal of helping students to become inquirers, working in a fluid way toward discovery in the scientific realm.

The impetus for this movement grows out of an urgent need to have science experienced as a changing field, as it is in the modern world, rather than as a closed book of already discovered facts. The possession of a body of knowledge *about* science is not an adequate achievement for the student today. Hence the aim is to get the student away from the misleading image of science as absolute, complete, and permanent (Schwab, 1960). Suchman (1961, 1962) is one of those who has given rather specific details regarding the manner in which this aim can be implemented. In trying to strengthen the autonomous processes within the learner he advocates a new approach in which special training is necessary for teachers of science. The teacher sets the stage of inquiry by posing the problems, creating an environment responsive to the learner, and giving assistance to the students in the investigative operations. This makes it possible for pupils to achieve autonomous discoveries and to engage in self-directed learning. They become scientists *themselves*, on a simple level, seeking answers to real questions, discovering for themselves the pitfalls and the joys of the scientist's search. They may not learn as many scientific "facts," but they develop a real appreciation of science as a never-ending search, a recognition that there is no closure in any real science.

It is obvious that if prospective teachers are to engage in this kind of stimulation of inquiry among their pupils, they must have experienced it themselves. It is therefore clear that courses in the teacher-training institution must be taught in the same fashion as Suchman describes if teachers themselves are to experience the satisfaction of self-initiated discovery in the scientific realm. This new development in the area of science constitutes a deep challenge to present concepts of teaching. Current educational practice tends, according to the evidence, to make children less autonomous and less empirical in their search for knowledge and understanding as they move through the elementary grades. This is strictly at variance with the aim of those who focus on inquiry. When children are permitted to think their way through to new understandings, the concepts they derive in the process have greater depth, understanding, and durability. They have become more autonomous and more solidly based in an empirical approach.

Like any of the methods described in this chapter, the procedures involved in developing an inquiring state of mind can themselves become routinized and simply another means of imposing a teacher-directed curriculum on the students. I have known this to happen. It cannot be stressed strongly enough that none of the *methods* mentioned in this chapter will be effective unless the teacher's genuine desire is to create a climate in which there is freedom to learn.

SIMULATION AS A TYPE OF EXPERIENTIAL LEARNING

The trend toward a more experiential type of learning shows up in the increasing use of simulation as a device for use in the classroom. "A 'simulation' is a social system in miniature; a model of an organization, a nation, or a world—a 'laboratory analogue' by which a wide variety of social situations can be replicated" (Sprague, 1966). Thus far, more experimental work has been done on the simulation of international relationships than on any other single social system (Alger, 1963; Solomon, 1963; Guetzkow, 1963) but there have been some pilot studies simulating families, school systems, political parties, corporations, legislatures, and pressure groups. Any simulation is quite complex, since the participants must first have considerable knowledge about the system and some training in their function in the system.

Sprague (1966) describes an international relations simulation which has been used rather extensively with high school students.

> The Inter-Nation Simulation (the INS) models a "world" consisting of several "nations." Each is operated by a certain number of "decision-makers" who try to maintain themselves in office under a variety of "international" and "domestic" pressures. Supplied with a history of their world, and information as to the economic, military, and political characteristics of their nations, the decision-makers allocate basic resources for defense, development, foreign aid and trade, for the satisfaction of citizens' needs for consumer goods, domestic stability, and protection from foreign threats. They must cope with wars and threats of war, demands for military and economic aid, bloc-rivalries, and domestic opposition or insurrection. The course of events is determined partly by the social, economic, and political characteristics built into the system by the experimenter, and partly by the responses and decisions of the participants themselves.

> "Time" is highly compressed; each fifty-minute period of the simulation represents a year, and a single simulation "run" may contain up to twenty periods. But how does a simulation "work"? How do the decision-makers know the consequences of their decisions, and whether their decisions were good or bad?

> In the INS, the consequences of decisions are calculated according to mathematical formulae, and given numerical values. For example, a formula is used to determine the relationship between the amount of basic resources devoted to producing consumer goods, on the one hand, and the degree of citizen-satisfaction with the resulting standard of living, on the other. If too little is invested in consumer goods, the standard of living falls; the citizenry become dissatisfied; if their dissatisfaction, measured by another formula, falls below a certain level, the Central Decision-Maker loses office.

> Another formula is used to calculate the relative military and defensive strength of each nation and of multi-nation blocs. If defense needs have been slighted because too much of the nation's resources have been devoted to consumer goods ("guns versus butter"), the citizenry is likely to be dissatisfied with the nation's

security—and again, the Central Decision-Maker is in danger of losing office. Great ingenuity has been used in developing these formulae which provide a means of giving participants clear and realistic feedback each time they make a set of decisions.

Other aspects of the international system are modeled, particularly those having to do with communications. Barriers to inter-nation communications, intelligence leaks and espionage, false information, the difficulties of explicit communication under tension, the effects of diplomatic vagueness, the use and misuse of the international press, the problems of face-to-face communication among national leaders or in a world organization—all these must be coped with in the simulation.

What are the types of learning that follow from the use of such a simulation experience? They provide the student with first hand experience of various processes which occur in real life: with decision-making based upon incomplete and changing information, made urgent by deadlines; with the difficulties of communication, the sometimes disastrous results of misunderstandings and crossed messages, or the discrepancy between verbal communication and actual behavior; with the handling of interpersonal relationships in negotiation, bargaining, and "deals." Throughout the experience the student (who becomes deeply involved) not only takes action, but bears the personal responsibility for the decisions and actions he takes. There develops a disciplined commitment to information-gathering, decision, action. Such an experience tends to develop a positive, constructive type of learning rather than the negative, critical traits so often encouraged in current education.

Though research on the outcomes of simulation is in its infant stages, there is no doubt that students become enthusiastically in-volved, and (in a simulation such as INS) feel that they learn a great deal about international relations, about human behavior, and about the difficulties of communication (Sprague, 1966). They also clearly prefer it to the lecture system (Alger, 1963). Another value, from my point of view, is that although the teacher introduces the simulation to the group, it is the class and the individual students who assume the responsibility for running it, thus gaining much in the way of self-initiated learning.

PROGRAMMED INSTRUCTION AS
EXPERIENTIAL LEARNING

As educators well know, there has been a vast and explosive development in this field (Skinner, 1961; Fry, 1963; Gage, 1963; Pressey, 1963). This is not the place to review these developments or the theory of operant conditioning upon which this work is based. It is appropriate, however, to point out that programmed instruction may be used in a variety of ways. It can be seen as potentially providing for all learning or it may be seen as one new and very useful tool in the facilitation of learning. As Skinner has pointed out, "To acquire behavior the student must engage in behavior" (1961, p. 389).

It is of particular interest to note that in the development of programmed instruction there is a tendency toward shorter "plug-in" programs, rather than toward the development of whole courses covering a total field of knowledge. To me, the development of these shorter programs suggests the most fruitful way in which the student may be involved in the use of so-called "teaching machines." When learning is being facilitated, the student will frequently come across gaps in his knowledge, tools which he lacks, information which he needs to meet the problem he is confronting. Here the flexibility of programmed instruction is invaluable. A pupil who needs to know how to use a microscope can find a program covering this knowledge. The student who is planning to spend three months in France can utilize programmed instruction in conversational French. The pupil who needs algebra, whether for the solution of problems of interest to him or simply to get into college, can work on a program of instruction in algebra.

Used in these ways there is no doubt that a competently developed program gives the student immediate experiences of satisfaction, enables him to learn a body of knowledge when he needs it for his own functioning, gives him the feeling that any content is learnable, and a recognition that the process of education is an intelligible and comprehensible one. He can work at his own rate and finds that the carefully designed program presents him with coherent, interrelated steps. Its stress on immediate reinforcement and reward rather than on punitive or evaluative measures is another factor in its favor. If programmed learning is used flexibly it can constitute a large forward step in meeting the massive needs for functional learning of subject matter as the number of pupils grows by leaps and bounds.

Programmed learning is spreading into new and unexpected fields. Berlin & Wyckoff (1963) have developed programs for the improvement of interpersonal relationships in which two people work together at mutual tasks, assigned by the programmed text, learning not only some of the cognitive concepts in regard to interpersonal relationships but gradually experiencing deeper and deeper communication with each other. Both industry and educational institutions have begun to make use of this developing series of programs, impressed by the fact that the learnings involve both feelings and intellect, and that they have significant personal meaning for the learner.

It goes without saying that programmed learning has great potential risks if it is unwisely used. If it becomes a substitute for thinking in larger patterns and gestalts, if it becomes a way of stressing factual knowledge as over against creativity, then real damage may be done. But if it is perceived as an instrument which may be used by educators to achieve flexibility in education, then it is readily evident that it is one of the most powerful tools which psychology has as yet contributed to the field.

THE BASIC ENCOUNTER GROUP

A very important example of a new development which fosters a climate for significant learning is the basic encounter group or so-called "sensitivity training." We have already seen this utilized in Chapter 3 in the course which I conducted. This is an approach which is of help in educating not only students but teachers and administrators for the newer goals in education. It has as much relevance for them as for the classroom situation.

Since we have already seen an instance of this approach in operation and since it will be discussed in greater depth in a later chapter, only the briefest description will be given here.

The encounter group is not yet widely used in educational institutions, and relatively few teachers or administrators have had experience with it. There has, however, been a burgeoning use of the intensive group experience in the development of business executives and government administrators. Under a variety of labels—T-Group, the Laboratory Group, the Sensitivity Training Course, the intensive Workshop in Human Relations, the Basic Encounter Group—this approach has become an important part of the development of leaders in both their personal and professional functioning. (See Bradford, Gibb, & Lippitt, 1956).

It is difficult to describe briefly the nature of such a group experience, especially since it varies greatly from group to group and from leader to leader. (See Wechsler & Reisel, 1959, for one description.) Essentially, the group begins with little imposed structure, so that the situation and the purposes are ambiguous, and up to the group members to decide. The leader's function is to facilitate expression, and to clarify or point up the dynamic pattern of the group's struggle to work toward a meaningful experience. In such a group, after an initial "milling around," personal expressiveness tends to increase. This also involves an increasingly free, direct and spontaneous communication between members of the group. Façades become less necessary, defenses are lowered, basic encounters occur as individuals reveal hitherto hidden feelings and aspects of themselves, and receive spontaneous feedback—both negative and positive—from group members. Some or many individuals become much more facilitative in relationships to others, making possible greater freedom of expression.

In general, when the experience is a fruitful one, it is a deeply personal experience resulting in more direct person-to-person communication, sharply increased self-understanding, more realness and independence in the individual, and an increased understanding and acceptance of others. While much still remains to be learned about the intensive group experience in all its forms, it is already clear that it helps to create in most members of the group attitudes which, among other things, are highly conducive to experiential learning.

SELF-EVALUATION

The evaluation of one's own learning is one of the major means by which self-initiated learning becomes also responsible learning. It is when the individual has to take the responsibility for deciding what criteria are important to him, what goals he has been trying to achieve, and the extent to which he has achieved those goals, that he truly learns to take responsibility for himself and his directions. For this reason it seems important that some degree of self-evaluation be built into any attempt to promote an experiential type of learning.

In the first three chapters of this book we have already seen a number of ways of implementing this. Miss Shiel settled the problem of grades by mutual discussion with her pupils. Faw gave the students a good deal to think about in terms of what evaluation means and encouraged them to evaluate the sub-sections of their own work but he himself took the responsibility for their grade. In my class the students were primarily responsible both for the criteria and for the grade assigned. In classes like Professor Combs', fulfillment of the contract is itself a completion of the self-evaluation which began with the contract. Professor Shofstall provides for his students summaries of learnings and self evaluations made by previous students so that they can have some notion of the task. During the whole course the student makes an analysis of his strengths and weaknesses. He checks these with the other members of his small group in order to have feedback from his colleagues as well as his own personal evaluation of himself. The final grades are decided upon by representatives selected by each group who meet with the instructor to make their recommendations.

It is obvious that there are many patterns for the student to follow in making an appraisal of his own efforts and his own learning. The particular pattern is far less important than that he should feel responsible for intelligently pursuing the aims he wishes to pursue. One student may choose a very rigid goal such as simply amassing a certain amount of testable information in the field of study. Another may use a course to become more spontaneous in his learning, more open to a wide range of stimuli, or free to be himself in reacting to the resources which have been made available to him. Obviously the criteria will be very different for these two individuals. Yet each has functioned as a responsible learner and in much the same fashion as a responsible professional person functions in society.

METHODS WHICH ARE NOT EMPLOYED

When the leader concentrates on creating a facilitative climate there are a number of traditional methods which he does not use and perhaps a very brief mention of these would be useful. He does *not set lesson tasks*. He does *not assign readings*. He does *not lecture or expound* (unless requested to). He does *not evaluate and criticize* unless a student wishes his judgment on a product. He does *not give required examinations*. He does *not take sole responsibility for grades*.

Perhaps this brief list will make it clear that a facilitator is not a teacher and is not simply giving lip service to a different approach to learning. He is actually operationally giving his students the opportunity to learn to be responsibly free.

CONCLUDING REMARKS

The person who is desirous of creating the conditions for self-initiated, self-directed learning finds that there are a number of methods already at hand which are congenial to this approach. It has been the purpose of this chapter to present a few of these methods and the ways in which they might be used. It has by no means been a complete or exhaustive list. It has been intended rather as a stimulus to the facilitator, a hopefully suggestive list of approaches which he may try or adapt to his own personality and style. As more teachers endeavor to create a classroom climate of freedom, there will be many more procedures used which achieve this aim. Those mentioned in this chapter are simply a small beginning.

References

Alger, C. Use of the inter-nation simulation in undergraduate teaching. In H. Guetzkow (Ed.), *Simulation in internation relations.* Englewood Cliffs, New Jersey: Prentice-Hall, 1963. Pp. 150-189.

Berlin, J. I., & Wyckoff, L. B. *Relationship Improvement Programs.* Atlanta: Human Development Institute, Inc., 1963.

Bradford, L., Gibb, J., & Lippitt, R. *Explorations in human relations training.* Washington, D.C.: National Training Laboratory in Group Development, National Educational Association, 1956.

Fry, E. *Teaching machines and programmed instruction.* New York: McGraw-Hill, 1963.

Gage, N. L. (Ed.), *Handbook of research on teaching.* Chicago: Rand McNally, 1963.

Guetzkow, H. (Ed.), *Simulation in internation relations.* Englewood Cliffs, New Jersey: Prentice-Hall, 1963.

Pressey, S. Teaching machine (and learning theory) crisis. *Journal of Applied Psychology*, 1963, *47*, 1-6.

Rogers, C. R. To facilitate learning. In M. Provus (Ed.), *Innovations for time to teach.* Washington, D.C.: National Educational Association, 1966. Pp. 4-19.

Rogers, C. R. The facilitation of significant learning. In L. Siegel (Ed.), *Contemporary theories of instruction.* Chandler Publishing Co., 1967.

Schwab, J. J. Inquiry, the science teacher and the educator. *School Review*, 1960, *68*, 176-195.

Shofstall, W. P. Training high school facilitators of learning. Unpublished manuscript, Tempe, Arizona: Arizona State University, 1966.

Skinner, B. F. Why we need teaching machines. *Harvard Educational Review*, 1961, *31*, 377-398.

Solomon, L. N. Reducing tensions in a test-tube world. *War/Peace Report*, July 1963, *3* (7), 10-12.

Sprague, H. T. Using simulations to teach international relations. La Jolla, California: Western Behavioral Sciences Institute Report, Unpublished manuscript, 1966.

Suchman, J. R. Inquiry training: Building skills for autonomous discovery. *Merrill-Palmer Quarterly of Behavior and Development*, 1961, 7, 147-169.

Suchman, J. R. *The elementary school training program in scientific inquiry.* Urbana: University of Illinois, 1962.

Wechsler, I. R., & Reisel, J. *Inside a sensitivity training group.* Los Angeles: Institute of Industrial Relations, UCLA, 1959.

part III

Some Assumptions

Introduction to Part III

This section of the book will give the reader much more of an opportunity to see whether he agrees with the principles and assumptions which underlie the approach which has been presented. Some readers will find them shocking and will disagree violently. Others will find them confirmed by their own experience. At any rate, I have tried to state them straightforwardly so that each can form his own conclusions for himself.

Two of the chapters deal ostensibly with graduate education, but I give full assurance that this relationship is in appearance only. Actually all but a few sentences apply to all levels of education and the high school teacher may, for example, see himself more truly when he thinks that he is looking at the graduate school professor and discovers that he is looking obliquely at a mirror image of himself. Such is my hope.

Thus, here are my perceptions of the way students *learn*, of what present education is *really* like, of what it *might* be, and of what educational administration might be.

6

Personal Thoughts on
Teaching and Learning

This brief chapter contains a distillation of the convictions which I have drawn from my experience as a teacher and it has, in the past, been successful in provoking thought. So, though it was written more than fifteen years ago, I present it in this book intended for today.

I wrote this paper as a concise statement of my own views, in order to stimulate discussion. I wrote it while in Mexico, far away from the academic world. If the style, and the attempt to be as honest as possible, smacks of Kierkegaard, this is not a coincidence. I had spent much of my time on this trip reading, digesting, and appreciating his work.

This statement catches very well the surprise that I felt as I discovered the directions in which my thinking was taking me. I did not start out to be an educational heretic, and I was inwardly astonished at the fact that when I tried honestly to review my experience, teaching *seemed of such little importance, and* learning *so vastly important. As I have continued to live with this emphasis, it no longer seems so startling as it did at that time.*

The paper was presented to a Harvard Conference on "Classroom Approaches to Influencing Behavior," made up of forward-looking college teachers, many of whom were using discussion methods in their classes. Consequently, I was foolish enough to expect an understanding and acceptant audience. The response instead was furiously critical for the most part, with only a few soft-spoken individuals speaking up, with gradually increasing force, to indicate that their experience had led them to somewhat similar conclusions, which they had never dared to voice.

This material has been printed before.[1] Indeed the ideas in it have been presented much more fully, and much more ade-

[1] "Personal Thoughts about Teaching and Learning," *Merrill-Palmer Quarterly*, Summer, 1957, 3, 241-243. Reprinted with permission.

*quately (I hope) in the chapters which precede and follow it in
this book. Why then do I include it? It is because it was the
first germinal credo of my thinking about the difference between teaching and learning, and crude as it is, brief as it is,
it may encourage some reader to put down for himself some
deep but very uncertain beliefs of his own about the educational process. It is these deep, tentative, uncertain, frightening
formulations which are the heart of creativity and if only one
reader risks himself in this way, the inclusion of this chapter
will have served its purpose.*

I wish to present some very brief remarks, in the hope that if
they bring forth any reaction from you, I may get some new light
on my own ideas.

I find it a very troubling thing to *think*, particularly when I think
about my own experiences and try to extract from those experiences
the meaning that seems genuinely inherent in them. At first, such
thinking is very satisfying, because it seems to discover sense and
pattern in a whole host of discrete events. But then it very often
becomes dismaying, because I realize how ridiculous these thoughts,
which have so much value to me, would seem to most people. My
impression is that if I try to find the meaning of my own experience it leads me, nearly always, in directions regarded as absurd.

So in the next few minutes, I will try to digest some of the
meanings which have come to me from my classroom experience
and the experience I have had in individual therapy and group
experience. They are in no way intended as conclusions for someone else, or a guide to what others should do or be. They are the
very tentative meanings, as of April 1952, which my experience has
had for me, and some of the bothersome questions which their
absurdity raises. I will put each idea or meaning in a separate
lettered paragraph, not because they are in any particular logical
order, but because each meaning is separately important to me.

a.) I may as well start with this one in view of the purposes of
this conference. *My experience has been that I cannot teach another
person how to teach.* To attempt it is for me, in the long run, futile.

b.) *It seems to me that anything that can be taught to another
is relatively inconsequential and has little or no significant influence*

on behavior. That sounds so ridiculous I can't help but question it at the same time that I present it.

c.) *I realize increasingly that I am only interested in learnings which significantly influence behavior.* Quite possibly this is simply a personal idiosyncrasy.

d.) *I have come to feel that the only learning which significantly influences behavior is self-discovered, self-appropriated learning.*

e.) *Such self-discovered learning, truth that has been personally appropriated and assimilated in experience, cannot be directly communicated to another.* As soon as an individual tries to communicate such experience directly, often with a quite natural enthusiasm, it becomes teaching, and its results are inconsequential. It was some relief recently to discover that Søren Kierkegaard, the Danish philosopher, had found this too, in his own experience, and stated it very clearly a century ago. It made it seem less absurd.

f.) As a consequence of the above, *I realize that I have lost interest in being a teacher.*

g.) When I try to teach, as I do sometimes, I am appalled by the results, which seem a little more than inconsequential, because sometimes the teaching appears to succeed. When this happens I find that the results are damaging. It seems to cause the individual to distrust his own experience, and to stifle significant learning. *Hence I have come to feel that the outcomes of teaching are either unimportant or hurtful.*

h.) When I look back at the results of my past teaching, the real results seem the same—either damage was done—or nothing significant occurred. This is frankly troubling.

i.) As a consequence, *I realize that I am only interested in being a learner, preferably learning things that matter, that have some significant influence on my own behavior.*

j.) *I find it very rewarding to learn,* in groups, in relationships with one person as in therapy, or by myself.

k.) *I find that one of the best, but most difficult, ways for me to learn is to drop my own defensiveness, at least temporarily, and to try to understand the way in which his experience seems and feels to the other person.*

l.) *I find that another way of learning for me is to state my own uncertainties, to try to clarify my puzzlements, and thus get closer to the meaning that my experience actually seems to have.*

m.) This whole train of experiencing, and the meanings that I have thus far discovered in it, seem to have launched me on a process which is both fascinating and at times a little frightening. *It seems to mean letting my experiences carry me on, in a direction which appears to be forward, toward goals that I can but dimly define, as I try to understand at least the current meaning of that experience.* The sensation is that of floating with a complex stream of experience, with the fascinating possibility of trying to comprehend its ever-changing complexity.

I am almost afraid I may seem to have gotten away from any discussion of learning, as well as teaching. Let me again introduce a practical note by saying that by themselves these interpretations of my experience may sound queer and aberrant, but not particularly shocking. It is when I realize the *implications* that I shudder a bit at the distance I have come from the commonsense world that everyone knows is right. I can best illustrate this by saying that if the experiences of others had been the same as mine, and if they had discovered similar meanings in it, many consequences would be implied:

a.) Such experience would imply that we would do away with teaching. People would get together if they wished to learn.

b.) We would do away with examinations. They measure only the inconsequential type of learning.

c.) We would do away with grades and credits for the same reason.

d.) We would do away with degrees as a measure of competence partly for the same reason. Another reason is that a degree marks an end or a conclusion of something, and a learner is only interested in the continuing process of learning.

e.) We would do away with the exposition of conclusions, for we would realize that no one learns significantly from conclusions.

I think I had better stop there. I do not want to become too fantastic. I want to know primarily whether anything in my inward thinking, as I have tried to describe it, speaks to anything in your experience of the classroom as you have lived it, and if so, what the meanings are that exist for you in *your* experience.

7

Regarding Learning
and Its Facilitation

How does a person learn? How can important learnings be facilitated? What basic theoretical assumptions are involved? In this chapter I have tried to answer these questions in a "bare-bones" fashion, simply stating the core of my views on these questions.

It is customary to begin a presentation with theoretical and general principles, and then to indicate the way in which these principles might be carried out in practice. I have followed the opposite course in this book. I have endeavored to present a wealth of practical experience and descriptions of methods, all of which have been used to set students free for self-initiated, self-reliant learning. Now I would like to make a succinct general statement of some of the principles (or hypotheses) which can reasonably be abstracted, it seems to me, from these and other similar experiences. I will be drawing on my own experience, on the work of many other facilitators of learning who have sent me accounts of their work and its outcomes, and upon relevant research, some of which has been reported in earlier chapters.

LEARNING

Here are a number of the principles which can, I believe, be abstracted from current experience and research related to this newer approach:

1.) *Human beings have a natural potentiality for learning.* They are curious about their world, until and unless this curiosity is blunted by their experience in our educational system. They are ambivalently eager to develop and learn. The reason for the ambivalence is that any significant learning involves a certain amount of pain, either pain connected with the learning itself or distress connected with giving up certain previous learnings. The first type of ambivalence is illustrated by the small child who is learning to walk. He stumbles, he falls, he hurts himself. It is a painful process. Yet, the satisfactions of developing his potential far outweigh the bumps and bruises. The second type of ambivalence is evident when a student who has been absolutely tops in every way in his small town high school enrolls in a superior college or university where he finds that he is simply one of many bright students. This is a painful learning to assimilate, yet in most instances he does assimilate it and goes forward.

This potentiality and desire for learning, for discovery, for enlargement of knowledge and experience, can be released under suitable conditions. It is a tendency which can be trusted, and the whole approach to education which we have been describing builds upon and around the student's natural desire to learn.

2.) *Significant learning takes place when the subject matter is perceived by the student as having relevance for his own purposes.* A somewhat more formal way of stating this is that a person learns significantly only those things which he perceives as being involved in the maintenance of or the enhancement of his own self. Think for a moment of two students taking a course in statistics. One is working on a research project for which he definitely needs the material of the course in order to complete his research and move forward in his professional career. The second student is taking the course because it is required. Its only relationship to his own purposes or the enhancement of himself is simply that it is necessary for him to complete the course in order to stay in the university. There can hardly be any question as to the differences in learning which ensue. The first student acquires a functional learning of the material; the second learns how to "get by."

Another element related to this principle has to do with the speed of learning. When an individual has a goal he wishes to achieve and he sees the material available to him as relevant to achieving that goal, learning takes place with great rapidity. We need only to recall what a brief length of time it takes for an adolescent to learn to drive a car. There is evidence that the time for learning various subjects would be cut to a fraction of the time currently allotted if the material were perceived by the learner as related to his own purposes. Probably one third to one fifth of the present time allotment would be sufficient.

3.) *Learning which involves a change in self organization—in the perception of oneself—is threatening and tends to be resisted.* Why has there been so much furor, sometimes even lawsuits, concerning an adolescent boy who comes to school with long hair? Surely the length of his hair makes little objective difference. The reason seems to be that if I, as a teacher or administrator, accept the value which he places on non-conformity then it threatens the value which I have placed on conforming to social demands. If I permit this contradiction to exist I may find myself changing, because I will be forced to a reappraisal of some of my values. The same thing applies to the former interest in "beatniks" and the current interest in "hippies." If their rejection of almost all middle class values is permitted to stand, then an individual's acceptance of middle class values as a part of himself is deeply threatened, since to most people it seems that to the degree *others* are right, *they* are wrong.

Sometimes these painful and threatening learnings have to do with contradictions within oneself. An example might be the person who believes "every citizen in this country has equal right to any opportunity which exists." He also discovers that he has the conviction, "I am unwilling for a Negro to live in my neighborhood." Any learning which arises from this dilemma is painful and threatening since the two beliefs cannot openly co-exist, and any learning which emerges from the contradiction involves a definite change in the structure of self.

4.) *Those learnings which are threatening to the self are more easily perceived and assimilated when external threats are at a minimum.* The boy who is retarded in reading already feels threatened and inadequate because of this deficiency. When he is forced to attempt to read aloud in front of the group, when he is ridiculed for his efforts, when his grades are a vivid reflection of his failure, it is no surprise that he may go through several years of school with no perceptible increase in his reading ability. On the other hand, a supportive, understanding environment and a lack of grades, or an encouragement of self evaluation, remove the external threats and permit him to make progress because he is no longer paralyzed by fear. This is also one of the great advantages of the teaching machine, when properly used. Here the poor reader can begin at his own level of achievement and practically every minute step he makes is marked by reward and a feeling of success.

It is fascinating to me how completely we have tended to disregard the evidence which clearly supports this principle. Nearly forty years ago Herbert Williams,[1] then a teacher, was put in charge of a classroom in which all of the most serious delinquents in a large school system were brought together. They were the "worst boys" in a city of 300,000. He could not hope to carry on much individualized instruction, and the boys were at all levels of school achievement. As might be expected, they were retarded intellectually (average I. Q. 82) as well as in their school achievement. He had very little special equipment. Besides the usual desks and blackboards, there was a large table in the room on which he placed picture books, readers, story books, and textbooks in various subjects, appropriate to all levels of reading achievement. There were also art materials available. There were but two rules. A boy must keep busy doing something, and no boy was permitted to annoy or disturb others. Each child was told, without criticism, of his results on an achievement test. Encouragement and suggestions were given only after an activity had been self initiated. Thus, if a boy had worked along artistic lines he might be given assistance in getting into a special art class. If activities in mathematics or mechanics had engaged his interest, arrangements might be made for him to attend courses in these subjects. The group remained together for four months. During this period the measured educational achievement (on the Stanford Achievement Test) of those who had been in the group for the major part of this period increased fifteen months on the average, and this improvement was evident in reading, arithmetic, and other subjects. The increase was more than four times the normal expectation for a group with this degree of retardation, and this in spite of the fact that reading and other educational disabilities abounded. This incredible improvement came about through informal, self-directed, activity. It is my belief that studies such as this have been disregarded

---

[1] H. D. Williams, "Experiment in Self-directed Education," *School and Society*, 1930, *31*, 715-718.

primarily because they provide a threat to the teacher. Here is evidence that the most unpromising students learn rapidly when they are simply given opportunities to learn and when no attempt is made to teach them. This must seem to many teachers that they might be deprived of their jobs and hence the information is simply not assimilated.

One reason for the success of this highly unorthodox and inexpensive venture must have been the attitude of Mr. Williams himself. He surmises that his interest in each child's home conditions, neighborhood, health, and in each boy individually may have stimulated the youngsters. He states that he wanted to get acquainted with each boy, and spent his time in this sort of activity rather than in teaching. That he had a strong and sympathetic interest in, and belief in, juvenile delinquents is shown by the fact that he went on to become superintendent of a highly progressive institution for delinquents.

5.) *When threat to the self is low, experience can be perceived in differentiated fashion and learning can proceed.* In a sense this is only an extension of, or an explanation of, the preceding principle. The poor reader is a good illustration of what is involved in this principle. When he is called upon to recite in class the internal panic takes over and the words on the page become less intelligible symbols than they were when he was sitting at his seat before he was called upon. When he is in an environment in which he is assured of personal security and when he becomes convinced that there is no threat to his ego, he is once more free to perceive the symbols on the page in a differentiated fashion, to recognize the differing elements in similar words, to perceive partial meanings and try to put them together—in other words, to move forward in the process of learning. Any sort of learning involves an increasing differentiation of the field of experience and the assimilation of the meanings of these differentiations. Such differentiations, it seems to me, are most effectively made under two sharply differing kinds of conditions. They may occur when the threat to the *organism* is intense, but such threats are quite different than threats to the *self* as perceived. The combat soldier, for example, learns very quickly to distinguish the shriek of a shell going high overhead from the whine of one which is coming in his direction. He learns to discrimi-

nate very readily a normal footpath from one whose surface has
been disturbed, since the latter may be a land mine. He is, in these
instances, responding to threat of a very serious nature, but this
is threat to his organism and not a threat to the self he perceives
himself to be. In fact the more quickly he can learn these discrimi-
nations the more his self is enhanced. In the ordinary educational
situation, however, such realistic life and death threats are rare
and when these exist pupils respond well to them. Children learn
traffic rules, for example, quite readily and comfortably. But humiliation, ridicule, devaluation, scorn and contempt—these are threats
to the person himself, to the perception he has of himself and as
such interfere strongly with learning. On the other hand, as
described above, when threat to the self is minimized, the individual
makes use of opportunities to learn in order to enhance himself.

6.) *Much significant learning is acquired through doing.* Placing
the student in direct experiential confrontation with practical
problems, social problems, ethical and philosophical problems,
personal issues, and research problems, is one of the most effective
modes of promoting learning. Illustrations range from the class
group which becomes involved in a dramatic production, selecting
the play and the cast, designing and making the scenery and
costumes, coaching the actors, and selling tickets, to much more
sophisticated confrontations. I have always been impressed with the
fact that brief intensive courses for individuals on the firing line
facing immediate problems—teachers, doctors, farmers, counselors
—are especially effective because the individuals are trying to cope
with problems which they are currently experiencing.

7.) *Learning is facilitated when the student participates responsibly in the learning process.* When he chooses his own directions,
helps to discover his own learning resources, formulates his own
problems, decides his own course of action, lives with the consequences of each of these choices, then significant learning is maximized. There is evidence from industry as well as from the field
of education that such participative learning is far more effective
than passive learning.

8.) *Self-initiated learning which involves the whole person of the
learner—feelings as well as intellect—is the most lasting and pervasive.* We have discovered this in psychotherapy, where it is the

totally involved learning of oneself by oneself which is most effective. This is not learning which takes place "only from the neck up." It is a "gut level" type of learning which is profound and pervasive. It can also occur in the tentative discovery of a new self-generated idea or in the learning of a difficult skill, or in the act of artistic creation—a painting, a poem, a sculpture. It is the whole person who "lets himself go" in these creative learnings. An important element in these situations is that the learner *knows* it is his own learning and thus can hold to it or relinquish it in the face of a more profound learning without having to turn to some authority for corroboration of his judgment.

9.) *Independence, creativity, and self-reliance are all facilitated when self-criticism and self-evaluation are basic and evaluation by others is of secondary importance.* The best research organizations, in industry as well as in the academic world, have learned that creativity blossoms in an atmosphere of freedom. External evaluation is largely fruitless if the goal is creative work. The wise parent has learned this same lesson. If a child is to grow up to be independent and self reliant he must be given opportunities at an early age not only to make his own judgments and his own mistakes but to evaluate the consequences of these judgments and choices. The parent may provide information and models of behavior, but it is the growing child and adolescent who must evaluate his own behaviors, come to his own conclusions, and decide on the standards which are appropriate for him. The child or adolescent who is dependent both at school and at home upon the evaluations of others is likely to remain permanently dependent and immature or explosively rebellious against all external evaluations and judgments.

10.) *The most socially useful learning in the modern world is the learning of the process of learning, a continuing openness to experience and incorporation into oneself of the process of change.* The point has been made in preceding chapters that a static kind of learning of information may have been quite adequate in previous times. If our present culture survives it will be because we have been able to develop individuals for whom *change* is the central fact of life and who have been able to live comfortably with this central fact. It means that they will not be concerned, as so many are today, that their past learning is inadequate to enable them to cope with current situations. They will instead have the comfortable expectation that it will be continuously necessary to incorporate new and challenging learnings about ever-changing situations.

FACILITATION

So much has been presented in preceding chapters about various methods of facilitating learning and various qualities of the facilitator that only the briefest summary of some of the guidelines which can be abstracted will be presented here.

1.) *The facilitator has much to do with setting the initial mood or climate of the group or class experience.* If his own basic philosophy is one of trust in the group and in the individuals who compose the group, then this point of view will be communicated in many subtle ways.

2.) *The facilitator helps to elicit and clarify the purposes of the individuals in the class as well as the more general purposes of the group.* If he is not fearful of accepting contradictory purposes and conflicting aims, if he is able to permit the individuals a sense of freedom in stating what they would like to do, then he is helping to create a climate for learning. There is no need for him to try to manufacture one unified purpose in the group if such a unified purpose is not there. He can permit a diversity of purposes to exist, contradictory and complementary, in relationship to each other.

3.) *He relies upon the desire of each student to implement those purposes which have meaning for him, as the motivational force behind significant learning.* Even if the desire of the student is to be guided and led by someone else, the facilitator can accept such a need and motive and can either serve as a guide when this is desired or can provide some other means, such as a set course of study, for the student whose major desire is to be dependent. And for the majority of students he can help to utilize the individual's own drives and purposes as the moving force behind his learning.

4.) *He endeavors to organize and make easily available the widest possible range of resources for learning.* He endeavors to make available writings, materials, psychological aids, persons, equipment, trips, audio-visual aids—every conceivable resource which his students may wish to use for their own enhancement and for the fulfillment of their own purposes.

5.) *He regards himself as a flexible resource to be utilized by the group.* He does not downgrade himself as a resource. He makes himself available as a counselor, lecturer, and advisor, a person with experience in the field. He wishes to be used by individual students, and by the group, in the ways which seem most meaningful to them insofar as he can be comfortable in operating in the ways they wish.

6.) *In responding to expressions in the classroom group, he accepts both the intellectual content and the emotionalized attitudes, endeavoring to give each aspect the approximate degree of emphasis which it has for the individual or the group.* Insofar as he can be genuine in doing so, he accepts rationalizations and intellectualizing, as well as deep and real personal feelings.

7.) *As the acceptant classroom climate becomes established, the facilitator is able increasingly to become a participant learner, a member of the group, expressing his views as those of one individual only.*

8.) *He takes the initiative in sharing himself with the group— his feelings as well as his thoughts—in ways which do not demand nor impose but represent simply a personal sharing which students may take or leave.* Thus, he is free to express his own feelings in giving feedback to students, in his reaction to them as individuals, and in sharing his own satisfactions or disappointments. In such expressions it is his "owned" attitudes which are shared, not judgments or evaluations of others.

9.) *Throughout the classroom experience, he remains alert to the expressions indicative of deep or strong feelings.* These may be feelings of conflict, pain, and the like, which exist primarily within the individual. Here he endeavors to understand these from the person's point of view and to communicate his empathic understanding. On the other hand, the feelings may be those of anger, scorn, affection, rivalry, and the like—interpersonal attitudes among members of the group. Again he is as alert to these as to the ideas being expressed and by his acceptance of such tensions or bonds he helps to bring them into the open for constructive understanding and use by the group.

10.) *In his functioning as a facilitator of learning, the leader endeavors to recognize and accept his own limitations.* He realizes that he can only grant freedom to his students to the extent that he is comfortable in giving such freedom. He can only be understanding to the extent that he actually desires to enter the inner world of his students. He can only share himself to the extent that he is reasonably comfortable in taking that risk. He can only participate as a member of the group when he actually feels that he and his students have an equality as learners. He can only exhibit trust of the student's desire to learn insofar as he feels that trust. There will be many times when his attitudes are not facilitative of learning. He will find himself being suspicious of his students. He will find it impossible to accept attitudes which differ strongly from his own. He will be unable to understand some of the student feelings which are markedly different from his own. He may find himself angry and resentful of student attitudes toward him and angry at student behaviors. He may find himself feeling strongly judgmental and evaluative. When he is experiencing attitudes which are non-facilitative, he will endeavor to get close to them, to be clearly aware of them, and to state them just as they are within himself. Once he has expressed these angers, these judgments, these mistrusts, these doubts of others and doubts of himself, as something coming from within himself, not as objective facts in outward reality, he will find the air cleared for a significant interchange between himself and his students. Such an interchange can go a long way toward resolving the very attitudes which he has been experiencing, and thus make it possible for him to be more of a facilitator of learning.

CONCLUSION

It is hoped that this chapter may provide a view of the skeleton of hypotheses and principles which underlie the practices and methods of the individuals and groups whose experience has been described in earlier chapters.

8

Current Assumptions in Graduate Education: A Passionate Statement

Over the past decade I have become more and more keenly disturbed by the damage which is done to students during their graduate training in the various professional fields. In 1963 I attempted to document my concern in a paper, "Graduate Education in Psychology: A Passionate Statement." It was submitted to the leading professional journal in psychology, but was rejected because it was too controversial and might have a divisive effect upon the science and profession of psychology! I let it be known that the document existed, and since then thousands of copies have been distributed upon request to individuals in a variety of fields. I suspect it has become one of the most widely read unpublished papers of the past decade. This is its first appearance in print.

The letters I have received in response make it clear that the fallacious assumptions I see in graduate education in psychology exist also in other fields. This is especially borne out in the article by Arrowsmith (1966), "The Shame of the Graduate Schools." His ringing protest is against education in the humanities, *and he rather blithely assumes that all is well in graduate education in the sciences.*

Hence, though the content of this chapter deals with the graduate education of psychologists, since that is the field I know intimately, it is my firm belief that the statements in it apply equally to most secondary schools, to most undergraduate education, and indeed to almost every phase of our vast educational enterprise.

So I simply suggest that educators at every level ask themselves, "Do the assumptions listed here apply to any degree to the educational program in which I am involved?" If the answer is "No," they are indeed fortunate.

I wish in this paper to express a strong and growing personal concern about the educational policies which are operative in most departments of psychology in their graduate training programs. Very briefly, the theme of my statement is that we are doing an unintelligent, ineffectual, and wasteful job of preparing psychologists, to the detriment of our discipline and society.

My concern has its basis in the knowledge that the future of civilization may depend on finding the solutions to psychological problems. It is a truism that man has made great progress in solving many of the material problems of his existence, but that he may well be defeated, and perhaps annihilated, by his failure to solve the *psychological* problems which face him—interpersonal, interracial, and international frictions, delinquency, the disturbances labelled "mental illness," the growing loss of a sense of purpose, and the inability to learn at a rate which will keep up with our expanding knowledge. Thus, the logic of our culture *demands* that the behavioral sciences play an increasingly important part in the foreseeable future of our society as it confronts these problems.

Obviously this situation constitutes a challenge to psychology and the other behavioral sciences. We should be selecting and training individuals for creative effectiveness in seeking out and discovering the significant new knowledge which is needed. Furthermore, since psychology, more than the other sciences, has access to the cumulating research knowledge regarding learning, creativity, and the development of autonomous persons, it would seem that our programs for the preparation of psychologists should be superior to programs in other fields.

Is this the case? I fear not. As Sigmund Koch has recently said of psychologists, "We are not known for our readiness to be in the wavefront of history." Granting that American psychologists have not been noted as pioneers, it seems to me unnecessary that in our graduate programs we should so frequently display timid or reactionary patterns which put us in the backwaters rather than the wavefront of history.

In recent years I have had opportunity to observe a number of psychology departments. I have gathered material from graduate students in widely divergent places. For me these observations and this material raise profound and disturbing questions about the general pattern of scientific and professional education in our discipline. When we examine what we *do*, rather than what we *profess* in this area, the picture which emerges is, in my estimation, a sorry one.

I am well aware that members of other sciences and professions often feel similarly critical of graduate education in their own areas. I am limiting my remarks to the field of psychology for two reasons. It is the only field in which I can speak from firsthand knowledge. It is also the science which should be leading the way in preparation of new members of its science and profession.

IMPLICIT ASSUMPTIONS

I believe that we may best consider our programs of graduate education by examining the implicit assumptions on which they appear to be based. I will present these assumptions as I see them, and some of the evidence which challenges them. I trust the reader will think of these statements in relation to some departmental situation he knows and see to what extent they apply.

IMPLICIT ASSUMPTION 1: *The student cannot be trusted to pursue his own scientific and professional learning.*

This is an extremely pervasive assumption in the great majority of departments. One might suppose that the graduate student who has chosen to become a psychologist could be trusted to pursue that purpose, and that the function of the faculty would be to give help in fulfilling his aim of learning the material of his science and profession. Instead, it is almost uniformly true that the faculty attitude is one of mistrustful guidance. Work must be assigned; the completion of this work must be supervised; students must be continually guided and then evaluated. It is very rare indeed that the graduate student finds his program to be an experience in which he is *set free* to pursue the learnings which are of importance to himself.

Many years ago I endeavored to state the divergent views on this point:

> Many believe that the goals of graduate education can best be reached by requiring students to work through a carefully guided program in which the content to be required, the credits to be gained, and the courses to be taken, are quite carefully and clearly defined. They believe that a carefully planned curriculum which sets forth the knowledge and skills to be acquired is perhaps our best method of achieving such a goal.

Others believe that quite a different method is called for in achieving these goals. To them it seems that the best education, and particularly the best graduate education, is that which frees the student to pursue the knowledge, skills, attitudes and experiences which seem to him related to his own goals of ultimate professional and scientific competence. To this second group this seems to be more in accord with what we know of the laws of learning and the principles of individual development and growth.

A graduate student discusses the same issue with more feeling. She says:

> The general attitude in higher education today is one of student *vs.* faculty, rather than student *with* faculty. I wonder if this "opposing attitude" in education doesn't go back to the system of learning in the primary and elementary system. Here the student is asked to memorize rules rather than to understand intrinsically the basic concepts and reasons for these rules. One is "taken to" learning by the hand, rather than "guided toward" knowledge by desire. Professors have learned this way, and the majority of them carry this "opposition learning" to the student. It is what they have experienced, and thus, it is what they transfer to the next fellow.

Later in her statement she gives an appealing view of the alternative possibility:

> In my mind, the two most basic, and at the same time, most general, qualities that should exist in learning, are freedom and responsibility. Freedom of time and freedom of thought, allowing students to relax and become "swept up" by a stimulating environment; to become involved, to be able to give to as well as take from. Responsibility should be felt and accepted by the student—a responsibility to himself, and to his field; to learn, to be involved, to question what he does and thinks and what others do and think.

Her statement is strongly echoed by a distinguished group of nine psychologists who spent four weeks in formulating the principles by which graduate education in psychology might lead to more initiative for research, and more significant research. They say:

> The attitudes, the independence of thought, and the willingness to persist in one's own interest and beliefs that characterize good research work are often the very traits that lead an individual to

resist actively pressures toward conformity to a given pattern of study, toward mastery of given areas of knowledge, or toward acceptance of given ways of thinking. Consequently, the imposition of standardized patterns may often operate to exclude individuals with traits desirable for research (*American Psychologist* 1959, p. 173).

Thus, there seems reason to believe that trusting the student would be a much sounder assumption than the present attitude of mistrust which has a definitely damaging effect upon self-confidence. MacKinnon, in studying creativity in architects, gives a list of the factors in the early life of these men which are highly associated with their present creativeness (as judged by their fellows). The first such background factor is: "An extraordinary respect for the child and confidence in his ability to do what was appropriate" (1963, p. 20).

We might try extending such respect and confidence to our graduate students.

IMPLICIT ASSUMPTION 2: *Ability to pass examinations is the best criterion for student selection and for judging professional promise.*

The best candidate to be selected for training as a psychologist is one who has passed examinations in the past. The most promising graduate student is the one who best passes the examinations in this department.

This assumption, again implicit in the great majority of departments, leads to a heavy stress on the academic record and the grade point average in the process of selecting graduate students. It also leads to the use of measures such as the Graduate Record Examination and the Miller Analogies Test, in the hope that they will predict "academic success," that is, the ability to pass courses similar to undergraduate courses. It also, of course, leads to the use of examinations as the primary criterion for assessing the promise of those students who have been selected for graduate work.

While it is clear that examination-passing ability is a useful skill, and has a place in professional training, it almost certainly emphasizes rote learning and mental agility rather than originality of thought and scientific curiosity, traits which in the long run are more valuable. Guilford has pointed out that education ...

. . . has emphasized abilities in the areas of convergent thinking and evaluation, often at the expense of development in the area of divergent thinking. We have attempted to teach students how to arrive at "correct" answers that our civilization has taught us are correct. This is convergent thinking. . . . Outside the arts we have generally discouraged the development of divergent thinking abilities, unintentionally but effectively (1957, p. 19).

Likewise, in terms of the research by Getzels and Jackson, it would appear that our present methods of selection and assessment tend to place value on what they term the high-I.Q. individual rather than the creative individual. It is useful to think of our usual assessment procedures in the light of their comments about these two types of student:

It seems to us that the essence of the performance of our creative adolescents lay in their ability to produce new forms, to risk conjoining elements that are customarily thought of as independent and dissimilar, to "go off in new directions." The creative adolescent seemed to possess the ability to free himself from the usual, to "diverge" from the customary. He seemed to enjoy the risk and uncertainty of the unknown. In contrast, the high-I. Q. adolescent seemed to possess to a high degree the ability and the need to focus on the usual, to be "channeled and controlled" in the direction of the right answer—the customary. He appeared to shy away from the risk and uncertainty of the unknown and to seek out the safety and security of the known (1963, p. 172).

The effect of this second assumption is that students who are selected and valued as psychologists-to-be tend to excel in examination passing, rather than in those qualities which would give them promise as independent discoverers of new knowledge.

IMPLICIT ASSUMPTION 3: *Evaluation is education; education is evaluation.*

It is incredible the way this preposterous assumption has become completely imbedded in graduate education in the United States. Examinations have become the beginning and the end of education. They are a way of life for the graduate student, and a more stultifying way of life could hardly be imagined. In one university the graduate student in psychology is faced with these major evaluation hurdles:

1.) Examination in first foreign language
2.) Examination in second foreign language
3.) First six hour qualifying examination
4.) Second six hour qualifying examination (both of these in the first graduate year)
5.) Three hour examination in methodology and statistics
6.) Four hour examination in a chosen major field of psychology
7.) Two hour examination in a minor field
8.) Oral examination on Master's thesis
9.) Committee evaluation of Ph.D. proposal
10.) Committee evaluation of Ph.D. thesis
11.) Oral examination on Ph.D. thesis

Since 10 to 50 per cent of those taking any of these examinations are failed on the first attempt, the actual number of examinations taken is considerably greater than indicated above. Understandably, the anxiety on the second attempt is considerably (sometimes unbearably) greater. Furthermore, these examinations are so spaced out that during the four to seven years of his graduate work the student's main concern is with the next sword of Damocles which hangs over his career. As if the above list were not enough, it should be made clear that these major examinations are *in addition to* any quizzes, mid-semester and final examinations given in his courses.

Obviously the student cannot possibly have the sense of fully independent freedom which is clearly at the base of creative professional work. Small wonder that a graduate student leaving this program wrote:

> I don't mind a certain amount of academic hazing of graduate students by the faculty. I know that they feel that they must "get tough." But at this university the point is never reached at which the student feels, "The department is now behind me in my endeavor to get a degree."[1]

The way in which examinations stultify real learning is indicated by a student from another university who writes:

---

[1] It is important to note that all of the graduate students quoted in this paper are doing highly creditable graduate work. One holds a National Science Foundation Fellowship; others hold other national fellowships based on merit. One is known to have a straight A graduate record. None of the quotations are "gripes" from marginal or failing students. For reasons of diplomacy, the authors of the quotations prefer not to be identified.

A lot of people are never sure when they write an exam what grade range they are in. The grade on the exam depends upon whether you have hit the point or points that the professor is looking for. In class you have to tune your mind into the wave length of the instructor. You would like to understand what he is getting at but this is barred by trying to determine what he wants fed back on an exam (Clark, 1962, p. 42).

Another graduate student in still another university expresses something of the bitterness which this approach engenders:

One leaves the course knowing gobs of jargon, and most of "the" answers. He has filled all the pages of his notebook with the professor's speeches, and on the final exam, he has hopefully given back to the professor most of the important facts and basic ideas. The professor looks for and expects a blind acceptance; he wants back what he gave you, not giving you the opportunity for digestion and reaction. There is little chance for synthesis. The student is requested to conform to the instructor's view, and no reward is given for creative thought and individual reaction to the material. The subject is presented as black and white, and one-dimensional. As I write this I feel frustrated. It is a feeling of bitterness, a rebellion, feeling all steamed up inside, but without a hole in the kettle spout to let out some steam; it is a burning steam.

Frequently, for the major examinations, the student is given almost no clues as to what the examination will cover. It will simply be an examination in "general psychology" or "social psychology," or some other field. But since the student knows that the examination questions will be formulated by Professors X and Y, he does not waste his time concentrating on what for him is important in general or social psychology. He focuses instead on learning the interests and prejudices of the two professors. One student, commenting on this aspect, says:

One spends so much time trying to "second guess" what exam questions will be that he has no time to learn what he wants to learn.

Lest one feel that these are merely the rantings of callow graduate students, let me add one more quotation from a scientist looking back on some of his experience:

This coercion had such a deterring effect (upon me) that, after I had passed the final examination, I found the consideration of any problem distasteful for me for an entire year.

This is a statement by Albert Einstein. It portrays very well the impact of an evaluative system upon a sensitive, inquiring, and creative mind. A less restrained statement is said to have been made by another mature scientist, a noted astronomer. He states that real advances in knowledge come from people who are doing what they like to do. We all know the effect on children of compulsory spinach and compulsory rhubarb. It is the same with compulsory learning. They say "It's spinach and to hell with it." Though I cannot prove the authenticity of this statement it certainly expresses the same point of view as is held by most scientists.

It is difficult to exaggerate the damage done to promising graduate students by this completely fallacious assumption that they learn by being threatened, time after time, with catastrophic failure. While I am sure most faculty members would deny that they hold to this assumption, their behavior shows all too clearly that this is the operational principle by which they work.

IMPLICIT ASSUMPTION 4: *Presentation equals learning: What is presented in the lecture is what the student learns.*

It scarcely seems possible that intelligent men could hold to this assumption. Yet one has only to observe a hard-working, serious-minded committee of faculty members arguing over the topics to be included in a graduate survey course in psychology to realize that in their view of the course, what is "covered" (a marvelous term!) is what is learned.

Here is the reaction of a graduate student in the midst of taking such a carefully planned course:

Worst of all, I think, is the fact that not many of the students feel that they are learning anything at all. They feel that it is just a continuation of the idiocy of undergraduate school in which huge amounts of material are thrown at you and you are expected to regurgitate most of it on a test, and then supposedly you have learned something. You may indeed have gained some separated facts about psychology, but none of them can be integrated in any coherent way.

The assumption that learning is equivalent to hearing a lecture is closely tied in with the preceding assumption that education is evaluation. They are both closely related to the next assumption.

IMPLICIT ASSUMPTION 5: *Knowledge is the accumulation of brick upon brick of content and information.*

One might think that psychology, of all the scientific disciplines, would be the least likely to hold this implicit assumption. It is psychologists who have shown that learning takes place primarily and significantly when it is directly related to the meaningful purposes and motives of the individual. Yet most graduate departments proceed upon the conviction that there are a series of fundamental building blocks in the science of psychology which must be mastered sequentially by the student, whether or not they fit in with his current interests.

Some of the best minds in psychology know differently. The Conference on Education for Research in Psychology, mentioned previously, makes these important observations:

> A knowledge of facts of psychology is important for research. How much of this is to be imparted during graduate study, however, is not easy to determine. Much of the factual knowledge of the mature scientist has been accumulated during the course of his career and probably cannot be duplicated by explicit instruction. Moreover, substantive courses inevitably compete for the student's time with practical experience in the methods and art of research. For all these reasons, we urge caution against the overloading of an individual's graduate program with substantive courses, either as the result of department requirements or as the result of choice by the student (*American Psychologist*, 1959, p. 172).

> In general, we question the assumption that the more formal preparation the individual has for research, the more productive and creative he will be in reseach. Specifically, we doubt that the more complete the individual's mastery of statistical and other tools, the more effective he will be in research; we doubt that the greater his scholarly knowledge of the literature, the more likely he will be to contribute to that knowledge; we doubt that the value of theory in research increases continuously as it becomes more formalized and detailed (*American Psychologist*, 1959, p. 170).

I believe it is pertinent to note that Harvard and a number of other leading medical schools have done away with the pre-med undergraduate major, a requirement based on the "brick-by-brick" philosophy. Harvard found that by the third year of medical school those without the pre-med major were doing slightly better in their grades than those with such a major, besides having greater breadth and greater promise.

IMPLICIT ASSUMPTION 6: *The truths of psychology are known.*

In some departments with which I am acquainted this assumption of an orthodoxy of knowledge is quite evident. In other departments there is much more acceptance of divergence. To the extent that there is only one acceptable view, this seems most unfortunate in a developing science. One graduate student describes his experience:

> There is an orthodoxy here. [He then describes the ritual and dogma of his particular department in terms which might be identifying.] . . . Here, it seems, one speaks only in imitation of one's elders. The result is a "new scholasticism"; stultifying repetition of the thoughts and prejudices of the faculty.
>
> One related procedure, which struck me most forcefully in my first class session, is what I call "study-citing behavior," name-dropping about any member whatsoever of certain approved classes of research. It is behavior well calculated to gain the favor of the faculty; it serves the further end of eliminating any necessity for the citer having to think and is also effective in cutting off an opponent in argument. While appeal to research findings can have value if it does not itself become an authoritarianism, it is indicative of the closed-mindedness of the department that only certain brands of research have approved citing status. . . . One learns here rather quickly what is expected of him.

There is no point in belaboring this issue. Often faculty members talk critically about dogmatism, yet display an extreme degree of it in their behavior. Sometimes the orthodoxy is in regard to method, and it is the "truth methods" of scientific psychology that are regarded as immutable. In any event, where attitudes such as those described above exist in a department, the atmosphere is opposed to any true scientific endeavor. Only a pseudo-science can result.

IMPLICIT ASSUMPTION 7: *Method is science.*

Here is an assumption which I find particularly widespread in American psychology. A rigorous procedure is often considered (if one may judge by faculty behavior) as far more important than the ideas it is intended to investigate. A meticulous statistics and a sophisticated research design seem to carry more weight than significant observations of significant problems.

Here again, when prominent scientists in the field of psychology think together about graduate training, they resolutely reject such an assumption:

> Education for research must do more than develop competence in designing, executing, and interpreting experimental or other studies. Development of such competence is important, but much more important is the development of the individual's creativeness —his ability to discover new relations, to reformulate or systematize known facts, to devise new techniques and approaches to problems (*American Psychologist*, 1959, p. 170).

IMPLICIT ASSUMPTION 8: *Creative scientists develop from passive learners.*

A number of the preceding assumptions make it evident that many departments believe, operationally, that the student who absorbs and then gives back on examinations is the one on whom they are placing their bets for the future. Yet I know of no studies in the field which would support this assumption. Anne Roe, from her extensive work in studying leading scientists comes to the conclusion that some of the factors in our educational procedures which adversely affect students in their development as scientists are the following:

1. Insufficient valuation of problem solving attitudes in the school.
2. The general tendency of teachers to sweeping devaluation of "wild" or "silly" ideas.
3. Restriction upon curiosity (1963).

Similarly a broadly based study of several hundred colleges by Thistlethwaite (1963) shows that vigorous class discussions and flexibility of a curriculum are significantly associated with the number of Ph.D.'s in the social sciences produced by these colleges, relative to enrollment. Interestingly enough these same elements are somewhat negatively associated with the production of Ph.D.'s in the natural sciences. Here is an issue worth further study.

MacKinnon, from his extensive work in the investigation of creativity, points up a fact which is too little considered. He says:

> . . . *ledge*, the second element in the word *knowledge*, means sport. Knowledge is the result of playing with what we know, that is, with our facts. A knowledgeable person in science is not, as we are often wont to think, merely one who has an accumulation of facts, but rather one who has the capacity to have sport with what he knows, giving creative rein to his fancy in changing his world of phenomenal appearances into a world of scientific constructs (1963, p. 23).

I think I know what would happen, in most departments, to the graduate student who gave "creative rein to his fancy!"

Yet when students are *taught* to defer judgments about ideas, and are encouraged in a permissive atmosphere simply to *produce* ideas no matter how unreasonable they may seem, they are found to produce a greater quantity and a higher quality of problem-solving ideas than a control group, as research by Parnes and Meadow (1963) has shown.

In my judgment, in our insecurity as a profession, we attach enormous importance to turning out "hardheaded" scientists, and strongly punish any of the sensitive, speculative, sportive openness which is the essence of the real scientist. What departments of psychology of your acquaintance would value these qualities in their graduate students?

> Students who are "unusually appreciative of the intuitive and non-rational elements of their nature; distinguished by their pro-found commitment to the search for esthetic and philosophic meaning in all experience" (Taylor and Barron, 1963, p. 386.)

> Students who exhibit "an openness to their own feelings and emotions, esthetic interests, and a sensitive awareness of self and others" (MacKinnon, 1963, p. 36).

Yet these statements are taken from summaries of the objective characteristics of outstanding young scientists and outstandingly creative professional men. They are, however, the type of personal qualities which many psychologists fear in themselves and in their students.

IMPLICIT ASSUMPTION 9: *"Weeding out" a majority of the students is a satisfactory method of producing scientists and clinicians.*

To me it seems a scandalous waste of manpower that of the carefully selected graduate students whom we take into our programs, only a small proportion ever obtain their degrees. It is indicative of the irresponsible attitude of our discipline that most departments have no idea of what percentage of their students obtain a Ph.D. It appears that in fortunate departments perhaps one out of two students is successful. In some departments only one out of five, or even one out of seven of those who start actually obtain the degree. Usually this is regarded as evidence that the department maintains "high standards." I know of no other field of work in which such an attitude would be taken. Medicine has long ago recognized that when they select a talented group as medical students, the profession has an obligation to conserve this potentiality. Failure is seen as being as much a reflection upon the medical school as upon the student. Industry, too, realizes that it must conserve talented manpower. But in psychology it is not so.

The shameful attrition rate referred to above occurs in part because students fail some of the numerous evaluative hurdles previously mentioned and are eliminated from the program or discouraged from continuing. But it also occurs in considerable part because students with an original turn of mind become disenchanted with the sterility of a program based on the assumptions outlined in these pages and leave for other fields. As I have watched this process it is my conviction that among the students who leave our psychology departments one would find both the least promising and the most promising of our potential future psychologists. Any system of continuous evaluation weeds out some of the less competent or less intelligent. Yet, it also tends very definitely to eliminate the most unique and creative of our students who simply refuse to, as they say, "put up with all that Mickey Mouse."

All in all, it seems clear that most departments are quite satisfied with a weeding out process which wastes the vast majority (from 50 to 85 per cent) of the graduate students who have been so carefully selected. The thought that the profession has a responsibility to "grow psychologists" out of the talented individuals they select, seems scarcely to have entered our thinking. In my opinion, every student who leaves a department should be considered as a possible failure on the part of the department, either in selection, in teaching, in faculty-student relationship, or in the provision of a stimulating professional and scientific climate. His leaving should be carefully considered from each of these angles, in order that deficiencies may be corrected. Industry endeavors to learn from its "exit interviews." Psychology might do likewise.

IMPLICIT ASSUMPTION 10: *Students are best regarded as manipulable objects, not as persons.*

Certainly in a number of departments the relationship between students and faculty is remote and impersonal. This seems to grow out of two causes. In the first place the current ultra-behavioristic philosophy which underlies today's psychology tends to see all individuals simply as machines, managed by reward and punishment. Hence students are dealt with on this same basis. Since students do not like to be treated as objects, the net effect is low morale. Students even tend to treat each other in the same fashion. In some departments where there is a very heavy stress on evaluation, student A will not give help to student B because any improvement in B's showing will automatically put A lower "on the curve." This seems to be a vicious sort of attitude for a professional person who will later be expected to be a part of a scientific or professional team.

There is another factor in this remoteness of faculty-student relationship. It is that it is almost impossible to be close to a student if one's primary relationship to him is that of a judge and evaluator. This is hinted at by a graduate student who describes the faculty-student relationship at his university:

> I see . . . instructors hiding behind a mask of impersonal, "scientific" objectivity in order to avoid the risk involved in *personal* interpersonal relationships, and perhaps out of distaste for the evaluative task they have imposed upon themselves.

In some instances faculty members put the student in a real "double bind" situation by giving him a contradictory message. It is as if the faculty member said: "I welcome you to a warm and close interpersonal relationship—and when you come close I will clobber you with my evaluation." The analogy to the parents of schizophrenics is painfully clear.

Again, solid evidence exists to contradict this tenth assumption. Thistlethwaite, in a study referred to previously, found that faculty "informality and warmth of student-faculty contacts" in the institution is significantly related to the rate of production of Ph.D.'s in the natural sciences, and also in the arts, humanities and social sciences (1963). Psychology may be hurting its own future by its insistence that the individual is nothing more than a machine.

WHY THESE ASSUMPTIONS?

Why is it that departments cling to these behaviors and their underlying assumptions, when even a casual study would expose their fallacies? Why is it that advancement and prestige in departments of psychology depends on adherence to these shaky assumptions? Why is it, for example, that a faculty member who fails half his students on an examination is likely to be regarded as a better (because more "tough-minded") instructor than his colleague who fails none? Why is it that the man who treats his students as persons, as human beings, as junior colleagues, is apt to be looked on with some suspicion by his fellows? How is it that the behaviors described have been so rewarding that they have become embedded in American psychology, in spite of their fallacious base?

I can only speculate. No doubt one reason is that students, consciously or unconsciously, after sixteen years of academic spoon-feeding, tend to demand more of the same. Another reason may be that original, curious, autonomous students, pursuing their own goals, are nearly always disturbing to have around. They challenge pet beliefs and fixed ways of doing things, and, hence, as faculty members we may tend to avoid producing them. Still another reason is that as Research has become an end rather than a means, various results follow. Teaching is devalued, purity of research design becomes all important, and students are a means of getting research done. There is little concern with the true nurture of young scientists. Most important of all, perhaps, is that the philosophical views of psychologists regarding education and the nature of man seem not to have caught up with the advances in their own field. These are only possibilities. The question needs a great deal more investigation. There must be a rational explanation for the stubborn way in which psychology departments cling to these outmoded ideas.

THE OTHER SIDE OF THE COIN

I am well aware that not all of the teaching which goes on in graduate programs operates on the assumptions I have listed. One graduate student, after making a number of complaints, writes:

> More rarely, I will leave a class feeling inspired, excited, and stimulated. Here is the rare professor who encourages freedom of thought. He does not yield to the pressures of having to see his students pass the "finish line," but realizes that there is no finish line. A questioning, thought-provoking atmosphere exists. The student has the opportunity to react openly and honestly, and to lend his own creative thoughts to the subject. The professor does not want his students to take what he says for granted, but rather he encourages them to think about what he says; to think, to react, to question; to accept, to reject, to incorporate.

It is the good fortune of psychology to have a number of such teachers, operating on a very different set of hypotheses, whose open-minded venturesome honesty leads to scientific curiosity and excitement in their students.

Although the operational procedures in most of our graduate programs tend to be in line with the assumptions I have listed, it would not be too difficult to implement a vastly improved program, based upon sharply different principles. Many of the elements of such a program have already been set forth in the report on "Education for Research in Psychology" to which I have made several references. I shall endeavor to spell out such a program in the next chapter.

A FINAL CHALLENGE

If the day comes when psychology wishes to make a thoughtful appraisal of its methods of professional preparation, it will, I believe, throw out most of its current assumptions and procedures. I have tried to indicate, however, that lying all about, in the research literature of psychology itself, are the facts and findings upon which we could build a graduate program of which we could be proud—a program productive of freely independent, openly curious psychologists, unafraid in their search for genuinely new and deeply significant approximations to the truth.

References

American Psychologist. Education for research in psychology. (Report of a seminar group sponsored by the Education and Training Board of the American Psychological Association), 1959, *14*, 167-179.

Arrowsmith, W. The shame of the graduate schools. *Harpers Magazine*, March, 1966, *232* (1390), 51-59.

Clark, J. V. Education for the use of behavioral science. Los Angeles: Institute of Industrial Relations, UCLA, 1962.

Getzels, J. W. & Jackson, P. W. The highly intelligent and the creative adolescent. In C. Taylor & F. Barron (Ed.), *Scientific creativity: Its recognition and development.* New York: John Wiley and Sons, 1963.

Guilford, J. P. A revised structure of intellect. *Reports from the Psychological Lab.*, #19, Los Angeles: University of Southern California, 1957.

MacKinnon, D. W. The nature of creativity. In *Creativity and college teaching.* Proceedings of a conference held at the University of Kentucky. Bulletin of the Bureau of School Service, 1963. *35*, #4, College of Education, University of Kentucky, Lexington, Kentucky.

Parnes, S. J. & Meadow, A. Development of individual creative talent. In C. Taylor and F. Barron (Ed.), *Scientific creativity: Its recognition and development.* New York: John Wiley and Sons, 1963.

Roe, Anne. Personal problems and science. In C. Taylor and F. Barron (Ed.), *Scientific creativity: Its recognition and development.* New York: John Wiley and Sons, 1963.

Taylor, C. & Barron, F. (Ed.), *Scientific creativity: Its recognition and development.* New York: John Wiley and Sons, 1963.

Thistlethwaite, D. The college environment as a determinant of research potentiality. In C. Taylor & F. Barron (Ed.), *Scientific creativity: Its recognition and development.* New York: John Wiley and Sons, 1963.

9

A Revolutionary Program
for Graduate Education

I regret the fact that the preceding chapter is composed almost entirely of negative criticisms aimed at what exists. I want to formulate a statement which will present a feasible substitute and which will encompass the values which I regard as important in both higher and graduate education. This chapter is such an attempt. It is pertinent to this discussion because it seems to me its general pattern is as feasible for professional training in education as it is for the preparation of behavioral scientists.

I wish to put forward some tentative suggestions for a program for graduate level learners in the various behavioral sciences. In spite of their tentative nature these proposals would, if taken seriously, bring about a decided upheaval in present graduate school practices. Because I am a psychologist and an educator, my suggestions will undoubtedly be flavored by experience in those fields. Nonetheless, it is my belief that the suggestions made would be relevant not only to the various social and behavioral sciences but to other fields as well. They also could be adapted, with appropriate changes, to lower levels of education. Indeed the most serious attempts actually to carry through somewhat similar programs have been made and found effective at both the elementary and college levels. Why then do I select graduate education as the target of my remarks? In the first place, it is because I have more experience and competence at that level and feel much more comfortable speaking from experience. The second reason is that I believe that of all the various levels of education, from nursery school to post-doctoral work, graduate education is frequently the furthest behind the main stream of our culture and is the least educational in any true sense. The third reason is that I would like to put forth some positive proposals because I believe the educational world is becoming increasingly ripe for the sorts of changes I propose.

PURPOSES

The major purpose of the program which will be described would be to set up an environment in which freely self-directed and creative learning could take place. Though this may sound simple, it is in direct contradiction to the environment created in most graduate programs in the behavioral sciences.

This general purpose can be broken down into a number of more specific aims which are, I believe, consistent. Thus we could say that the purpose of the whole program is to provide a situation which:

- will restore, stimulate, and enhance the unquenchable curiosity which the student has as a small child. Customarily, by the time he reaches graduate school this curiosity has been dulled and blunted into a passive conformity;

- will encourage the student to choose his own interests and to develop these into mature and growth-promoting professional goals;

- will provide all types of resources—the written word, the laboratory, the equipment for programmed learning, the informed human being, the relevant organizational experience, the relevant community experience—with which the student may nurture his interests. Thus there will be included resources which give the student experience in working on human problems as they exist in their natural context as well as in the classroom and laboratory;

- will permit the student to make responsible choices as to his directions and to live responsibly with the consequences of his mistaken choices as well as his sound ones;

- will give the student a participative role in forming and building the whole graduate program of which he is a part;

- will be primarily oriented toward the future problems of the science and profession rather than its past history or even the present accumulation of so-called "facts";

- will be oriented toward a focus on the solution of *significant* scientific and professional problems rather than primarily upon methodological training in a discipline. The solution of significant problems always leads to interdisciplinary learnings where breakthroughs and advances are most likely;

- will provide close, human, communicative interaction between real persons—student and student, student and faculty, faculty and student;

- will, through such interaction, focus on the real problems—personal and emotional as well as intellectual and professional—which confront the student in his work;

- will develop the student as a self-disciplined and critical learner able to evaluate his own contributions as well as those of others. Thus the student will work, not for the approval of others, but in terms of his own socialized and self-actualizing purposes;

- will enable the student to adapt intelligently, flexibly, and creatively to new problem situations in the future, problems undreamed of at the time of his graduate work;

- will enable the student to make continuing, creative contributions to the solution of the human problems which at this point threaten to abolish the human race. These contributions may be through the approach of pure science or through professional practice or through a combination of both;

- will enable the student to win acceptance as one of the group of qualified professionals who are attempting to cope with these significant scientific and human concerns.

SELECTION OF STUDENTS

I would propose a rigorous selection system, which would weed out, so far as possible, those who seem unlikely to become creative scholars or practitioners. Part of my reasoning is that being refused admission to a program is not a serious blow to a student's personality. It is a rejection which can be rationalized relatively easily. But once *in* the program, the student should not be rejected except for very grave cause. Instead, it should be the task of the staff to develop *all* the selected students as competent professional individuals. They should not be harassed at every turn with requirements and examinations whose major effect is to destroy self confidence and curiosity. Any failure of a student to achieve a Ph.D. should be seen for what it is—a failure for which *both* the staff and student are responsible.

I would like to suggest three criteria for selection. The first would be "intelligence," perhaps more specifically defined as a high degree of ability in problem solving. My reason for this criterion is simply that, in general, intelligence "pays off." Of two professional individuals completely equal in every other respect, the brighter one of the two is probably more likely to make a lasting contribution.

The second criterion may seem surprising—it would be the degree of empathic understanding of which the individual is capable. At present there are no fully satisfactory instruments for measuring empathic ability, but some are being constructed, and it is not an impossible task. There are two reasons for selecting this criterion. In the behavioral sciences the ability truly to understand, accurately and sensitively, the private world of another person, is one of the major sources of information on which both scientific and professional activities can be based. The second reason is that empathic ability is, as Dr. John Shlien pointed out to me many years ago, one of the best single indices of psychological maturity. The immature person cannot permit himself to understand the world of another because it is different from his own and therefore threatening. Hence he cannot help but distort the thoughts and feelings of the other to make it less threatening to him. Only the individual who is reasonably secure in his own identity and self-hood can permit the other person to be different and unique, and can understand and appreciate that uniqueness. So I regard empathic ability as an important criterion for these two quite different reasons.

The third and final criterion is still more difficult to assess but not, I believe, impossible. It is the degree of spontaneous curiosity and originality which the individual exhibits. The person who is genuinely curious, with a childlike desire to *find out*—about his field, about other areas of knowledge, about practical affairs, mechanical devices, new approaches to learning, about all of the universe which surrounds him—is also, I believe, the person most likely to become creative. Indeed the present tests for creativity (which I would suggest using, along with an interview) are partially based on measuring curiosity, and partly upon a closely related element, the originality or uniqueness of response to a new situation. I think of Dr. L. L. Thurstone's informal way of tapping this quality by asking such posers as this: "Suppose that water shrank and became heavier, rather than expanding and becoming lighter, when it freezes. List as many as possible of the effects that this change would produce." Obviously, only the mind well informed by an imaginative and wide-ranging curiosity, unafraid of expressing tentative but unique ideas, could do well with this task. It is this double quality which I would regard as important in a graduate student.

These three would constitute my only criteria. The reason for not including college grades, graduate record examinations, and other criteria which have been shown to have some predictive power in regard to graduate work, is that they have a fundamental deficiency. Essentially, by measuring how well the student has jumped through hoops at the undergraduate level, one can hopefully predict how well he will jump through hoops at the graduate level. But since, in the program I will describe, there are none of the customary hoops, I regard these measures as unhelpful.

ELEMENTS OF THE PROGRAM

It is obvious that since both faculty and graduate students would participate in the planning and implementation of the program, and since different departments would organize their work somewhat differently, what follows is a series of suggestions which would be modified for use in different university situations. The ideas are perhaps best stated as a series of general instructions and information to be given to the incoming student.

PRESENTATION OF THE PROGRAM TO THE STUDENT

Here is a very general description to give you, the incoming student, an overall notion of the opportunities which will be available to you as you study for your doctoral degree in the behavioral sciences. There are, of course, many questions unanswered in this description, but perhaps this statement will be sufficient to give you a general orientation.

A. You are given freedom to use the next four years to become the most competent behavioral scientist you are capable of becoming.

B. You are free to use the courses in this department and other departments; the faculty members of this department and others; the laboratories, the libraries, the clinics, the internship possibilities which are available in, or in connection with the university to develop your own scientific and professional education. The only limit is that in many of these instances permission of the faculty member or of the person in charge must be *earned* in order to take advantage of a given kind of opportunity. Naturally this will be up to you.

The opportunities within the larger community are as important as the opportunities within the university. You may wish to travel to other centers where they are doing research of a type in which you are interested. You may want to find opportunities to observe or serve in clinics, schools, neighborhoods, industries, laboratories, or research institutions which exist in the enlarged community. Everything possible will be done to help you utilize the opportunities you desire.

C. During the first few weeks of your stay here you will have an opportunity to meet in small groups with every faculty member in the department (and perhaps with faculty members from other related departments if you so desire). These meetings will be opportunities for each faculty member to tell you of his own work and interests, the research he is currently involved in, the opportunities that might be available in working with him, the scientific or professional directions in which he is moving, and his hopes and expectations for the future. The purpose of these meetings is to give you the opportunity to make an initial clarification of your own field of interest and to form some impression of the faculty members with whom you will be working.

D. You are to select, as soon as you are ready, a sponsor and at least two additional faculty members to consult with you regarding your work. The choice of sponsor and the composition of this group is entirely up to you, providing only that you can obtain the consent of the faculty members to serve. The function of your sponsor and of this committee is to consult with you on any problems you present to them; to keep you informed of resources of which you may not be aware; to point out what they regard as weaknesses in the program you are developing and to discuss with you the various possibilities you are considering for your own work. The final responsibility for what you do lies with you, the student, not with this committee. They give no formal approval or disapproval to your plan. Their function is to consult with you and to give you every help they can in developing, enriching and improving your own program of work.

There is no need that this group should continue to work with you throughout your four years. If your interests change you may desire to select a different sponsor and a different group of consultants. This is your privilege.

E. Much of your work will naturally be composed of independent study. It is probable, however, that you will wish to work in a tutorial group with your sponsor and he is prepared to accept this responsibility. For some periods of time you may find it more profitable to work in a tutorial group with some other faculty member whose interests enrich your own.

Whether you concentrate entirely on independent study, or work in a tutorial group, or divide your time between these types of effort, you are primarily responsible for planning and carrying out your program. You are to submit to your sponsor and your committee at the beginning of each quarter (or semester) your tentative plans for the work you expect to do during that period. At the end of each period you are to submit a description of what you have done and your own evaluation of your progress and achievements, or lack of same, during that period. In making such an evaluation you are to describe the criteria by which you are judging your own work.

F. You will have the opportunity of joining a basic encounter group composed of several of your fellow students and several faculty members. It is intended that each group will contain from six to eight graduate students and four to six faculty members. Insofar as possible each student will be in a group with his sponsor and at least some of the faculty members on his committee. This group will be quite different from the tutorial group. It will be an opportunity to meet with each other as persons; to explore the feelings and attitudes which exist between individuals; to become more aware of yourself, and more aware of the impact you have on others. It will also be an opportunity for mutual feedback in which others can give you information on the way in which they see your weaknesses and strengths and you can do the same for them. This applies both to faculty and students. The primary purpose of this encounter group is to give all of its members an opportunity to improve their interpersonal communication and to grow and develop as persons. This group will meet initially for one full weekend and then at intervals thereafter as you yourselves desire and plan. In general, it is the expectation that you will have an experience in some encounter group during each of the years that you are in the university. The encounter group is not a requirement but it is believed that most students will wish to take advantage of this opportunity.

G. During the next four years you will submit evidence which by the end of the four year period should be proof that you are an informed and competent behavioral scientist who is capable of doing creative research work and capable of sound professional functioning, and that you are worthy of being granted a doctoral degree.

This evidence will be cumulative and will include your reports of work during each period and your evaluation of that work. It should also include the very first things you undertake, even though these may be seen later as being rather crude efforts. You may, for example, want to survey a field in which you think you have some interests. Very well, make such a survey and write it up and submit it for the folder which will be established for you. Keep one copy for yourself so that you will always have in your own hands all of the evidence which is also in the hands of the university.

To carry the example further, perhaps out of your survey of a given field will come some interest in doing a small research study in that field. You will consult with the members of your committee on the design of this research and the means for carrying it out. Once it is completed you will write it up and submit it for your folder.

You may be interested in a different type of survey, namely, observing the practices of a mental health clinic or a school system or an industry. In that case the write-up of your observations can be filed. Later you may undertake some project in a school, an industry or within the community. This, too, can be a portion of the evidence. As time goes on you may find yourself writing theoretical papers or case reports or reports of your internship experience, or further and more elaborate research studies. Some of these should be of a quality worthy of publication and it is expected that you will submit them for publication to a suitable journal. Here, too, consultation with your sponsor may help in improving the paper and in locating a proper channel for its publication.

It is hoped that this makes clear in general the way in which you will build up the evidence which shows that you are a competent and productive professional person and scientist.

H. The evaluation of this evidence and the decision as to your fitness for a doctoral degree will be made by a group of five. This examining committee will be selected by the departmental staff and at least a majority of the committee will be behavioral scientists from outside of this university. You and your committee may nominate individuals whom you feel would be competent members of such a committee, but the final decision will be made by the faculty of the department.

The function of this committee is to examine the evidence which has accumulated in your folder and to conduct additional oral or written examinations to determine whether your contribution to knowledge in the behavioral sciences has been sufficient to justify the awarding of a doctoral degree.

I. The criteria upon which the committee will evaluate your work is as follows:

(1) *Ability and promise shown in your contributions to knowledge.* Judgment on this criteria will be based on research work you have submitted and also significant theoretical contributions. Consideration will be given to the quality of creative theoretical thinking which has gone into your projects; the adequacy of the scientific methodology and the degree of significant contribution to tested knowledge.

(2) *Professional competence and promise.* The methods used by the committee in this area will have to vary somewhat with your field of specialization. There will be material in your folder bearing on this topic. Judgment will also be based upon written evaluation made by those who are well acquainted with your professional functioning—for instance colleagues and superiors with whom you have worked if you are in the clinical field, colleagues and supervisors from the educational or industrial or computer fields if you have specialized in such areas. Insofar as they are appropriate to your field of specialization, such elements as the following will be taken into consideration: your skills in your professional field; the likelihood that you will be a productive leader in this field; your attitude toward yourself, toward your work and toward others; your effectiveness in interpersonal relationships, to the extent that this is involved in your professional work; and your independent grasp of the professional problems that face the practitioner in your area.

In case you are specializing in a field of professional application such as industrial, clinical or child psychology, or teaching, the interest of society will be protected by an oral or written examination designed to test the type of knowledge which is necessary to carry on such professional functioning in a responsible way.

(3) *The breadth and depth of your learning in your own field.*
Evaluation in terms of this criterion will be largely based upon
a study of the evidence which you have submitted and placed
in your folder—the various papers, exhibits, observations, sur-
veys, research reports—as well as upon the oral examination.

J. During the course of the four years you may take course
examinations if they are offered. You may ask your sponsor
to give you doctoral preliminary examinations which have
been offered in previous years, or you may request special
written or oral examinations at any reasonable time during
your progress to assist you in the evaluation of your own
development. These will be graded or evaluated and the
evaluations given to you for your own use. They do not constitute a part of the final evaluation of your work. They are
entirely diagnostic in their purpose, aiming to indicate to you
the areas of strength and weakness in your own preparation.
It is strongly suggested, for example, that you undergo a
"trial assessment" by members of your committee and other
faculty members, several months prior to your examination by
an outside committee. This too will be diagnostic in its purpose. Following this trial assessment you may consult, col-
lectively or individually, with the faculty members who
conducted it, finding out the areas in which you seem deficient, and the ways in which you might present yourself and
your work more adequately.

K. In payment for your professional education you are to pay
tuition for the usual number of graduate courses which would
be taken by a full-time student completing his doctoral degree.

THE RATIONALE OF THE PROGRAM

Much of the basic rationale, and the assumptions on which the
program is built, are clearly implicit in the program itself. Yet it
may be well to state these assumptions explicitly as well.

Most significantly the plan is built on the hypothesis that *the
student has the potentiality and the desire to learn*, providing that a

suitable environment can be established. Very few educators believe this, yet there is research evidence even in lower forms of life to support this view. Both rats and flatworms choose more complex environments, with more difficult problems to solve, when they are given the choice. Thus in this program the student is continually working on the unsolved problems which he perceives as relevant to his own purposes and development. He is trying to solve the problems he is able to recognize. Hobbs states this well when he says that the goal of the faculty member is "by example and design, to get his students into trouble . . . to teach his students the art of precipitating themselves into just manageable difficulties of their own choosing."[1]

The learning of the student is *rooted in reality* from the very first. Whether he works in a school, a clinic, an industry or a laboratory—whether he is only an observer or a working participant in these situations— he faces from the first, on an experiential level, the real problems which cry out for solution. He is not simply working at "problems" set for him by others.

It is clear that the program focuses on learning, *meaningful learning*, by the student. It is not accidental that nothing has been said about teaching. Teaching, in its customary sense of lecturing and imparting unrequested knowledge, is irrelevant to this program.

The focus of the program is on providing *a psychological climate suitable for self-directed and significant learning*. This means freedom to think unusual thoughts without being squelched. It means the availability of a tremendous range of stimulating resources—community situations, teaching machines, laboratory opportunities, human beings in creative action, as well as the more usual resources of books, films, tapes and the like. Freedom, stimulation, human understanding of one's purposes and frustrations—these constitute a suitable climate for the sort of learning which makes a difference.

In all this the faculty member has a role just as difficult as, but very different from, the conventional professorial role. He is imaginative about providing the resources mentioned above—one of these resources being himself—as these resources are appropriate

---

[1] Nicholas Hobbs "The Professor and the Student." Paper presented at the American Council on Education, October, 1965.

to, and desired by, the student. He encounters the student as a person, and reacts himself as a person. He is more free to do the latter because he has no power over the student. He can relax his façade and be *himself* to the student, a person with attitudes, interests, feelings, biases and purposes.

The program as outlined relies fundamentally on *self-criticism* and *self-evaluation*, thus promoting true creativity. It is not however an insulated or autistic self-evaluation, for continuing feedback from other students and faculty gives a reality dimension to the student's appraisal of himself. Nevertheless, the student is the final judge, and can embark, if he chooses, on a course of study and action which everyone else regards as absurd.

The program does away entirely with all the horrible machinery of tests, examinations and evaluation which have unfortunately become the central feature and hallmark of American education. Thus the student can read a book for what it contributes to his learning, not simply to pick out the items which are likely to be asked on an examination. He is forced to develop his own inner directions, and to discover directions which are *rewarding* to *him*, instead of relying passively on the rewards he will receive in the way of grades.

The program as outlined aims to develop the whole person—not simply someone informed from the neck up, but someone who exists in a significant relationship to others and to himself. In the encounter groups the student has the opportunity to become more of a *person*—more self-aware, and more understanding of others. He will not become simply a wooden technician, an outcome all too evident in many of the graduate programs in science, but an outcome especially tragic in the behavioral sciences.

One of the aspects of the program which may be puzzling to many readers is the use (largely or wholly) of outside evaluators in making the decision as to whether the candidate has earned a Ph.D. I have no special brief for outside evaluation, which can be as faulty as evaluation by one's own faculty. But it has the enormous advantage of permitting the faculty member to be a *friend* to his junior colleague, the student. The faculty member will be eager for him to do well, will help him with counsel and advice—instead of periodically trying to trap him in examinations, or trying to weed him out of the program to show that he, the faculty member, is "tough-minded." It will rescue the professor from the intolerable double bind in which he currently lives—on the one hand his desire to be a helpful human being to his students, and on the other hand the continuing necessity of being a judge and executioner at the same time. It releases the faculty member to undertake one task only— that of facilitating the learning of his students.

Finally, the program permits the student to *become* a fully professional person—a scientist, a practitioner, a facilitator of learning— not at some future date, after he has received his degree, but during every day and year of his graduate work. He is learning by being and doing, and for me this constitutes the best type of learning.

POSTSCRIPT

To many, the program I have outlined may seem impractical, far-out, oblivious of the realities of higher education. Yet the ferment which is now so evident in industrial organizations, and in such stable institutions as the Roman Catholic Church, is beginning to touch education—our most conservative institution—as well. And so perhaps these proposals may strike a more responsive chord now than they would have earlier.

10

Some Thoughts About Educational Administration

There can be no doubt that the point of view presented in this book is infectious and pervasive. If the classrooms of a school become permeated by this point of view, questions will soon be raised as to the administration of the school. Is it possible that it could be conducted in the same way? I have felt compelled to formulate a brief statement on this complex topic. I hope that it will at least be suggestive, and helpful to those who carry this burden, increasingly difficult in modern times.

Since I have never been responsible for the administration of an educational institution or an educational system, this chapter will be brief. I do not wish to write in areas where I have not had direct experience. Yet I have been responsible for a large counseling center, and for various research groups, and I have learned many things about administration the hard way. I have made my full share of mistakes. I have also had the very rewarding experience of watching both an institution, and the individuals who constitute it, grow and flourish. At such times I believe I have had a part in "growing people," which to me is the most important function of an administrator.

Much of the point of view which I have come to hold regarding administration has been stated by others. Gordon (1955) gives a thoughtful analysis and two case histories. An excellent presentation has also been made by the late Douglas McGregor more than a decade ago (published in 1961). I particularly appreciated his statement because it put into words what I felt I had been learning in my own attempts to lead an organization.

McGregor develops a "Theory X" which gives the basis of much of current executive behavior. He also puts forth a "Theory Y" which is based on the experience and research in the social and behavioral sciences which underlie all of this book. His own writing about these theories was directed toward industrial organizations. I should like to paraphrase his ideas, putting them in an educational context. In doing so, I am drawing heavily on his writing.

THE CONVENTIONAL VIEW

The educational administrator who follows the usual pattern in carrying responsibility for his school (McGregor's "Theory X") sees his task as that of harnessing the energy of faculty and students so that the goals and requirements of the educational system will be met. In the first place he sees himself as responsible for organizing the available money, equipment, and people in such a way as to achieve the educational goal which he has in view. This means that he must motivate and direct his faculty, and through them the students. It means that one of his main functions is to control the actions and to modify the behavior of all members of the school in such ways that the educational goal will be achieved. Central to his policies is the view that both faculty and students would be, if left to their own devices, apathetic to, or resistant to, the educational goal. Consequently, they must be rewarded, punished, persuaded— through use of both the carrot and the stick—so that they work toward the goal which the administrator, or his board of trustees, or the state, has defined as "being educated."

This usual approach to educational administration has implicit in it a rather definite view of the nature of the human being. It is implied that both teacher and student are naturally apathetic and tend to avoid any strenuous effort. Both teacher and student are seen as disliking responsibility and preferring to be guided or led. This view assumes that both teacher and student (but especially the student) are indifferent to achieving an educational goal and will only work toward this if a proper series of behavioral controls are instituted.

Since I have, in Chapter 8, spelled out in a more emotional way many of the assumptions which underlie this kind of an approach, I will not further enlarge on them here. I would only add that administrators and teachers who hold this theoretical approach may be "hard" or "soft." The person who is "hard," whose controls are largely of the coercive type, whose discipline is very strict, finds his view of people and hence his theory confirmed, because his subordinates are continually sabotaging his policies. For example, I recently heard of a principal who assigned each teacher to a numbered seat for faculty meetings so that roll could easily be taken, and pressure applied to those who failed to attend. Doubtless the principal was surprised, and certainly his view of human nature was confirmed, when he discovered that many of his policies were formally adopted, and then completely defeated by subtle and indirect means.

But the administrator who is "soft," whose desire is for harmony, who tries to be kindly and permissive, also finds himself defeated if he holds, and attempts to implement, this conventional theory. His persuasions often fall on deaf ears. He finds that his teachers (and students) take advantage of him. They ask for more and more, since he is a giving person, but *they* tend to give less and less in their own efforts. So again his view of the nature of both teachers and students is confirmed, and he is likely to become cynical. Frequently in his cynicism he veers toward the "hard" approach.

Though the practices of a large number of educational administrators (probably a majority) would fall under this conventional approach to administration, it is a point of view which is increasingly challenged by the experience and research of the behavioral sciences, and by the experience of a growing number of forward-looking and successful industries. Let us take a look at an alternative approach.

A MODERN VIEW

The grounds for the theory of administration which McGregor calls "Theory Y" have been exemplified in all of the preceding chapters of this book. The assumptions on which this theory is based, the kinds of evidence from the behavioral sciences which support it, the view of human nature which permeates it, constitute the backbone of what I have set forth. Consequently, a very brief presentation of my version of the theory as it affects educational administration should suffice.

In terms of this theory the educational administration is responsible for organizing the resources of the institution—the teachers, the students, the funds, the equipment and materials in such a way that all of the persons involved can work together toward defining and achieving *their own* educational goals. The mainspring of the organization is the motivation for development and learning which is inherent in each person. The task of the administrator is to so arrange the organizational conditions and methods of operation that people can best achieve their own goals by also furthering the jointly defined goals of the institution. The administration finds that his work consists primarily of removing obstacles such as "red tape", of creating opportunities where teachers and students and administrators (including himself) can freely use their potential, of encouraging growth and change, and of creating a climate in which each person can *believe* that his potential is valued, his capacity for responsibility is trusted, his creative abilities prized.

It should be clear from the above that responsibility and authority and initiative would be diffused throughout the group, in order to make the best use of all available knowledge, skill and originality, and thus to maximize the soundness of decisions. By following such a policy the development of the individuals involved is also maximized.

The administrator has the task of using himself in just as fulfilling a way as he makes possible for his staff and students. He does not submerge himself, but uses his leadership qualities, his vision, his wider information, all the characteristics which have led to his being placed in a position of responsibility, as positive input in a living and changing organization. Part of his function is to serve as a catalyst in releasing the capacity of others, but he is failing in his task if he does not release and develop his own potential as well. He is in the business of growing persons, but he himself is one of those persons.

In-service training in such an educational system would see its most important problem as "How may we generate or develop more facilitative leaders?" The aim would be to bring such leaders into being at the administrative, faculty, and student levels—individuals who could listen, understand, accept, clarify, communicate—who could help either an individual or a group to experience more clearly its own current and changing aims, difficulties, desires, frustrations, antagonisms, so that he or they could be more effectively self-directing. This type of training is difficult because it is not enough to pick up certain tricks of method or procedure. The leader needs to grow into a person who can *actually* understand,

and *actually* accept very diverse views and feelings, and can express his own views and feelings without imposing them on others. Hence the in-service training would be essentially concerned with providing growth opportunities for persons who could then facilitate growth in other individuals or groups.

This, in brief, is the theory of administration which is most consonant with the point of view expressed in this book. But thus far it has been stated only in abstract terms. Perhaps an example will help to remedy this.

A SMALL ILLUSTRATION

During the dozen years that I was the leader of the Counseling Center at the University of Chicago, the organization grew until there were approximately fifty members. I was endeavoring to build organizational procedures which would be consistent with the view of human potential which pervaded our counseling work. Though we made many mistakes, we functioned well in our unorthodox fashion, and I think it is fair to say that we were decidedly successful in growing persons. I have known few organizations where the staff exhibited such dedicated loyalty to the group, and were so productive. Working hours meant nothing, and on evenings, weekends, and holidays, staff members could be found at the Center working on their self-assigned tasks.

I am pleased that in the midst of our groping toward more effective organizational procedures, I wrote down a number of the questions I felt I must continually be asking myself. Administrators of schools and educational systems may gain some fresh stimulation, and perhaps some challenge, from reading these questions. They are presented here in the form in which I wrote them in 1948.

An Administrator's Musings

1.) Do I trust the capacities of the group, and of the individuals in the group, to meet the problems with which we are faced, or do I basically trust only myself? I find that when I take the risk, the gamble, of resting my confidence in the group, ingenuity, responsibility, and strength are multiplied. If I am fearful of doing that, and rely on myself, this produces in the group passivity, a willing-

ness to sit back and criticize, and dries up initiative and constructive effort.

2.) Do I free the group for creative discussion by being willing
to understand, accept and respect *all* attitudes, or do I find myself
trying subtly to manipulate group discussion so that it comes out
my way? I find that this tests my basic philosophy very deeply. . . .
When there is a genuine willingness for all attitudes to be expressed
—critical and hostile as well as constructive—then the group senses
the fact that it is *their* organization, and they respond with vigor,
with loyalty, and with responsibility. When the clerical staff is
as free to contribute attitudes as the professional staff, then perhaps
this principle is most deeply operative. On the other hand, if the
freedom is of the "pseudo" variety, then suspicion develops.

3.) Do I, as leader, participate by honest expression of my own
attitudes but without trying to control the attitudes of others? . . .
In a situation such as a staff group, where I am most certainly
ego-involved, it is as important that I express my feeling as that
the next person does. But this will again test deeply the leader's
philosophy. He can express his attitude in such a way as to imply
"and you had better think the same," or his expression can on the
other hand imply, "this is just one feeling, and others may have
very different attitudes."

4.) Do I rely upon basic attitudes for motivation, or do I think
surface procedures motivate behavior? It has been our experience
that when a problem is felt by the group, and freely and openly
considered, and a way of meeting it is discovered and experienced
by the group, action along those lines follows. If this process has
not been achieved, no amount of formal agreement will bring
constructive action. . . . The group seems to be an organism, and
when it feels itself to be clearly integrated, action follows inevitably. When it is in conflict, action is confused or conflicting, and
no amount of neatly typed policy will make it otherwise.

5.) Am I willing to be responsible for those aspects of action which
the group has delegated to me? If I do not wish the responsibility I
should say so. If I accept it, I am obliged to carry it out.

6.) Do I trust the individual to do his job? Here we plunge
directly into the question of what is supervision. If supervision
is the task of an overseer, directing the individual as to how he does
his work, then I think much of what I have described is negated.

We have come to put new meaning into the term supervision. We regard supervisory contact as the opportunity which the individual has to think through more clearly the problems he is meeting on his job—the unpleasant demands made upon him, and the way he will adjust to those; the failure experiences he is having in his counseling; the problems he may feel in his personal orientation to the staff. We find that the more the individual is given the responsibility for his job, the more deeply he accepts it, but when someone else assumes that responsibility then his attitude is, "I just work here."

7.) When tensions occur, do I try to make it possible for them to be brought out into the open? I think administrators tend to think they are doing well if no tensions are evident. On the basis of our experience it seems much sounder to accept the fact of tension as basic and to learn to deal with it. People, because they are living people, are bound to be at times dissatisfied, to feel out of line with the group, to feel jealous, to feel critical of others, etc. We have come to believe that it is only when a tension is displaced in its object that it is dangerous. If the staff feels I have been too dictatorial or have played favorites in some action of mine, only constructive thinking accrues if that is told to me. The experience may be painful, but it results in growth. But if it is bottled up, and expressed only in opposition to some new policy proposal of mine, then it does not dissolve, but tends to become heightened. . . So we have found it highly important to try to create an atmosphere in which real attitudes can be expressed toward their real objects. When this occurs, tension is reduced, and almost inevitably perceptions (and hence behaviors) are altered. In such an atmosphere morale is not always superficially sweet, but it is sound and real, and experienced as a significant anchorage (Rogers, 1948).

COMMENT

Both before and since the writing of these questions I have held responsibility for the leadership of various groups, with varying degrees of success. With one group I believe that I was a failure as a leader, and some of the events which occurred were disastrous. As I have endeavored to understand this painful failure, I have concluded that it came about because my behavior was such that I could not have given affirmative answers to the seven questions listed above. I was in too great a hurry for "results," the net outcome being that I and all the members of the group were decidedly unhappy with the results. I felt there was "not enough time" for a complete trust in the capacity of the group, nor for permitting tensions to be openly worked out. As a result the trust I put in the group was to some extent incomplete, and the psychological climate to some extent a pseudo-freedom. The experience is a painful one to recall, and I can scarcely believe that I could have failed so significantly to implement what I so deeply believe.

The experience has taught me one firm lesson. If one is going to exercise *control* of the group, and to follow "Theory X," then it is highly important to do so *openly*. Many organizations function quite effectively under a hierarchial type of controlling authority. This is definitely preferable to an organization which functions under "Theory Y" in a *pseudo*-fashion. As in setting the conditions for a classroom, genuineness is perhaps the most important ingredient of success. If an administrator can grant only a small sector of freedom to the members of his organization, he should be completely open about the control he intends to exercise over the remaining sectors of their functioning. This at least I feel I have learned from my painful experience of failure.

CONCLUSION

An educational administrator can function in a fashion which is consistent with the whole approach of this book. He can operate in a way which involves his staff as participants, which draws upon their knowledge and abilities, which relies upon the basic human trend toward learning and self-fulfillment. To do so is not easy, and the extent to which it can be achieved depends primarily upon the attitude of the administrator. Yet it is worth the risk, since only in this way can the exciting potential of the group be utilized to carry the organization—and its constituent members—forward.

References

Gordon, T. *Group-centered leadership.* Boston: Houghton Mifflin, 1955.

McGregor, D. M. The human side of enterprise. In W. G. Bennis, K. D. Benne, & R. Chin (Ed.), *The planning of change.* New York: Holt, Rinehart, & Winston, 1961. Pp. 442-431. (Originally a convocation talk at Massachusetts Institute of Technology in 1957.)

Rogers, C. R. Some implications of client-centered counseling for college personnel work. *Educational* & *Psychological Measurement*, 1948, *8*, 540-549.

part **IV**

The Philosophical and Value Ramifications

Introduction to Part IV

It will already be clearly evident that the orientation which pervades this book is not a technique nor a method of facilitating learning. The whole approach obviously exists in a personal context, a philosophical context, a context of values, a view as to the goal of personal development. This has, I believe, been implicit throughout. But it seems only fair to the reader that these basic background elements should be made explicit also.

So, in this fourth portion of the book, I shall first try to set forth some of my most basic beliefs about persons and the capacities they have for living and being in relationships. This material is expressed from a very personal point of view. The chapter which follows presents a line of thought and theory as to how modern man, living in his constantly changing environment, with institutions crumbling all around him, can possibly find and determine the values by which he can live in this highly existential world. The next question which is faced is one basically raised by the behavioral sciences; is there any such thing as freedom in human beings who are, according to most psychologists, completely determined by their environment? The final chapter in this part faces a question rarely raised. If the whole point of view and philosophy of this book were to be successfully achieved, what kind of person would emerge? Would we like that person? Would we choose him as the goal toward which we move and strive?

But what does all this have to do with education? Education, in the eyes of most, has to do with curricula, with methods, with administration, with teaching. It is my contention that tomorrow's educator, whether the humblest kindergarten teacher, or the president of a great university, must know, at the deepest personal level, the stance he takes in regard to life. Unless he has true convictions as to how his values are arrived at, what sort of an individual he hopes will emerge from his educational organization, whether he is manipulating human robots, or dealing with free individual persons, and what kind of a relationship he is striving to build with these persons, he will have failed not only his profession, but his culture. So it is without apology that I present my tentative answers to these deeply vexing questions. I do not ask the reader to agree, for some of my thoughts are far from conventional. I ask only that he think through these issues *for himself*, to a point that he knows *where* he stands, and *why*, because his students and his public will increasingly be challenging him on just such issues.

II

Being in Relationship

This chapter is a revised version of a highly personal talk I gave to a recent conference of the American Personnel and Guidance Association in Dallas. I was dumbfounded that the auditorium, holding several thousand persons, was crammed full at 8:30 in the morning (!) to hear a talk on interpersonal relationships. I believe it presents important elements of me, and thus may contribute to an understanding of the chapters which precede and those which follow it in this book.

Just as it was an awesome thing to face a sea of a thousand faces so early in the morning, so I have the same feeling, something akin to panic, whenever I start a chapter for this book. What possible way is there in which I can make real *contact* with a multitude of unknown readers, whose background, expectations, and attitudes are all unknown to me? Especially is this concern a deep one when I want to talk about interpersonal relationships. I don't believe a scholarly, abstract chapter will make that contact. Furthermore, I have no desire to instruct my readers, or impress you with my knowledge in this field. I have no desire to tell you what you should think or feel or do. How can I meet this dilemma?

The only solution I have come up with is that perhaps I can share something of myself, something of *my* experience in interpersonal relationships, something of what it has been like to be me, in communication with others. This is not an easy thing to do. But if I can do it, if I can share something of myself, then I think you can take what I say, or leave it alone. You can decide whether it is relevant to your own job, your career, your profession, your life. You can respond to it with the reaction, "That's just what *I've* felt and what *I've* discovered," or equally valuably, "I feel *very* differently. My experience has taught me something entirely different." In either case, it may help you to define *yourself* more clearly, more openly, more surely. That I *do* regard as worthwhile, and as something I hope I can facilitate.

221

So I'm going to share with you a somewhat miscellaneous bag of learnings, things I have learned or am learning about this mysterious business of relating with other human beings, about communication between persons. I'm going to share some of my satisfactions and my dissatisfactions in this area. The reason I call it a mysterious business is that interpersonal communication is almost never achieved except in part. You probably never feel fully understood by another, and neither do I. Yet I find it extremely rewarding when I have been able, in a particular instance, truly to communicate myself to another. I find it very precious when, for some moment in time, I have felt really close to, fully in touch with, another person.

I LIKE TO HEAR

So the first simple feeling I want to share with you is my enjoyment when I can really *hear* someone. I think perhaps this has been a long standing characteristic of mine. I can remember this in my early grammar school days. A child would ask the teacher a question and the teacher would give a perfectly good answer to a completely different question. A feeling of pain and distress would always strike me. My reaction was, "But you didn't *hear* him!" I felt a sort of childish despair at the lack of communication which was (and is) so common.

I believe I know why it is satisfying to me to hear someone. When I can really hear someone it puts me in touch with him. It enriches my life. It is through hearing people that I have learned all that I know about individuals, about personality, about psychotherapy, and about interpersonal relationships. There is another peculiar satisfaction in it. When I really hear someone it is like listening to the music of the spheres, because beyond the immediate message of the person, no matter what that might be, there is the universal, the general. Hidden in all of the personal communications which I really hear there seem to be orderly psychological laws, aspects of the awesome order which we find in the universe as a whole. So there is both the satisfaction of hearing this particular person and also the satisfaction of feeling oneself in some sort of touch with what is universally true.

When I say that I enjoy hearing someone I mean, of course, hearing deeply. I mean that I hear the words, the thoughts, the feeling tones, the personal meaning, even the meaning that is below the conscious intent of the speaker. Sometimes, too, in a message which superficially is not very important, I hear a deep human cry, a "silent scream," that lies buried and unknown far below the surface of the person.

So I have learned to ask myself, can I hear the sounds and sense the shape of this other person's inner world? Can I resonate to what he is saying, can I let it echo back and forth in me, so deeply that I sense the meanings he is afraid of yet would like to communicate, as well as those meanings he knows?

I think, for example, of an interview I had with an adolescent boy, the recording of which I listened to only a short time ago. Like many an adolescent today he was saying at the outset of the interview that he had no goals. When I questioned him on this he made it even stronger that he had no goals whatsoever, not even one. I said, "There isn't anything you want to do?" "*Nothing* . . . Well, yeah, I want to keep on living." I remember very distinctly my feeling at that moment. I resonated very deeply to this phrase. He might simply be telling me that, like everyone else, he wanted to live. On the other hand he might be telling me, and this seemed to be a distinct possibility, that at some point the question of whether or not to live had been a real issue with him. So I tried to resonate to him at all levels. I didn't know for certain what the message was. I simply wanted to be open to any of the meanings that this statement might have, including the possible meaning that he might have at one time considered suicide. I didn't respond verbally at this level. That would have frightened him. But I think that my being willing and able to listen to him at all levels is perhaps one of the things that made it possible for him to tell me, before the end of the interview, that not long before he had been on the point of blowing his brains out. This little episode constitutes an example of what I mean by wanting to really hear someone at all the levels at which he is endeavoring to communicate.

I find, in therapeutic interviews, and in the intensive group experiences which have come to mean a great deal to me in recent years, that hearing has consequences. When I do truly hear a person and the meanings that are important to him at that moment, hearing not simply his words, but *him*, and when I let him know that I have heard his own private personal meanings, many things happen. There is first of all a grateful look. He feels released. He wants to tell me more about his world. He surges forth in a new sense of freedom. I think he becomes more open to the process of change.

I have often noticed, both in therapy and in groups, that the more deeply I can hear the meanings of this person the more there is that happens. One thing I have come to look upon as almost universal is that when a person realizes he has been deeply heard, there is a moistness in his eyes. I think in some real sense he is weeping for joy. It is as though he were saying, "Thank God, *somebody* heard me. Someone knows what it's like to be me." In such moments I have had the fantasy of a prisoner in a dungeon, tapping out day after day a Morse code message, "Does anybody hear me? Is there anybody there? Can anyone hear me?" And finally one day he hears some faint tappings which spell out "Yes." By that one simple response he is released from his loneliness, he has become a human being again. There are many, many people living in private dungeons today, people who give no evidence of it whatever on the outside, where you have to listen very sharply to hear the faint messages from the dungeon.

If this seems to you a little too sentimental or overdrawn, I would like to share with you an experience I had recently in a basic encounter group with fifteen persons in important executive posts. Early in the very intensive sessions of the week they were asked to write a statement of some feeling or feelings which they had which they were *not* willing to tell in the group. These were anonymous statements. One man wrote, "I don't relate easily to people. I have an almost impenetrable façade. Nothing gets in to hurt me but nothing gets out. I have repressed so many emotions that I am close to emotional sterility. This situation doesn't make me happy but I don't know what to do about it." This is clearly a message from a dungeon. Later in the week a member of my group identified himself as the man who had written that anonymous message, and filled out in much greater detail his feelings of isolation, of complete coldness. He felt that life had been so brutal to him that he had been forced to live a life without feeling, not only at work, but in social groups, and saddest of all, with his family. His gradual achievement of greater expressiveness in the group, of less fear of being hurt, of more willingness to share himself with others, was a very rewarding experience for all of us who participated.

I was both amused and pleased when, in a letter a few weeks later he included this paragraph. "When I returned from (our group) I felt somewhat like a young girl who had been seduced but still wound up with the feeling that it was exactly what she had been waiting for and needed! I am still not quite sure who was responsible for the seduction—you or the group, or whether it was a joint venture, I suspect it was the latter. At any rate I want to thank you for what was an intensely meaningful experience." I think it is not too much to say that because several of us in the group were able genuinely to hear him, he was released from his dungeon and has come out, at least to some degree, into the sunnier world of warm interpersonal relationships.

I LIKE TO BE HEARD

Let me move on to a second learning which I would like to share with you. I like to *be heard*. A number of times in my life I have felt myself bursting with insoluble problems, or going round and round in tormented circles or, during one period, overcome by feelings of worthlessness and despair, sure I was sinking into psychosis. I think I have been more lucky than most in finding at these times individuals who have been able to hear me and thus to rescue me from the chaos of my feelings. I have been fortunate in finding individuals who have been able to hear my meanings a little more deeply than I have known them. These individuals have heard me without judging me, diagnosing me, appraising me, evaluating me. They have just listened and clarified and responded to me at all the levels at which I was communicating. I can testify that when you are in psychological distress and someone really hears you without passing judgment on you, without trying to take responsibility for you, without trying to mold you, it feels *damn good*. At these times, it has relaxed the tension in me. It has permitted me to bring out the frightening feelings, the guilts, the despair, the confusions that have been a part of my experience. When I have been listened to and when I have been heard, I am able to reperceive my world in a new way and to go on. It is amazing that feelings which were completely awful, become bearable when someone listens. It is astonishing how elements which seem insoluble become soluble when someone hears; how confusions which seem irremediable turn into relatively clear flowing streams when one is understood. I have deeply appreciated the times that I have experienced this sensitive, empathic, concentrated listening.

I have been very grateful that by the time I quite desperately needed this kind of help, I had trained and developed therapists, persons in their own right, independent and unafraid of me, who were able to go with me through a dark and troubled period in which I underwent a great deal of inner growth. It has also made me sharply aware that in developing my style of therapy for others, I was without doubt, at some unconscious level, developing the kind of help I wanted and could use myself.

WHEN I CAN NOT HEAR

Let me turn to some of my dissatisfactions in this realm. I dislike it in myself when I can't hear another, when I do not understand him. If it is only a simple failure of comprehension or a failure to focus my attention on what he is saying, or a difficulty in understanding his words, then I feel only a very mild dissatisfaction with myself.

But what I really dislike in myself is when I cannot hear the other person because I am so sure in advance of what he is about to say that I don't listen. It is only afterward that I realize that I have only heard what I have already decided he is saying. I have failed really to listen. Or even worse are those times when I can't hear because what he is saying is too threatening, might even make me change my views or my behavior. Still worse are those times when I catch myself trying to twist his message to make it say what I want him to say, and then only hearing that. This can be a very subtle thing and it is surprising how skillful I can be in doing it. Just by twisting his words a small amount, by distorting his meaning just a little, I can make it appear that he is not only saying the thing I want to hear, but that he is the person I want him to be. It is only when I realize through his protest or through my own gradual recognition that I am subtly manipulating him that I become disgusted with myself. I know too from being on the receiving end of this how frustrating it is to be received for what you are not, to be heard as saying something which you have not said and do not mean. This creates anger and bafflement and disillusion.

WHEN OTHERS DO NOT UNDERSTAND

The next learning I want to share with you is that I am terribly frustrated and shut into myself when I try to express something which is deeply me, which is a part of my own private, inner world, and the other person does not understand. When I take the gamble, the risk, of trying to share something that is very personal with another individual and it is not received and not understood, this is a very deflating and a very lonely experience. I have come to believe that it is that experience which makes some individuals psychotic. They have given up hoping that anyone can understand them and once they have lost that hope then their own inner world, which becomes more and more bizarre, is the only place where they can live. They can no longer live in any shared human experience. I can sympathize with them because I know that when I try to share some feeling aspect of myself which is private, precious, and tentative, and when this communication is met by evaluation, by reassurance, by denial, by distortion of my meaning, I have very strongly the reaction, "Oh, what's the use!" At such a time one knows what it is to be *alone*.

So, as you can see, a creative, active, sensitive, accurate, empathic, non-judgmental listening, is for me terribly important in a relationship. It is important for me to provide it. It has been extremely important especially at certain times in my life to receive it. I feel that I have grown within myself when I have provided it. I am very sure that I have grown and been released and enhanced when I have received this kind of listening.

I WANT TO BE REAL

Moving on to another area of my learnings, I find it very satisfying when I can be real, when I can be close to whatever it is that is going on within me. I like it when I can listen to myself. To really know what I am experiencing in the moment is by no means an easy thing but I feel somewhat encouraged because I think that over the years I have been improving at it. I am convinced, however, that it is a life-long task and that none of us ever is really able to be comfortably close to *all* that is going on within his own experience.

In place of the term *realness* I have sometimes used the word *congruence*. By this I mean that when my experiencing of this moment is present in my awareness, and when what is present in my awareness is present in my communication, then each of these three levels matches or is congruent. At such moments I am integrated or whole, I am completely in one piece. Most of the time of course I, like everyone else, exhibit some degree of incongruence. I have learned, however, that realness, or genuineness, or congruence—whatever term you wish to give to it—is a fundamental basis for the best of communication, the best of relationships.

What do I mean by being real? I could give many examples from many different fields. But one meaning, one learning is that there is basically nothing to be afraid of when I present myself as I *am*, when I can come forth nondefensively, without armor, just me. When I can accept the fact that I have many deficiencies, many faults, make lots of mistakes, am often ignorant where I should be knowledgeable, often prejudiced when I should be openminded, often have feelings which are not justified by the circumstances, then I can be much more real. And when I can come out wearing no armor, making no effort to be different from what I am, I learn so much more—even from criticism and hostility—and I am so much more relaxed, and I get so much closer to people. Besides, my willingness to be vulnerable brings forth so much more real feeling from other people who are in relationship to me, that it is very rewarding. So I enjoy life *much* more when I am not defensive, not hiding behind a façade, just trying to be and express the real me.

COMMUNICATING THE REALNESS IN ME

I feel a sense of satisfaction when I can dare to communicate the realness in me to another. This is far from easy partly because what I am experiencing keeps changing in every moment, partly because feelings are very complex. Usually there is a lag, sometimes of moments, sometimes of days, weeks, or months, between the experiencing and the communication. In these cases, I experience something, I feel something, but only later do I become aware of it, only later do I dare to communicate it, when it has become cool enough to risk sharing it with another. Yet it is a most satisfying experience when I can communicate what is real in me at the moment that it occurs. Then I feel genuine, and spontaneous, and alive.

Such real feelings are not always positive. One man, in a basic encounter group of which I was a member, was talking about himself in ways which seemed to me completely false, speaking of the pride he took in maintaining his front, his pretense, his façade, how skillful he was in deceiving others. My feeling of annoyance rose higher and higher until finally I expressed it by simply saying, "Oh, nuts!" This somehow pricked the bubble. From that time on he was a more real and genuine person, less a braggadocio, and our communication improved. I felt good for having let him know my own real angry feeling as it was occurring.

I'm sorry to say that very often, especially with feelings of anger, I'm only partly aware of the feeling at the moment, and full awareness comes later. I only learn afterward what my feeling *was*. It is only when I wake up in the middle of the night, finding myself angrily fighting someone, that I realize how angry I was at him the day before. Then I know, seemingly too late, how I might have been my real feeling self; but, at least, I have learned to go to him the next day, if need be, to express my anger, and gradually I'm learning to be more quickly acquainted with it inside myself. In the last basic encounter group in which I participated, I was at different times very angry with two individuals. With one, I wasn't aware of it until the middle of the night and had to wait until morning to express it. With the other, I was able to realize it and express it in the session in which it occurred. In both instances, it led to real communication, to a strengthening of the relationship, and gradually to a feeling of genuine liking for each other. But I am a slow learner in this area.

ENCOUNTERING REALNESS IN OTHERS

It is a sparkling thing when I encounter realness in another person. Sometimes in the basic encounter groups which have been a very important part of my experience these last few years, someone says something which comes from him transparently and whole. It is so obvious when a person is not hiding behind a façade but is speaking from deep within himself. When this happens I leap to meet it. I want to encounter this real person. Sometimes the feelings thus expressed are very positive feelings. Sometimes they are decidedly negative ones. I think of a man in a very responsible position, a scientist at the head of a large research department in a huge electronics firm, very "successful." One day in such a basic encounter group he found the courage to speak of his isolation, to tell us that he had never had a single friend in his life. There were plenty of people whom he knew but not one he could count as a friend. "As a matter of fact," he added, "there are only two individuals in the world with whom I have even a reasonably communicative relationship. These are my two children." By the time he finished he was letting loose some of the tears of sorrow for himself which I am sure he had held in for many years. But it was the honesty and realness of his loneliness which caused every member of the group to reach out to him in some psychological sense. It was also most significant that his courage in being real enabled all of us to be more genuine in our communications, to come out from behind the façades we ordinarily use.

MY FAILURES TO BE REAL

I am disappointed when I realize—and of course this realization always comes afterward, after a lag of time—that I have been too frightened or too threatened to let myself get close to what I am experiencing and that consequently I have not been genuine or congruent. There immediately comes to mind an instance which is somewhat painful to reveal. Some years ago I was invited to spend a year as a Fellow at the Center for Advanced Study in the Behavioral Sciences at Stanford, California. The Fellows are a group chosen because they are supposedly brilliant and well-informed scholars. It is doubtless inevitable that there is a considerable amount of one-upsmanship, of showing off one's knowledge and achievements. It seems important for each Fellow to impress the others, to be a little more assured, to be a little more knowledgeable than he really is. I found myself several times doing this same thing—playing a role of greater certainty and of greater competence than I really felt. I can't tell you how disgusted with myself I was as I realized what I was doing. I was not being me; I was playing a part.

I regret it when I suppress my feelings too long and they burst forth in ways that are distorted or attacking or hurtful. I have a friend whom I like very much but who has one particular pattern of behavior that thoroughly annoys me. Because of the usual tendency to be nice, polite, and pleasant I kept this annoyance to myself for too long a time. When it finally burst its bounds it came out not only as annoyance but as an attack on him. This was hurtful and it took us some time to repair the relationship.

I am inwardly pleased when I have the strength to permit another person to be his own realness and to be *separate* from me. I think that is often a very threatening possibility. In some ways I have found it sort of an ultimate test of staff leadership and of parenthood. Can I freely permit this staff member or my client or my son or my daughter to become a separate person with ideas, purposes, and values which may not be identical with my own? I think of Kahlil Gibran's poem on marriage,[1] which includes the lines:

> Let there be spaces in your to-
> getherness,
>   And let the winds of the heavens
> dance between you.
>   Love one another, but make not a
> bond of love:
>   Let it rather be a moving sea between
> the shores of your souls. . . .
>
>   Give your hearts, but not into each
> other's keeping.
>   For only the hand of Life can contain
> your hearts.
>   And stand together yet not too near
> together:
>   For the pillars of the temple stand
> apart,
>   And the oak tree and the cypress grow
> not in each other's shadow.

[1] Reprinted from *The Prophet*, by Kahlil Gibran with permission of the publisher, Alfred A. Knopf, Inc. Copyright 1923 by Kahlil Gibran; renewal copyright 1951 by Administrators C.T.A. of Kahlil Gibran Estate, and Mary G. Gibran.

From a number of these things I have been saying I trust it is clear that when I can permit realness in myself or sense it or permit it in the other, I find it very satisfying. When I cannot permit it in myself or fail to permit a separate realness in another it is to me very distressing and regrettable. I find that when I am able to let myself be congruent and genuine it often helps the other person. When the other person is transparently real and congruent it often helps me. In those rare moments when a deep realness in one meets a deep realness in the other it is a memorable "I-thou relationship," as Martin Buber, the existential Jewish philosopher, would call it. Such a deep and mutual personal encounter does not happen often but I am convinced that unless it happens occasionally we are not human.

UNLEASHING FREEDOM FOR OTHERS

There's another learning. I like it when I can permit freedom to others, and in this I think I have learned, and developed considerable ability. I am frequently, though not always, able to take a group, a course, or a class of students, and to set them psychologically free. I can create a climate in which they can be and direct themselves. At first, they are suspicious; they're sure that the freedom I'm offering them is some kind of a trick, and then they bring up the question of grades. They can't be free because in the end I will evaluate them and judge them. When we have worked out some solution, in which we have all participated, to the absurd demand of the University that learning is measured by grades, then they begin to feel that they are really free. Then curiosity is unleashed. Individuals and groups start to pursue their own goals, their own purposes. They become explorers. They can try to find the meaning of their lives in the work they're doing. They work twice as hard in such a course where nothing is required as in courses with requirements. I can't always achieve this atmosphere and when I cannot, I think it is because of some subtle holding back within myself, some unwillingness for the freedom to be complete. But when I can achieve it, then education becomes what it should be, an exciting quest, a searching, not an accumulation of facts soon to be out-dated and forgotten. These students become persons living in process, able to live a changing life. Of all the learnings I have developed, I think this climate of freedom which I can frequently create, which I can often somehow carry with me and around me, is to me one of the most precious parts of myself.

ACCEPTING AND GIVING LOVE

Another area of my learning in interpersonal relationships has been slow and painful for me. It is most warming and fulfilling when I can let in the fact, or permit myself to feel, that someone cares for, accepts, admires, or prizes me. Because, I suppose, of elements in my past history it has been very difficult for me to do this. For a long time I tended almost automatically to brush aside any positive feelings which were turned in my direction. I think my reaction was, "Who, me? You couldn't possibly care for me. You might like what I have done or my achievements but not *me*." This is one respect in which my own therapy helped me very much. I am not always able even now to let in such warm and loving feelings from others, but I find it very releasing when I can do so. I know that some people flatter me in order to gain something for themselves. Some people praise me because they are afraid to be hostile. Some people, in recent years, admire me because I'm a "great name," or an "authority." But I have come to recognize the fact that some people genuinely appreciate *me*, like me, love me, and I want to sense that fact and let it in. I think I have become less aloof as I have been able really to take in and soak up those loving feelings.

I have found it to be a very enriching thing when I can truly prize or care for or love another person and when I can let that feeling flow out to him. Like many others, I used to fear that I would be trapped by this. "If I let myself care for him he can control me, or use me, or make demands on me." I think that I have moved a long way in the direction of being less fearful in this respect. Like my clients I, too, have slowly learned that tender, positive feelings are *not* dangerous either to give or receive.

Here I could give examples from my own experiences, but, as I thought this over, it seemed to me that it would be almost too personal and might reveal the identities of others, so I'm going to give an illustration in which I have helped two other people to go even further than I could, I think, in the giving of love. The story has to do with two friends, both of them priests, whom I will call

Joe and Andy. Joe participated in a basic encounter group that I conducted and he was deeply affected by it. Later, Andy was also a member of a group with which I was associated. Some months later, I received this letter from Andy. It said:

> Dear Carl: I've been trying to get a letter off to you ever since the workshop. I keep thinking I'm going to have some leisure time when I can sit down and really collect my many impressions of those three days. I can see that the leisure time is a dream so I'd like to get at least a note to you.
>
> Perhaps, I can best tell you what that workshop meant by describing an incident that happened not too long after.
>
> Joe [the other priest] had been working with a severely neurotic woman with schizophrenic tendencies, very suicidal and very guilty. She had spent a fortune on psychiatrists and psychologists. One afternoon he asked me to come down to her home with him to meet her, sing and play my guitar and talk. As Joe hoped, it turned into a basic encounter. At one point, she said that her hands really contained her. When she is angry, her hands are angry; when she is happy, her hands are happy; when she is dirty, her hands are dirty. As she was speaking and gesturing, she was sitting near me on the couch. I had the sudden urge to take her hand. I just couldn't buy the concept that she was dirty. So I did. Her first reaction was, "Thank you." Then she went into a type of seizure, shaking and crying. We learned later she was reliving a frightening and traumatic experience from her past. Joe had his arm around her shoulders. I held onto her hand for dear life. Finally, she relaxed. She put my hand in hers, turned it over and looked at it. She remarked, "It is not cracked and bleeding, is it?" I shook my head. "But it should be, I'm so dirty." About ten minutes later in the course of the encounter, she reached out and took my hand.
>
> A while later her little girl, a third grader, was screaming. The girl is very emotional and has a lot of problems. I excused myself and went in to see her. I sat on her bed, talked with her and sang. Before long I had her in my arms, holding her and kissing her and rocking her. When she quieted down, I put her under the covers and got her Mom. She told me later that when she kissed Mary good night, on a new inspiration, she leaned over and kissed her again on the cheek. "This was for Father Andy." Mary looked up, smiled, and said, "You know Mommy, he loves me kind of special, doesn't he?" Then she turned over and went to sleep.

I wanted to tell you about these incidents, Carl, as the workshop with you helped me to respond in each case freely and trustingly with my own instinctive reactions. I have had the words for years. In theory, I have strongly held that that is how I think a man—a Christian—a priest most truly acts. But I have had a hard struggle getting to the point where I could be that free, without hesitation or worry. I left your workshop *really* knowing that I couldn't just say to people that I love them or that they are loveable, especially when they need to be shown this. Since then, many times, I have in some way or another *shown* where before I would have *said*. This has brought much more joy and peace to many like this mother and daughter and to myself.

So often I think gratefully about our group. As you might imagine, I can quite vividly remember the love and warmth of the members of the group as I was struggling so hard to be truly honest with myself and you. For an experience like that, it is difficult to say thank you. May a life more free, more honest, and more loving say it for me. I still get tears in my eyes when I think of the last few hours, all of us sharing deeply and warmly, without any urgency, of ourselves. I can't ever remember being so deeply touched by anything—nor have I felt more true love for a group of people. I could go on but I think you see how truly grateful I am for the workshop, for the group, for you. I just pray that I can help give to others what you and the others gave me. Thank you.

I'm not at all sure that I could have gone as far as those two men did, but I'm very pleased that I have had a part in helping someone go beyond where I am. I think it is one of the exciting aspects of working with younger people.

It is also very meaningful to me that I can vouch for the truth of this account. Since the time of this letter I have come to know both Andy and Joe much better. I have also had the privilege of becoming acquainted with the woman whose psychological life they quite literally saved. So I feel confirmed in my view that prizing, loving feelings are *not* basically dangerous to give or receive, but are instead growth-promoting.

I AM MORE ABLE TO APPRECIATE OTHERS

Because of having less fear of giving or receiving positive feelings, I have become more able to *appreciate* individuals. I have come to believe that this is rather rare. So often, even with our children, we love them to control them rather than loving them because we appreciate them. I have come to think that one of the most satisfying experiences I know—and also one of the most growth-promoting experiences for the other person—is just fully to *appreciate* this individual in the same way that I appreciate a sunset. People are just as wonderful as sunsets if I can let them *be*. In fact, perhaps the reason we can truly appreciate a sunset is that we cannot control it. When I look at a sunset as I did the other evening I don't find myself saying, "Soften the orange a little on the right hand corner, and put a bit more purple along the base, and use a little more pink in the cloud color." I don't do that. I don't *try* to control a sunset. I watch it with awe as it unfolds. I like myself best when I can experience my staff member, my son, my daughter, my grandchildren, in this same way, appreciating the unfolding of a life. I believe this is a somewhat oriental attitude, but for me it is the most satisfying one.

So in this third area, prizing or loving and being prized or loved is experienced by me as very growth enhancing. A person who is loved appreciatively, not possessively, blooms, and develops his own unique self. The person who loves non-possessively is himself enriched. This at least has been my experience.

I VALUE INTERPERSONAL COMMUNICATION AND RELATIONSHIPS

Let me close this chapter by saying that in my experience real interpersonal communication and real interpersonal relationships are deeply growth-promoting. I enjoy facilitating growth and development in others. I am enriched when others provide a climate which makes it possible for me to grow and change.

So I value it very much when I am able sensitively to hear the pain and the joy, the fear, the anger, the confusion and despair, the determination and the courage to be, in another person. And I value more than I can say the times when another person has truly been able to hear those elements in me.

I prize it greatly when I am able to move forward in the never-ending attempt to be the real me in this moment, whether it is anger or enthusiasm or puzzlement which is real. I am so delighted when a realness in me brings forth more realness in the other, and we come closer to a mutual I-thou relationship.

And I am very grateful that I have moved in the direction of being able to take in, without rejecting it, the warmth and the caring of others, because this has so increased my own capacity for giving love, without fear of being entrapped and without holding back.

These, in my experience, are some of the elements which make communication between persons, and *being in* relationship to persons, more enriching and more enhancing. I fall *far* short of achieving these elements, but to find myself moving in these directions makes life a warm, exciting, upsetting, troubling, satisfying, enriching, and above all a worthwhile venture.

12

A Modern Approach
to the Valuing Process

The work of the teacher and educator, like that of the thera-pist, is inextricably involved in the problem of values. The school has always been seen as one of the means by which the culture transmits its values from one generation to the next. But now this process is in upheaval, with many of our young people declaring themselves "dropouts" from the confused and hypocritical value system which they see operating in the world. How is the educator—how is the citizen—to orient himself in relation to this complex and perplexing issue?

While on a vacation in Jamaica, some time ago, watching the abundant sea life through my snorkel, and the equally fascinat-ing development of three of our grandchildren, I attempted an essay on this problem based largely on my experience in psy-chotherapy.¹ When I had finished, I felt quite dissatisfied with it, but it has, for me, stood the test of time, and I now feel good about its venturesome quality. I feel in regard to it, as with a small number of other papers, that I was writing more than I consciously "knew," and that it took my intellect some time to catch up with what I had written. I have also found that it has had significant meaning for many other people.

I did not at that time foresee the multitude of young people who would declare an open *revolt against our system of values, but I did realize that the basis for such a revolt was present in the culture. I hope—and believe—that the way of valuing and living which is presented here has some relevance both to the "hippie" and the "square"—in short, to every citizen of this chaotic modern world. I do not anticipate that every citizen or every educator would* agree *with what I have to say here, but I believe the central theme may provide food for productive thought.*

---

¹ A condensed version of this chapter was first published as: "Toward a Modern Approach to Values," *Journal of Abnormal and Social Psychology*, 1964, *68*, 160-167.

There is a great deal of concern today with the problem of values. Youth, in almost every country, is deeply uncertain of its value orientation; the values associated with various religions have lost much of their influence; sophisticated individuals in every culture seem unsure and troubled as to the goals they hold in esteem. One does not have to look far to find the reasons. The world culture, in all its aspects, seems increasingly scientific and relativistic, and the rigid, absolute views on values which come to us from the past appear anachronistic. Even more important, perhaps, is the fact that the modern individual is assailed from every angle by divergent and contradictory value claims. It is no longer possible, as it was in the not too distant historical past, to settle comfortably into the value system of one's forebears or one's community or one's church and live out one's life without ever examining the nature and the assumptions of that system.

In this situation it is not surprising that value orientations from the past appear to be in a state of disintegration or collapse. Men question whether there are, or can be, any universal values. It is often felt that we may have lost, in our modern world, all possibility of any general or cross-cultural basis for values. One natural result of this uncertainty and confusion is that there is an increasing concern about, interest in, and searching for, a sound or meaningful value approach which can hold its own in today's world.

I share this general concern. I have also experienced the more specific value issues which arise in my own field, psychotherapy. The client's feelings and convictions about values frequently change during therapy. How can he or we know whether they have changed in a sound direction? Or does he simply, as some claim, take over the value system of his therapist? Is psychotherapy simply a device whereby the unacknowledged and unexamined values of the therapist are unknowingly transmitted to an unsuspecting client? Or should this transmission of values be the therapist's openly held purpose? Should he become the modern priest, upholding and imparting a value system suitable for today? And what would such a value system be? There has been much discussion of such issues, ranging from thoughtful and empirically based presentations such as that of Glad (1959), to more polemic statements. As is so often true, the general problem faced by the culture is painfully and specifically evident in the cultural microcosm which is called the therapeutic relationship.

I should like to attempt a modest approach to this whole problem. I have observed changes in the approach to values as the individual grows from infancy to adulthood. I observe further changes when, if he is fortunate, he continues to grow toward true psychological maturity. Many of these observations grow out of my experience as a therapist, where I have had the rare opportunity of seeing the ways in which individuals move toward a richer life. From these observations I believe I see some directional threads emerging which might offer a new concept of the valuing process, more tenable in the modern world. I have made a beginning by presenting some of these ideas partially in previous writings (1951, 1959); I would like now to voice them more clearly and more fully.

I would stress that my vantage point for making these observations is not that of the scholar or philosopher: I am speaking from my experience of the functioning human being, as I have lived with him in the intimate experience of therapy, and in other situations of growth, change, and development.

SOME DEFINITIONS

Before I present some of these observations, perhaps I should try to clarify what I mean by values. There are many definitions which have been used, but I have found helpful some distinctions made by Charles Morris (1956). He points out that value is a term we employ in different ways. We use it to refer to the tendency of any living beings to show preference, in their actions, for one kind of object or objective rather than another. This preferential behavior he calls "operative values." It need not involve any cognitive or conceptual thinking. It is simply the value choice which is indicated behaviorally when the organism selects one object, rejects another. When the earthworm, placed in a simple Y maze, chooses the smooth arm of the Y, instead of the path which is paved with sandpaper, he is indicating an operative value.

A second use of the term might be called "conceived values." This is the preference of the individual for a symbolized object. Usually in such a choice there is anticipation or foresight of the outcome of behavior directed toward such a symbolized object. A preference for "Honesty is the best policy" is such a conceived value.

A final use of the term might be called "objective values." People use the word in this way when they wish to speak of what is objectively preferable, whether or not it is in fact sensed or conceived of as desirable. What I have to say involves this last definition scarcely at all. I will be concerned with operative values and conceptualized values.

THE INFANT'S WAY OF VALUING

Let me first speak about the infant. The living human being has, at the outset, a clear approach to values. He prefers some things and experiences, and rejects others. We can infer from studying his behavior that he prefers those experiences which maintain, enhance, or actualize his organism, and rejects those which do not serve this end. Watch him for a bit:

Hunger is negatively valued. His expression of this often comes through loud and clear.

Food is positively valued. But when he is satisfied, food is negatively valued, and the same milk he responded to so eagerly is now spit out, or the breast which seemed so satisfying is now rejected as he turns his head away from the nipple with an amusing facial expression of disgust and revulsion.

He values security and the holding and caressing which seem to communicate security.

He values new experience for its own sake, and we observe this in his obvious pleasure in discovering his toes, in his searching movements, and in his endless curiosity.

He shows a clear negative valuing of pain, bitter tastes, and sudden loud sounds.

All of this is commonplace, but let us look at these facts in terms of what they tell us about the infant's approach to values. It is first of all a flexible, changing, valuing *process*, not a fixed system. He likes food and dislikes the same food. He values security and rest, and rejects it for new experience. What is going on seems best described as an organismic valuing process, in which each element, each moment of what he is experiencing is somehow weighed, and selected or rejected, depending on whether, at that moment, it tends to actualize the organism or not. This complicated weighing of experience is clearly an organismic, not a conscious or symbolic function. These are operative, not conceived values. But this process can nonetheless deal with complex value problems. I would remind you of the experiment in which young infants had spread in front of them a score or more of dishes of natural (that is, unflavored) foods. Over a period of time they clearly tended to value the foods which enhanced their own survival, growth, and development. If for a time a child gorged himself on starches, this would soon be balanced by a protein "binge." If at times he chose a diet deficient in some vitamin, he would later seek out foods rich in this very vitamin. He was utilizing the wisdom of the body in his value choices, or perhaps more accurately, the physiological wisdom of his body guided his behavioral movements, resulting in what we might think of as objectively sound value choices.

Another aspect of the infant's approach to value is that the source or locus of the evaluating process is clearly within himself. Unlike many of us, he *knows* what he likes and dislikes, and the origin of these value choices lies strictly within himself. He is the center of the valuing process, the evidence for his choices being supplied by his own senses. He is not at this point influenced by what his parents think he should prefer, or by what the church says, or by the opinion of the latest "expert" in the field, or by the persuasive talents of an advertising firm. It is from within his own experiencing that his organism is saying in non-verbal terms—"This is good for me," "That is bad for me," "I like this," "I strongly dislike that." He would laugh at our concern over values, if he could understand it. How could anyone fail to know what he liked and disliked, what was good for him and what was not?

THE CHANGE IN THE VALUING PROCESS

What happens to this highly efficient, soundly based valuing process? By what sequence of events do we exchange it for the more rigid, uncertain, inefficient approach to values which characterizes most of us as adults? Let me try to state briefly one of the major ways in which I think this happens.

The infant needs love, wants it, tends to behave in ways which will bring a repetition of this wanted experience. But this brings complications. He pulls baby sister's hair and finds it satisfying to hear her wails and protests. He then hears that he is "a naughty, bad boy," and this may be reinforced by a slap on the hand. He is cut off from affection. As this experience is repeated, and many,

many others like it, he gradually learns that what "feels good" is often "bad" in the eyes of others. Then the next step occurs, in which he comes to take the same attitude toward himself which these others have taken. Now, as he pulls his sister's hair, he solemnly intones, "Bad, bad boy." He is introjecting the value judgment of another, taking it in as his own. To that degree he loses touch with his own organismic valuing process. He has deserted the wisdom of his organism, giving up the locus of evaluation, and is trying to behave in terms of values set by another, in order to hold love.

Or take another example at an older level. A boy senses, though perhaps not consciously, that he is more loved and prized by his parents when he thinks of being a doctor than when he thinks of being an artist. Gradually he introjects the values attached to being a doctor. He comes to want, above all, to be a doctor. Then in college he is baffled by the fact that he repeatedly fails in chemistry, which is absolutely necessary to becoming a physician, in spite of the fact that the guidance counselor assures him he has the ability to pass the course. Only in counseling interviews does he begin to realize how completely he has lost touch with his organismic reactions, how out of touch he is with his own valuing process.

Let me give another instance from a class of mine, a group of prospective teachers. I asked them at the beginning of the course, "Please list for me the two or three values which you would most wish to pass on to the children with whom you will work." They turned in many value goals, but I was surprised by some of the items. Several listed such things as "to speak correctly," "to use good English, not to use words like ain't." Others mentioned neatness—"to do things according to instructions"; one explained her hope that "When I tell them to write their names in the upper right-hand corner with the date under it, I want them to do it *that way*, not in some other form."

I confess I was somewhat appalled that for some of these adolescent young women the most important values to be passed on to pupils were to avoid bad grammar, or meticulously to follow teacher's instructions. I felt baffled. Certainly these behaviors had not been *experienced* as the most satisfying and meaningful elements in their own lives. The listing of such values could only be accounted for by the fact that these behaviors had gained approval—and thus had been introjected as deeply important.

Perhaps these several illustrations will indicate that in an attempt to gain or hold love, approval, esteem, the individual relinquishes the locus of evaluation which was his in infancy, and places it in others. He learns to have a basic *dis*trust for his own experiencing as a guide to his behavior. He learns from others a large number of conceived values, and adopts them as his own, even though they may be widely discrepant from what he is experiencing. Because these concepts are not based on his own valuing, they tend to be fixed and rigid, rather than fluid and changing.

SOME INTROJECTED PATTERNS

It is in this fashion, I believe, that most of us accumulate the introjected value patterns by which we live. In this fantastically complex culture of today, the patterns we introject as desirable or undesirable come from a variety of sources and are often highly contradictory in their meanings. Let me list a few of the introjections which are commonly held.

Sexual desires and behaviors are mostly bad. The sources of this construct are many—parents, church, teachers.

Disobedience is bad. Here parents and teachers combine with the military to emphasize this concept. To obey is good. To obey without question is even better.

Making money is the highest good. The sources of this conceived value are too numerous to mention.

Learning an accumulation of scholarly facts is highly desirable.

Browsing and aimless exploratory reading for fun is undesirable. The source of these last two concepts is apt to be the school, the educational system.

Abstract art is good. Here the people we regard as sophisticated are the originators of the value.

Communism is utterly bad. Here the government is a major source.

To love thy neighbor is the highest good. This concept comes from the church, perhaps from the parents.

Cooperation and teamwork are preferable to acting alone. Here companions are an important source.

Cheating is clever and desirable. The peer group again is the origin.

Coca-Colas, chewing gum, electric refrigerators, color TV, and automobiles are all utterly desirable. This conception comes not only from advertisements, but is reinforced by people all over the world. From Jamaica to Japan, from Copenhagen to Kowloon, the "Coca-Cola culture" has come to be regarded as the acme of desirability.

This is a small and diversified sample of the myriads of conceived values which individuals often introject, and hold as their own, without ever having considered their inner organismic reactions to these patterns and objects.

COMMON CHARACTERISTICS OF ADULT VALUING

I believe it will be clear from the foregoing that the usual adult—I feel I am speaking for most of us—has an approach to values which has these characteristics:

The majority of his values are introjected from other individuals or groups significant to him, but are regarded by him as his own.

The source or locus of evaluation on most matters lies outside of himself.

The criterion by which his values are set is the degree to which they will cause him to be loved or accepted.

These conceived preferences are either not related at all, or not clearly related, to his own process of experiencing.

Often there is a wide and unrecognized discrepancy between the evidence supplied by his own experience, and these conceived values.

Because these conceptions are not open to testing in experience, he must hold them in a rigid and unchanging fashion. The alternative would be a collapse of his values. Hence his values are "right" —like the law of the Medes and the Persians, which changeth not.

Because they are untestable, there is no ready way of solving contradictions. If he has taken in from the community the conception that money is the *summum bonum* and from the church the conception that love of one's neighbor is the highest value, he has no way of discovering which has more value for *him*. Hence a common aspect of modern life is living with absolutely contradictory values. We calmly discuss the possibility of dropping a hydrogen bomb on a country we regard as our enemy, but then find tears in our eyes when we see headlines about the suffering of one small child.

Because he has relinquished the locus of evaluation to others, and has lost touch with his own valuing process, he feels profoundly insecure and easily threatened in his values. If some of these conceptions were destroyed, what would take their place? This threatening possibility makes him hold his value conceptions more rigidly or more confusedly, or both.

THE FUNDAMENTAL DISCREPANCY

I believe that this picture of the individual, with values mostly introjected, held as fixed concepts, rarely examined or tested, is the picture of most of us. By taking over the conceptions of others as our own, we lose contact with the potential wisdom of our own functioning and lose confidence in ourselves. Since these value constructs are often sharply at variance with what is going on in our own experiencing, we have in a very basic way divorced ourselves from ourselves, and this accounts for much of modern strain and insecurity. This fundamental discrepancy between the individual's concepts and what he is actually experiencing, between the intellectual structure of his values and the valuing process going on unrecognized within him—this is a part of the fundamental estrangement of modern man from himself. This is a major problem for the therapist.

RESTORING CONTACT WITH EXPERIENCE

Some individuals are fortunate in going beyond the picture I have just given, developing further in the direction of psychological maturity. We see this happen in psychotherapy where we endeavor to provide a climate favorable to the growth of the person. We also see it happen in life, whenever life provides a therapeutic climate for the individual. Let me concentrate on this further maturing of a value approach as I have seen it in therapy.

In the first place let me say somewhat parenthetically that the therapeutic relationship is *not* devoid of values. Quite the contrary. When it is most effective, it seems to me, it is marked by one primary value: namely, that this person, this client, has worth. He as a person is valued in his separateness and uniqueness. It is when he senses and realizes that he is prized as a person that he can slowly begin to value the different aspects of himself. Most importantly, he can begin, with much difficulty at first, to sense and to feel what is going on within him, what he is feeling, what he is experiencing, how he is reacting. He uses his experiencing as a direct referent to which he can turn in forming accurate conceptualizations and as a guide to his behavior. Gendlin (1961, 1962) has elaborated the way in which this occurs. As his experiencing becomes more and more open to him, as he is able to live more freely in the process of his feelings, then significant changes begin to occur in his approach to values. It begins to assume many of the characteristics it had in infancy.

INTROJECTED VALUES IN RELATION TO EXPERIENCING

Perhaps I can indicate this by reviewing a few of the brief examples of introjected values which I have given, and suggesting what happens to them as the individual comes closer to what is going on within him.

> The individual in therapy looks back and realizes, "But I *enjoyed* pulling my sister's hair—and that doesn't make me a bad person."
>
> The student failing chemistry realizes, as he gets close to his own experiencing—"I *don't* value being a doctor, even though my parents do; I don't like chemistry; I don't like taking steps toward being a doctor; and I am not a failure for having these feelings."
>
> The adult recognizes that sexual desires and behavior may be richly satisfying and permanently enriching in their consequences, or shallow and temporary and less than satisfying. He goes by his own experiencing, which does not always coincide with the social norms.
>
> He considers art from a new value approach. He says, "This picture moves me deeply, means a great deal to me. It also happens to be an abstraction, but that is not the basis for my valuing it."
>
> He recognizes freely that this communist book or person has attitudes and goals which he shares as well as ideas and values which he does not share.
>
> He realizes that at times he experiences cooperation as meaningful and valuable to him, and that at other times he wishes to be alone and act alone.

VALUING IN THE MATURE PERSON

The valuing process which seems to develop in this more mature person is in some ways very much like that in the infant, and in some ways quite different. It is fluid, flexible, based on this particular moment, and the degree to which this moment is experienced as enhancing and actualizing. Values are not held rigidly, but are continually changing. The painting which last year seemed meaningful now appears uninteresting; the way of working with individuals which was formerly experienced as good now seems inadequate; the belief which then seemed true is now experienced as only partly true, or perhaps false.

Another characteristic of the way this person values experience is that it is highly differentiated, or as the semanticists would say, extensional. As the members of my class of prospective teachers learned, general principles are not as useful as sensitively discriminating reactions. One says, "With this little boy, I just felt I should be very firm, and he seemed to welcome that, and I felt good that I had been. But I'm not that way at all with the other children most of the time." She was relying on her experiencing of the relationship with each child to guide her behavior. I have already indicated, in going through the examples, how much more differentiated are the individual's reactions to what were previously rather solid, monolithic, introjected values.

In another way the mature individual's approach is like that of the infant. The locus of evaluation is again established firmly within the person. It is his own experience which provides the value information or feedback. This does not mean that he is not open to all the evidence he can obtain from other sources. But it means that this is taken for what it is—outside evidence—and is not as significant as his own reactions. Thus he may be told by a friend that a new book is very disappointing. He reads two unfavorable reviews of the book. Thus his tentative hypothesis is that he will not value the book. Yet if he reads the book his valuing will be based upon the reactions it stirs in him, not on what he has been told by others.

There is also involved in this valuing process a letting oneself down into the immediacy of what one is experiencing, endeavoring to sense and to clarify all its complex meanings. I think of a client who, toward the close of therapy, when puzzled about an issue, would put his head in his hands and say, "Now what *is* it that I'm feeling? I want to get next to it. I want to learn what it is." Then he would wait, quietly and patiently, trying to listen to himself, until he could discern the exact flavor of the feelings he was experiencing. He, like others, was trying to get close to himself.

In getting close to what is going on within himself, the process is much more complex than it is in the infant. In the mature person it has much more scope and sweep, for there is involved in the present moment of experiencing the memory traces of all the relevant learnings from the past. This moment has not only its immediate sensory impact, but it has meaning growing out of similar experiences in the past. It has both the new and the old in it. So when I experience a painting or a person, my experiencing contains within it the learnings I have accumulated from past meetings with paintings or persons, as well as the new impact of this particular encounter. Likewise the moment of experiencing contains, for the mature adult, hypotheses about consequences. "I feel now that I would enjoy a third drink, but past learnings indicate that I may regret it in the morning." "It is not pleasant to express forthrightly my negative feelings to this person, but past experience indicates that in a continuing relationship it will be helpful in the long run." Past and future are both in this moment and enter into the valuing.

I find that in the person I am speaking of (and here again we see a similarity to the infant) the criterion of the valuing process is the degree to which the object of the experience actualizes the individual himself. Does it make him a richer, more complete, more fully developed person? This may sound as though it were a selfish or unsocial criterion, but it does not prove to be so, since deep and helpful relationships with others are experienced as actualizing.

Like the infant, too, the psychologically mature adult trusts and uses the wisdom of his organism, with the difference that he is able to do so knowingly. He realizes that if he can trust all of himself, his feelings and his intuitions may be wiser than his mind, that as a total person he can be more sensitive and accurate than his thoughts alone. Hence he is not afraid to say—"I feel that this experience (or this thing, or this direction) is good. Later I will probably know *why* I feel it is good." He trusts the totality of himself.

It should be evident from what I have been saying that this valuing process in the mature individual is not an easy or simple thing. The process is complex, the choices often very perplexing and difficult, and there is no guarantee that the choice which is made will in fact prove to be self-actualizing. But because whatever evidence exists is available to the individual, and because he is open to his experiencing, errors are correctable. If this chosen course of action is not self-enhancing this will be sensed and he can make an adjustment or revision. He thrives on a maximum feedback interchange and thus, like the gyroscopic compass on a ship, can continually correct his course toward his true goal of self-fulfillment.

SOME PROPOSITIONS REGARDING THE VALUING PROCESS

Let me sharpen the meaning of what I have been saying by stating two propositions which contain the essential elements of this viewpoint. While it may not be possible to devise empirical tests of each proposition in its entirety, yet each is to some degree capable of being tested through the methods of science. I would also state that though the following propositions are stated firmly in order to give them clarity, I am actually advancing them as decidedly tentative hypotheses.

I. *There is an organismic base for an organized valuing process within the human individual.*

It is hypothesized that this base is something the human being shares with the rest of the animate world. It is part of the functioning life process of any healthy organism. It is the capacity for receiving feedback information which enables the organism continually to adjust its behavior and reactions so as to achieve the maximum possible self-enhancement.

II. *This valuing process in the human being is effective in achieving self-enhancement to the degree that the individual is open to the experiencing which is going on within himself.*

I have tried to give two examples of individuals who are close to their own experiencing: the tiny infant who has not yet learned to deny in his awareness the processes going on within; and the psychologically mature person who has relearned the advantages of this open state.

There is a corollary to this second proposition which might be put in the following terms. One way of assisting the individual to move toward openness to experience is through a relationship in which he is prized as a separate person, in which the experiencing going on within him is empathically understood and valued, and in which he is given the freedom to experience his own feelings and those of others without being threatened in doing so.

This corollary obviously grows out of therapeutic experience. It is a brief statement of the essential qualities in any growth-promoting relationship. There are already some empirical studies, of which the one by Barrett-Lennard (1962) is a good example, which give support to such a statement.

PROPOSITIONS REGARDING THE OUTCOMES OF THE VALUING PROCESS

I come now to the nub of any theory of values or valuing. What are its consequences? I should like to move into this new ground by stating bluntly two propositions as to the qualities of behavior which emerge from this valuing process. I shall then give some of the evidence from my own experience as a therapist in support of these propositions.

III. *In persons who are moving toward greater openness to their experiencing, there is an organismic commonality of value directions.*

IV. *These common value directions are of such kinds as to enhance the development of the individual himself, of others in his community, and to contribute to the survival and evolution of his species.*

It has been a striking fact of my experience that in therapy, where individuals are valued, where there is greater freedom to feel and to be, certain value directions seem to emerge. These are not chaotic directions but instead have a surprising commonality. This commonality is not dependent on the personality of the therapist, for I have seen these trends emerge in the clients of therapists sharply different in personality. This commonality does not seem to be due to the influences of any one culture, for I have found evidence of these directions in cultures as divergent as those of the United States, Holland, France, and Japan. I like to think that this commonality of value directions is due to the fact that we all belong to the same species—that just as a human infant tends, individually, to select a diet similar to that selected by other human infants, so a client in therapy tends, individually, to choose value directions similar to those chosen by other clients. As a species there may be certain elements of experience which tend to make for inner development and which would be chosen by all individuals if they were genuinely free to choose.

Let me indicate a few of these value directions as I see them in my clients as they move in the direction of personal growth and maturity.

They tend to move away from façades. Pretense, defensiveness, putting up a front, tend to be negatively valued.

They tend to move away from "oughts." The compelling feeling of "I ought to do or be thus and so" is negatively valued. The client moves away from being what he "ought to be," no matter who has set that imperative.

They tend to move away from meeting the expectations of others. Pleasing others, as a goal in itself, is negatively valued.

Being real is positively valued. The client tends to move toward being himself, being his real feelings, being what he is. This seems to be a very deep preference.

Self-direction is positively valued. The client discovers an increasing pride and confidence in making his own choices, guiding his own life.

One's self, one's own feelings come to be positively valued. From a point where he looks upon himself with contempt and despair, the client comes to value himself and his reactions as being of worth.

Being a process is positively valued. From desiring some fixed goal, clients come to prefer the excitement of being a process of potentialities being born.

Perhaps more than all else, the client comes to value an openness to all of his inner and outer experience. To be open to and sensitive to his own *inner* reactions and feelings, the reactions and feelings of others, and the realities of the objective world—this is a direction which he clearly prefers. This openness becomes the client's most valued resource.

Sensitivity to others and acceptance of others is positively valued. The client comes to appreciate others for what they are, just as he has come to appreciate himself for what he is.

Finally, deep relationships are positively valued. To achieve a close, intimate, real, fully communicative relationship with another person seems to meet a deep need in every individual, and is very highly valued.

These then are some of the preferred directions which I have observed in individuals moving toward personal maturity. Though I am sure that the list I have given is inadequate and perhaps to some degree inaccurate, it holds for me exciting possibilities. Let me try to explain why.

I find it significant that when individuals are prized as persons, the values they select do not run the full gamut of possibilities. I do not find, in such a climate of freedom, that one person comes to value fraud and murder and thievery, while another values a life of self-sacrifice, and another values only money. Instead there seems to be a deep and underlying thread of commonality. I dare to believe that when the human being is inwardly free to choose whatever he deeply values, he tends to value those objects, experiences and goals which contribute to his own survival, growth, and development, and to the survival and development of others. I hypothesize that it is characteristic of the human organism to prefer such actualizing and socialized goals when he is exposed to a growth-promoting climate.

A corollary of what I have been saying is that in *any* culture, given a climate of respect and freedom in which he is valued as a person, the mature individual would tend to choose and prefer these same value directions. This is a highly significant hypothesis which could be tested. It means that though the individual of whom I am speaking would not have a consistent or even a stable system of conceived values, the valuing process within him would lead to emerging value directions which would be constant across cultures and across time.

Another implication I see is that individuals who exhibit the fluid valuing process I have tried to describe, whose value directions are generally those I have listed, would be highly effective in the ongoing process of human evolution. If the human species is to survive at all on this globe, the human being must become more readily adaptive to new problems and situations, must be able to select that which is valuable for development and survival out of new and complex situations, must be accurate in his appreciation of reality if he is to make such selections. The psychologically mature person as I have described him has, I believe, the qualities which would cause him to value those experiences which would facilitate the survival and enhancement of the human race. He would be a worthy participant and guide in the process of human evolution.

Finally, it appears that we have returned to the issue of the universality of values, but by a different route. Instead of universal values "out there," or a universal value system imposed by some group—philosophers, rulers, or priests—we have the possibility of universal human value directions emerging from the experiencing of the human organism. Evidence from therapy indicates that both personal and social values emerge as natural, and experienced, when the individual is close to his own organismic valuing process. The suggestion is that though modern man no longer trusts religion or science or philosophy nor any system of beliefs to *give* him his values, he may find an organismic valuing base within himself which, if he can learn again to be in touch with it, will prove to be an organized, adaptive, and social approach to the perplexing value issues which face all of us.

SUMMARY

I have tried to present some observations, growing out of experience in psychotherapy, which are relevant to man's search for some satisfying basis for his approach to values.

I have described the human infant as he enters directly into an evaluating transaction with his world, appreciating or rejecting his experiences as they have meaning for his own actualization, utilizing all the wisdom of his tiny but complex organism.

I have said that we seem to lose this capacity for direct evaluation, and come to behave in those ways and to act in terms of those values which will bring us social approval, affection, esteem. To buy love we relinquish the valuing process. Because the center of our lives now lies in others, we are fearful and insecure, and must cling rigidly to the values we have introjected.

But if life or therapy gives us favorable conditions for continuing our psychological growth, we move on in something of a spiral, developing an approach to values which partakes of the infant's directness and fluidity but goes far beyond him in its richness. In our transactions with experience we are again the locus or source of valuing, we prefer those experiences which in the long run are enhancing, we utilize all the richness of our cognitive learning and functioning, but at the same time we trust the wisdom of our organism.

I have pointed out that these observations lead to certain basic statements. Man has within him an organismic basis for valuing. To the extent that he can be freely in touch with this valuing process in himself, he will behave in ways which are self-enhancing. We even know some of the conditions which enable him to be in touch with his own experiencing process.

In therapy, such openness to experience leads to emerging value directions which appear to be common across individuals and perhaps even across cultures. Stated in older terms, individuals who are thus in touch with their experiencing come to value such directions as sincerity, independence, self-direction, self-knowledge, social responsivity, social responsibility, and loving interpersonal relationships.

I have concluded that a new kind of emergent universality of value directions becomes possible when individuals move in the direction of psychological maturity, or more accurately, move in the direction of becoming open to their experiencing. Such a value base appears to make for the enhancement of self and others, and to promote a positive evolutionary process.

References

Barrett-Lennard, G. T. Dimensions of therapist response as causal factors in therapeutic change. *Psychological Monographs*, 1962, 76 (43, Whole No. 562).

Gendlin, E. T. Experiencing: A variable in the process of therapeutic change. *American Journal of Psychotherapy*, 1961, *15*, 233-245.

Gendlin, E. T. *Experiencing and the creation of meaning*. New York: The Free Press of Glencoe, Division of the Macmillan Co., 1962.

Glad, D. D. *Operational values in psychotherapy*. New York: Oxford University Press, 1959.

Morris, C. W. *Varieties of human value*. Chicago: University of Chicago Press, 1956.

Rogers, C. R. *Client-centered therapy*. Boston: Houghton Mifflin Co., 1951. Chapter XI (Pp. 522-524).

Rogers, C. R. A theory of therapy, personality and interpersonal relationships. In S. Koch (Ed.), *Psychology: A study of a science*, Vol. III. *Formulations of the person and the social context*. New York: McGraw Hill, 1959, Pp. 185-256.

13

Freedom and Commitment

"Freedom" to learn or choose; "self-directed" learning; these are completely untenable concepts in the minds of many behavioral scientists, who believe that man is simply the inevitable product of his conditioning. Yet these are terms which I have used freely in this book, as though they have real meaning.

I endeavored to face this discrepancy squarely in a talk I gave at the time I was honored as "Humanist of the Year" by the American Humanist Association.[1] I do not pretend that I resolved the age-old problem of freedom and determinism, but I have, for myself, formulated a way of living with it. Those who are perplexed by modern mechanistic-deterministic views on the one hand, and by the surging freedoms of students, underdeveloped nations, and "Black Power" on the other, may find this chapter of interest, and possibly of help.

One of the deepest issues in modern life, in modern man, is the question as to whether the concept of personal freedom has any meaning whatsoever in our present day scientific world. The growing ability of the behavioral scientist to predict and to control behavior has brought the issue sharply to the fore. If we accept the logical positivism and strictly behavioristic emphases which are predominant in the American psychological scene, there is not even room for discussion. The title of this chapter is then completely without meaning.

But if we step outside the narrowness of the behavioral sciences, this question is not only *an* issue, it is one of the primary issues which define modern man. Friedman in his book (1963, p. 251) makes his topic "the problematic of modern man—the alienation, the divided nature, the unresolved tension between personal free-

---

[1] "Freedom and Commitment," *The Humanist*, 1964, *24*, No. 2, 37-40.

dom and psychological compulsion which follows on 'the death of God.' " The issues of personal freedom and personal commitment have become very sharp indeed in a world in which man feels unsupported by a supernatural religion, and experiences keenly the division between his awareness and those elements of his dynamic functioning of which he is unaware. If he is to wrest any meaning from a universe which for all he knows may be indifferent, he must arrive at some stance which he can hold in regard to these timeless uncertainties.

So, writing as both a behavioral scientist and as one profoundly concerned with the human, the personal, the phenomenological and the intangible, I should like to contribute what I can to this continuing dialogue regarding the meaning of and the possibility of freedom.

MAN IS UNFREE

Let me explain, first of all, that to most psychologists and workers in the behavioral sciences, the title of this chapter would seem very strange indeed. In the minds of most behavioral scientists, man is not free, nor can he as a free man commit himself to some purpose, since he is controlled by factors outside of himself. Therefore, neither freedom nor commitment is even a possible concept to modern behavioral science as it is usually understood.

To show that I am not exaggerating, let me quote a statement from Dr. B. F. Skinner of Harvard, who is one of the most consistent advocates of a strictly behavioristic psychology. He says,

> The hypothesis that man is not free is essential to the application of scientific method to the study of human behavior. The free inner man who is held responsible for his behavior is only a pre-scientific substitute for the kinds of causes which are discovered in the course of scientific analysis. All these alternative causes lie *outside* the individual (1953, p. 477).

This view is shared by many psychologists and others who feel, as does Dr. Skinner, that all the effective causes of behavior lie outside of the individual and that it is only through the external stimulus that behavior takes place. The scientific description of behavior avoids anything that partakes in any way of freedom. For example, Dr. Skinner (1964, pp. 90-91) describes an experiment in which a pigeon was conditioned to turn in a clockwise direction. The behavior of the pigeon was "shaped up" by rewarding any movement that approximated a clockwise turn until, increasingly, the bird was turning round and round in a steady movement. This is what is known as operant conditioning. Students who had watched the demonstration were asked to write an account of what they had seen. Their responses included the following ideas: that the pigeon was conditioned to *expect* reinforcement for the right kind of behavior; that the pigeon *hoped* that something would bring the food back again; that the pigeon *observed* that a certain behavior seemed to produce a particular result; that the pigeon *felt* that food would be given it because of its action; that the bird came to *associate* his action with the click of the food dispenser. Skinner ridicules these statements because they all go beyond the observed behavior in using such words as *expect, hope, observe, feel,* and *associate.* The whole explanation from his point of view is that the bird was reinforced when it emitted a given kind of behavior; the pigeon walked around until the food container again appeared; a certain behavior produced a given result; food was given to the pigeon when it acted in a given way; and the click of the food dispenser was related in time to the bird's action. These statements describe the pigeon's behavior from a scientific point of view.

Skinner goes on to point out that the students were undoubtedly reporting what they would have expected, felt and hoped under similar circumstances. But he then makes the case that there is no more reality to such ideas in the human being than there is in the pigeon, that it is only because such words have been reinforced by the verbal community in which the individual has developed, that such terms are used. He discusses the fact that the verbal community which conditioned them to use such terms saw no more of their behavior than they had seen of the pigeon's. In other words the internal events, if they indeed exist, have no scientific significance.

As to the methods used for changing the behavior of the pigeon, many people besides Dr. Skinner feel that through such positive reinforcement human behavior as well as animal behavior can be "shaped up" and controlled. In his book, *Walden Two*, Skinner says,

> Now that we know how positive reinforcement works and how negative doesn't, we can be more deliberate and hence more successful in our cultural design. We can achieve a sort of control under which the controlled, though they are following a code much more scrupulously than was ever the case under the old system, nevertheless *feel free*. They are doing what they want to do, not what they are forced to do. That's the source of the tremendous power of positive reinforcement—there is no restraint and no revolt. By a careful cultural design we control not the final behavior but the *inclination* to behave—the motives, the desires, the wishes. The curious thing is that in that case *the question of freedom never arises* (1948, p. 218).

Another psychological experiment done by Dr. Richard Crutchfield at Berkeley (1955), again illustrates a way in which behavior may be controlled, in which it appears the individual is unfree. In this experiment five subjects at a time are seated side by side, each in an individual booth screened from one another. Each booth has a panel with various switches and lights. The subject can use the switches to signal his judgments on items that are projected on the wall in front of the group. The lights are signal lights which indicate what judgments the other four members are giving to the items. The subjects are told that they will be given identifying letters A, B, C, D, and E and are instructed to respond one at a time in that order. However, when they enter the cubicles, each discovers that he is letter E. They are not permitted to talk during the session.

Actually the lights in each booth are controlled by the experimenter and do not express the judgments of the other four members. Thus on those critical items where the experimenter wishes to impose group pressure, he can make it appear that all four members, A through D, agree on an answer which is clearly at variance with the correct answer. In this way each subject is confronted with a conflict between his own judgment and what he believes to be the consensus of the group. Thus, for example, the question may be, "Which of these two irregular figures is larger, X or Y?" The individual sees clearly that X is larger than Y, yet one after another the lights flash on indicating that all of the other four members regard Y as being the larger figure. Now it is his turn to decide. How will he respond? Which switch will he press? Crutchfield has shown that given the right conditions almost everyone will desert the evidence of his senses or his own honest opinion and conform to the seeming consensus of the group. For example, some high-level mathematicians yielded to the false group consensus on some fairly easy arithmetic problems, giving wrong answers that they would never have given under normal circumstances.

Here again there would seem to be evidence that the behavior of the individual is shaped by the outside stimulus, in this case a social stimulus, and that there is no such thing as freedom in choosing one's behavior. It helps to explain how Skinner in his book, *Walden Two*, can have his hero say:

> "Well, what do you say to the design of personalities? Would that interest you? The control of temperaments? Give me the specifications and I'll give you the man! What do you say to the control of motivation, building the interests which will make men most productive and most successful? Does that seem to you fantastic? Yet some of the techniques are available and more can be worked out experimentally. Think of the possibilities. . . . Let us control the lives of our children and see what we can make of them" (1948, p. 243).

An experience I had just a short time ago in a university on the West Coast further illustrates the unfreedom of man. Some psychologists were studying the ways in which individual patterns of behavior in a group can be changed. Four subjects are seated around a table. Each has in front of him a shielded light bulb invisible to the others. They are given a topic on which to talk. Notice is taken of the individual who seems least dominant in the group, who never takes a leadership role. Then for the second part of the experiment, this individual is given a paper in which he is told that the discussion is being listened to and observed by experts, and that when these experts think he is contributing usefully to the group process his light will blink. He will have to judge for himself what he is doing that is helpful. The other, more dominant, three are given similar sheets of instructions, except that each is told that his light will blink when he is *not* contributing helpfully. They are then given another question to discuss with the instruction that by the end of the half hour they are to try to arrive at conclusions in regard to this problem. Now, every time that the "shrinking violet" speaks, his light blinks. And whenever the others speak their lights also blink, but with the opposite meaning, that they are *not* contributing. After half an hour of such conditioning, the shy member is nearly always the perceived leader of the group. Furthermore, this pattern seems to carry over through an additional half hour in which no use is made of lights. The story is told of three mature scientists and one young graduate student who were put through this procedure. In the first session, the young student took almost no part. In the session with the blinking lights, he became so dominant that at the end when the group was asked for a summary of what had gone on, the older men turned to him and said, "Why don't you summarize it? You're the one best able to do that."

Here again it seems as though behavior is extremely manipulable, and that there is no such thing as freedom. The members of the group are behaving like puppets on a string, at the whim of the experimenters.

One more example of the degree of control which scientists have been able to achieve involves an experiment with rats. Years ago, Dr. James Olds (1955) found that he could implant tiny electrodes in the septal area of the brain of laboratory rats. When one of these animals presses a bar in his cage, it causes a minute current to pass through these electrodes. When the electrode has penetrated just the right area of brain tissue, this appears to be such a rewarding experience that the animal goes into an orgy of bar-pressing, often until he is exhausted. However, the subjective nature of the experience seems to be so satisfying that the animal prefers it to any other activity. Even after exhaustion, with a brief rest and a small bit of food and water, the rat returns to its orgy of pleasure. In one experiment, rats went on in this fashion for twenty-four hours a day for three weeks straight. Curiously enough, there seemed to be no physical or mental damage to the rats then or later. One can only speculate what this procedure might bring forth if applied fully to human beings.

As an article in *Life* magazine made clear to the general reader, there are not only experiments of this sort with animals, but there are beginning to be situations in which such electronic stimulation of the brain is utilized for a number of medical purposes in humans. Obviously there cannot be the experimentation with human beings that there has been with animals. Yet already we know that these tiny electronic currents passing through minute portions of the brain elicit feelings of happiness, rage or terror, and even depress feelings of extreme pain.

I think it is clear from all of this that man is a machine—a complex machine, to be sure, but one which is increasingly subject to scientific control. Whether behavior will be managed through operant conditioning as in *Walden Two* or whether we will be "shaped up" by the unplanned forms of conditioning implied in social pressure, or whether we will be controlled by electrodes in the brain, it seems quite clear that science is making out of man an object and that the purpose of such science is not only understanding and prediction but control. Thus it would seem to be quite clear that there could be no concept so foreign to the facts as that man is free. Man is a machine, man is unfree, man cannot commit himself in any meaningful sense; he is simply controlled by planned or unplanned forces outside of himself.

MAN IS FREE

I am impressed by the scientific advances illustrated in the examples I have given. I regard them as a great tribute to the ingenuity, insight, and persistence of the individuals making the investigations. They have added enormously to our knowledge. Yet for me they leave something very important unsaid. Let me try to illustrate this, first from my experience in therapy.

I think of a young man classed as schizophrenic with whom I had been working for a long time in a state hospital. He was a very inarticulate man, and during one hour he made a few remarks about individuals who had recently left the hospital; then he remained silent for almost forty minutes. When he got up to go, he mumbled almost under his breath, "If some of *them* can do it, maybe I can too." That was all—not a dramatic statement, not uttered with force and vigor, yet a statement of choice by this young man to work toward his own improvement and eventual release from the hospital. It is not too surprising that about eight months after that statement he was out of the hospital. I believe this experience of responsible choice is one of the deepest aspects of psychotherapy and one of the elements which most solidly underlies personality change.

I think of another young person, this time a young woman graduate student, who was deeply disturbed and on the borderline of a psychotic break. Yet after a number of interviews in which she talked very critically about all of the people who had failed to give her what she needed, she finally concluded: "Well, with that sort of a foundation, it's really up to *me*. I mean it seems to be really apparent to me that I can't depend on someone else to *give* me an education." And then she added very softly: "I'll really have to get it myself." She goes on to explore this experience of important and responsible choice. She finds it a frightening experience, and yet one which gives her a feeling of strength. A force seems to surge up within her which is big and strong, and yet she also feels very much alone and sort of cut off from support. She adds: "I am going to begin to do more things that I know I should do." And she did.

I could add many other examples. One young fellow talking about the way in which his whole life had been distorted and spoiled by his parents finally comes to the conclusion that, "Maybe now that I *see* that, it's up to *me*."

Let me spell out a trifle more fully the way such choosings occur in therapy. An immature, highly religious sixteen-year-old high school girl, brought up in a very strict family, had rather obviously been patterning herself upon a masculine ideal of work and scholarly achievements which was almost certainly beyond her abilities. The previous year she had had a "nervous breakdown" which overwhelmed her. Some months after her break, she came to me for help. To take just one theme of the many which she pursued through the interviews, I will focus on her views about being a woman, as quite fully reported in my notes. During the early interviews she made it clear that she disliked children, that she did not wish marriage, that she wished she were a man, or could act like a man. These feelings were accepted.

Later on she says, "I admire masculine qualities so much that I wish I could be a man. Maybe somebody ought to set me straight and show me that I could be a fine young woman." This more ambivalent attitude was again accepted as being her own.

Two interviews later she talks about her dislike for small children but adds thoughtfully, "Maybe my dislike has been more or less forced. Maybe I just thought I'd be that way."

In a later interview she talks rather freely of her fear of childbirth, her fear that marriage would interfere with a career, saying that she is still mixed up on all these issues, showing very definite ambivalence.

In one of the closing interviews she says, "You know I've thought about that femininity thing again and I'm going to see if I can put it into words. I'm a girl. I'm going to accept it, not as fate, not in a spirit of submission, but as meant for the best. I can probably do a lot more good by being myself and developing my own talent rather than trying to do something different. I'm going to accept it as a challenge. I feel that I've almost lost that feeling that I wanted to be masculine. I just want to be myself. Maybe before I get through I'll really be glad I'm feminine. I'm going to learn to cook and be a good cook and make an art out of it."

Here again we see a slowly growing experience of personal choice which appeared to be basic to all of the change in personality and behavior which occurred. She chose, freely, to perceive herself in a different way, and out of that different perception there flowed many changes in attitude and behavior.

Or perhaps I could somehow communicate best the significance of free and responsible choice by quoting one sentence from a confused, bitter, psychotic individual who had been in a state hospital for three admissions, the last admission having lasted two and one-half years at the time I began working with him. I think the changes which gradually took place were based on and epitomized by one sentence in one of his interviews when he was feeling particularly confused. He said, "I don't know *what* I'm gonna do; but *I'm* gonna do it." For me, that speaks volumes.

For those of you have seen the film *David and Lisa*—and I hope that you have had that rich experience—I can illustrate exactly what I have been discussing. David, the adolescent schizophrenic, goes into a panic if he is touched by anyone. He feels that "touching kills," and he is deathly afraid of it, and afraid of the closeness in human relationships which touching implies. Yet toward the

close of the film he makes a bold and positive choice of the kind
I have been describing. He has been trying to be of help to Lisa,
the girl who is out of touch with reality. He tries to help at first
in an intellectually contemptuous way, then increasingly in a
warmer and more personal way. Finally, in a highly dramatic
moment, he says to her, "Lisa, take my hand." He *chooses*, with
obvious conflict and fear, to leave behind the safety of his un-
touchableness, and to venture into the world of real human relationships where he is literally and figuratively in *touch* with another.
You are an unusual person if the film does not grow a bit misty
at this point.

Perhaps a behaviorist could try to account for the reaching out
of his hand by saying that it was the result of intermittent reinforcement of partial movements. I find such an explanation both
inaccurate and inadequate. It is the *meaning* of the *decision* which
is essential to understanding the act.

What I am trying to suggest in all of this is that I would be at
a loss to explain the positive change which can occur in psychotherapy if I had to omit the importance of the sense of free and
responsible choice on the part of my clients. I believe that this
experience of freedom to choose is one of the deepest elements
underlying change.

THE MEANING OF FREEDOM

Considering the scientific advances which I have mentioned,
how can we even speak of freedom? In what sense is a client
free? In what sense are any of us free? What possible definition
of freedom can there be in the modern world? Let me attempt
such a definition.

In the first place, the freedom that I am talking about is essentially an inner thing, something which exists in the living person
quite aside from any of the outward choices of alternatives which
we so often think of as constituting freedom. I am speaking of
the kind of freedom which Viktor Frankl vividly describes in his
experience of the concentration camp, when everything—pos-
sessions, status, identity—was taken from the prisoners. But even
months and years in such an environment showed only "that everything can be taken from a man but one thing: the last of the
human freedoms—to choose one's own attitude in any given set

of circumstances, to choose one's own way" (1959, p. 65). It is this inner, subjective, existential freedom which I have observed. It is the realization that "I can live myself, here and now, by my own choice." It is the quality of courage which enables a person to step into the uncertainty of the unknown as he chooses himself. It is the discovery of meaning from within oneself, meaning which comes from listening sensitively and openly to the complexities of what one is experiencing. It is the burden of being responsible for the self one chooses to be. It is the recognition of a person that he is an emerging process, not a static end product. The individual who is thus deeply and courageously thinking his own thoughts, becoming his own uniqueness, responsibly choosing himself, may be fortunate in having hundreds of objective outer alternatives from which to choose, or he may be unfortunate in having none. But his freedom exists regardless. So we are first of all speaking of something which exists within the individual, something phenomenological rather than external, but nonetheless to be prized.

The second point in defining this experience of freedom is that it exists not as a contradiction of the picture of the psychological universe as a sequence of cause and effect, but as a complement to such a universe. Freedom rightly understood is a fulfillment by the person of the ordered sequence of his life. The free man moves out voluntarily, freely, responsibly, to play his significant part in a world whose determined events move through him and through his spontaneous choice and will.

I see this freedom of which I am speaking, then, as existing in a different *dimension* than the determined sequence of cause and effect. I regard it as a freedom which exists in the subjective person, a freedom which he courageously uses to live his potentialities. The fact that this type of freedom seems completely irreconcilable with the behaviorist's picture of man is something which I will discuss a bit later.

FREEDOM MAKES A DIFFERENCE

Curiously enough, there is scientific evidence of the importance of this sense of freedom. For example, in the study done by Crutchfield (1955) which I mentioned earlier, I stated that under especially extreme circumstances, nearly everyone yielded in some degree to group pressure. Yet there were sharp individual differ-

ences, and these are found to be definitely correlated with personality characteristics. For example, the individuals who tended to
yield, agree, conform, the ones who could be controlled, gave
general evidence of incapacity to cope effectively with stress,
while the nonconformists did not tend to panic when placed under
pressure of conflicting forces.

The conformist also tended to have pronounced feelings of
personal inferiority and inadequacy, while the person who did
not yield to pressure had a sense of competence and personal
adequacy. He was more self-contained and autonomous in his
thinking. He was also a better judge of the attitudes of other people.

Most important of all for our purposes is the fact that those
who yielded, the conformists, tended to show a lack of openness and freedom in emotional processes. They were emotionally
restricted, lacking in spontaneity, tending to repress their own
impulses. The nonconformists, those who made their own choices,
were, on the other hand, much more open, free and spontaneous.
They were expressive and natural, free from pretense and unaf-
fected. Where the conformist tended to lack insight into his
own motives and behavior, the independent person had a good
understanding of himself.

What is the meaning of this aspect of Crutchfield's study? It
seems to imply that the person who is free within himself, who
is open to his experience, who has a sense of his own freedom and
responsible choice, is not nearly so likely to be controlled by his
environment as is the person who lacks these qualities.

Another story of research in this field, one with which I was
closely connected, had a very decided impact on me in the years
following the experience. A competent student doing his graduate
work under my supervision many years ago chose to study the
factors which would predict the behavior of adolescent delinquents.
He made careful objective ratings of the psychological environment
in the family, the educational experiences, the neighborhood and
cultural influences, the social experiences, the health history, and
the hereditary background of each delinquent. These external
factors were rated as to their favorableness for normal development on a continuum from elements destructive of the child's
welfare and inimical to healthy development to elements highly
conducive to healthy development. Almost as an afterthought, a
rating was also made of the degree of self-understanding, since

it was felt that although this was not one of the primary determining factors, it might play some part in predicting future behavior. This was essentially a rating of the degree to which the individual was open and realistic regarding himself and his situation, a judgment as to whether he was emotionally acceptant of the facts in himself and his environment.

These ratings on seventy-five delinquents were compared with ratings of their behavior and adjustment two to three years after the initial study. It was expected that the ratings on family environment and social experience with peers would be the best predictors of later behavior. To our amazement the degree of self-understanding was much the best predictor, correlating .84 with later behavior, while quality of social experience correlated .55 and family environment .36. We were simply not prepared to believe these findings and laid the study on the shelf until it could be replicated. Later it was replicated on a new group of seventy-six cases and all the essential findings were confirmed, although not quite so strikingly. Furthermore, the findings stood up even in detailed analysis. When we examined only the delinquents who came from the most unfavorable homes and who remained in those homes, it was still true that their future behavior was best predicted, not by the unfavorable conditioning they were receiving in their home environment, but by the degree of realistic understanding of themselves and their environment which they possessed (Rogers, Kell, McNeil, 1948).

The significance of this study was only slowly driven home to me. I began to see the significance of inner autonomy. The individual who sees himself and his situation clearly and who freely takes responsibility for that self and for that situation is a very different person from the one who is simply in the grip of outside circumstances. This difference shows up clearly in important aspects of his behavior.

THE EMERGENCE OF COMMITMENT

I have spoken thus far primarily about freedom. What about commitment? Certainly the disease of our age is lack of purpose, lack of meaning, lack of commitment on the part of individuals. Is there anything which I can say in regard to this?

It is clear to me that in therapy, as indicated in the examples that I have given, commitment to purpose and to meaning in life is one of the significant elements of change. It is only when the person decides, "I am someone; I am someone worth being; I am committed to being myself," that change becomes possible.

At a very interesting symposium at Rice University recently, Dr. Sigmund Koch sketched the revolution which is taking place in science, literature and the arts, in which a sense of commitment is again becoming evident after a long period in which that emphasis has been absent.

Part of what he meant by that may be illustrated by talking about Dr. Michael Polanyi, the philosopher of science, formerly a physicist, who has been presenting his notions about what science basically is. In his book, *Personal Knowledge*, Polanyi makes it clear that even scientific knowledge is personal knowledge, committed knowledge. We cannot rest comfortably on the belief that scientific knowledge is impersonal and "out there," that it has nothing to do with the individual who has discovered it. Instead every aspect of science is pervaded by disciplined personal commitment, and Polanyi makes the case very persuasively that the whole attempt to divorce science from the person is a completely unrealistic one. I think I am stating his belief correctly when I say that in his judgment logical positivism and all the current structure of science cannot save us from the fact that all knowing is uncertain, involves risk, and is grasped and comprehended only through the deep, personal commitment of a disciplined search.

Perhaps a brief quotation will give something of the flavor of his thinking. Speaking of great scientists, he says:

> So we see that both Kepler and Einstein approached nature with intellectual passions and with beliefs inherent in these passions, which led them to their triumphs and misguided them to their errors. These passions and beliefs were theirs, personally, even though they held them in the conviction that they were valid, universally. I believe that they were competent to follow these impulses, even though they risked being misled by them. And again, what I accept of their work today, I accept personally, guided by passions and beliefs similar to theirs, holding in my turn that my impulses are valid, universally, even though I must admit the possibility that they may be mistaken (1958, p. 145).

Thus we see that a modern philosopher of science believes that deep personal commitment is the only possible basis on which science can firmly stand. This is a far cry indeed from the logical positivism of twenty or thirty years ago, which placed knowledge far out in impersonal space.

Let me say a bit more about what I mean by commitment in the psychological sense. I think it is easy to give this word a much too shallow meaning, indicating that the individual has, simply by conscious choice, committed himself to one course of action or another. I think the meaning goes far deeper than that. Commitment is a total organismic direction involving not only the conscious mind but the whole direction of the organism as well.

In my judgment, commitment is something that one *discovers* within oneself. It is a trust of one's total reaction rather than of one's mind only. It has much to do with creativity. Einstein's explanation of how he moved toward his formulation of relativity without any clear knowledge of his goal is an excellent example of what I mean by the sense of commitment based on a total organismic reaction. He says:

> "During all those years there was a feeling of direction, of going straight toward something concrete. It is, of course, very hard to express that feeling in words but it was decidedly the case and clearly to be distinguished from later considerations about the rational form of the solution" (quoted in Wertheimer, 1945, p. 183-184).

Thus commitment is more than a decision. It is the functioning of an individual who is searching for the directions which are emerging within himself. Kierkegaard has said, "The truth exists only in the process of becoming, in the process of appropriation" (1941, p. 72). It is this individual creation of a tentative personal truth through action which is the essence of commitment.

Man is most successful in such a commitment when he is functioning as an integrated, whole, unified individual. The more that he is functioning in this total manner the more confidence he has in the directions which he unconsciously chooses. He feels a trust in his experiencing, of which, even if he is fortunate, he has only partial glimpses in his awareness.

Thought of in the sense in which I am describing it, it is clear that commitment is an achievement. It is the kind of purposeful and meaningful direction which is only gradually achieved by the individual who has come increasingly to live closely in relation-

ship with his own experiencing—a relationship in which his unconscious tendencies are as much respected as are his conscious
choices. This is the kind of commitment toward which I believe
individuals can move. It is an important aspect of living in a fully
functioning way.

THE IRRECONCILABLE CONTRADICTION

I trust it will be very clear that I have given two sharply
divergent and irreconcilably contradictory points of view. On
the one hand, modern psychological science and many other forces
in modern life as well, hold the view that man is unfree, that he
is controlled, that words such as purpose, choice, commitment
have no significant meaning, that man is nothing but an object
which we can more fully understand and more fully control.
Enormous strides have been and are being made in implementing
this perspective. It would seem heretical indeed to question
this view.

Yet, as Polanyi has pointed out in another of his writings (1957),
the dogmas of science can be in error. He says:

> In the days when an idea could be silenced by showing that it
> was contrary to religion, theology was the greatest single source
> of fallacies. Today, when any human thought can be discredited
> by branding it as unscientific, the power previously exercised by
> theology has passed over to science; hence science has become
> in its turn the greatest single source of error.

So I am emboldened to say that over against this view of man
as unfree, as an object, is the evidence from therapy, from subjective living, and from objective research as well, that personal
freedom and responsibility have a crucial significance, that one
cannot live a complete life without such personal freedom and
responsibility, and that self-understanding and responsible choice
make a sharp and measurable difference in the behavior of the
individual. In this context, commitment does have meaning. Commitment is the emerging and changing total direction of the
individual, based on a close and acceptant relationship between
the person and all of the trends in his life, conscious and unconscious. Unless, as individuals and as a society, we can make con-

structive use of this capacity for freedom and commitment, mankind, it seems to me, is set on a collision course with fate.

What is the answer to the contradiction I have described? For myself, I am content to think of it as a deep and lasting paradox. While paradoxes are often frustrating, they can still be very fruitful. In physics, there is the paradox that light is a form of wave motion and at the same time it can be shown to exist in quanta, the contradiction between the wave theory and the corpuscular theory of light. This paradox has been irreconcilable, and yet on the basis of it, physics has made important advances.

Friedman, the philosopher, believes that much the same point of view is necessary when man faces the philosophical issue of meaning. He says: "Today, meaning can be found, if at all, only through the attitude of the man who is willing to *live* with the absurd, to remain open to the mystery which he can never hope to pin down" (1963, p. 468).

I share this conviction that we must live openly with mystery, with the absurd. Let me put the whole theme of my discussion in the form of a contradiction.

A part of modern living is to face the paradox that, viewed from one perspective, man is a complex machine. We are every day moving toward a more precise understanding and a more precise control of this objective mechanism which we call man. On the other hand, in another significant dimension of his existence, man is subjectively free; his personal choice and responsibility account for the shape of his life; he is in fact the architect of himself. A truly crucial part of his existence is the discovery of his own meaningful commitment to life with all of his being.

If in response to this you say, "But these views *cannot* both be true," my answer is, "This is a deep paradox with which we must learn to live."

References

Crutchfield, R. S. Conformity and character. *American Psychologist*, 1955, *10*, 191-198.

Frankl, V. E. *From death camp to existentialism*. Boston: Beacon Press, 1959.

Friedman, M. *The problematic rebel*. New York: Random House, 1963.

Kierkegaard, S. *Concluding unscientific postscript*. Walter Lowre (Ed.), Princeton: Princeton University Press, 1941.

Olds, J. A physiological study of reward. In D. C. McClelland (Ed.), *Studies in motivation*. New York: Appleton-Century Crofts, 1955, Pp. 134-143.

Polanyi, M. Scientific outlook: Its sickness and cure. *Science*, 1957, *125*, 480-484.

Polanyi, M. *Personal knowledge*. Chicago: University of Chicago Press, 1958.

Rogers, C. R., Kell, B. L., & McNeil, Helen. The role of self understanding in the prediction of behavior. *Journal of Consulting Psychology*, 1948, *12*, 174-186.

Skinner, B. F. *Walden Two*. New York: Macmillan, 1948.

Skinner, B. F. *Science and human behavior*. New York: Macmillan, 1953.

Skinner, B. F. Behaviorism at fifty. In T. W. Wann (Ed.), *Behaviorism and Phenomenology: Contrasting bases for modern psychology*. University of Chicago Press, 1964, Pp. 90-91.

Wertheimer, M. *Productive thinking*. New York: Harper, 1945.

14

The Goal: The Fully Functioning Person

What are we striving for? Why is it that we desire the "best" (however we define that term) in family life, in the school, in the university, in the community? It is, I believe, because we hope to develop the "best" of human beings. But rarely do we give explicit thought to the exact meaning of this goal. What sort of human being do we wish to grow?

A number of years ago, writing as a psychotherapist, I tried to state my personal answer to this question.[1] I make no apology for the fact that this chapter is cast in the framework of therapy. To my mind the "best" of education would produce a person very similar to the one produced by the "best" of therapy. Indeed it may be of help to teachers and educators to think of this issue in a setting outside the school. It may make it easier for them to see, in sharper focus, those points where they agree with the picture I paint, and those points where they disagree.

I suspect that each one of us, from time to time, speculates on the general characteristics of the optimal person. If education were as completely successful as we could wish it to be in promoting personal growth and development, what sort of person would emerge? Or, speaking from the field in which I have had the most experience, suppose psychotherapy were completed in optimal fashion, what sort of person would have developed? What is the hypothetical end-point, the ultimate, of psychological growth and development? I wish to discuss this question from the point of view of therapy, but I believe the tentative answers which I formulate would be equally applicable to education, or to the family, or to any other situation which has as its aim the constructive development of persons. I am really raising the issue, what is the goal? What is the optimal person?

I have often asked myself this question and have felt an increasing dissatisfaction with the kind of answers which are current. They

---

[1] This chapter is a revised version of a paper first published as "The Concept of the Fully Functioning Person," *Psychotherapy: Theory, Research, and Practice,* 1963, *1*, No. 1, 17-26.

seem too slippery, too relativistic, to have much value in a developing science of personality. They often contain too, I believe, a concealed bias which makes them unsatisfactory. I think of the commonly held notion that the person who has completed therapy or is fully mature will be adjusted to society. But what society? Any society, no matter what its characteristics? I cannot accept this. I think of the concept, implicit in much psychological writing, that successful therapy means that a person will have moved from a diagnostic category considered pathological to one considered normal. But the evidence is accumulating that there is so little agreement on diagnostic categories as to make them practically meaningless as scientific concepts. And even if a person becomes "normal," is that a suitable outcome of therapy? Furthermore, the experience of recent years has made me wonder whether the term psychopathology may not be simply a convenient basket for all those aspects of personality which diagnosticians as a group are most afraid of in themselves. For these and other reasons, change in diagnosis is not a description of therapeutic outcome which is satisfying to me. If I turn to another type of concept, I find that the person whose psychological growth is optimal is said to have achieved a positive mental health. But who defines mental health? I suspect that the Menninger Clinic and the Center for Studies of the Person would define it rather differently. I am sure that the Soviet state would have still another definition.

Pushed about by questions such as these, I find myself speculating about the characteristics of the person who comes out of therapy, if therapy is maximally successful. I should like to share with you some of these tentative personal speculations. What I wish to do is to formulate a theoretical concept of the optimal end-point of therapy, or, indeed, of education. I would hope that I could state it in terms which would be free from some of the criticisms I have mentioned, terms which might eventually be given operational definition and objective test.

THE BACKGROUND FROM WHICH
THE PROBLEM IS APPROACHED

I shall have to make it clear at the outset that I am speaking from a background of client-centered therapy. Quite possibly all successful psychotherapy has a similar personality outcome, but I am less sure of that than formerly, and hence wish to narrow my field of consideration. So I shall assume that this hypothetical person whom I describe has had an intensive and extensive experience in client-centered therapy, and that the therapy has been as completely successful as is theoretically possible. This would mean that the therapist has been able to enter into an intensely personal and subjective relationship with this client—relating not as a scientist to an object of study, not as a physician expecting to diagnose and cure, but as a person to a person. It would mean that the therapist feels this client to be a person of unconditional self-worth; of value no matter what his condition, his behavior, or his feelings. It means that the therapist is able to let himself go in understanding this client; that no inner barriers keep him from sensing what it feels like to be the client at each moment of the relationship; and that he can convey something of his empathic understanding to the client. It means that the therapist has been comfortable in entering this relationship fully, without knowing cognitively where it will lead, satisfied with providing a climate which will free the client to become himself.

For the client, this optimal therapy has meant an exploration of increasingly strange and unknown and dangerous feelings in himself; the exploration proving possible only because he is gradually realizing that he is accepted unconditionally. Thus he becomes acquainted with elements of his experience which have in the past been denied to awareness as too threatening, too damaging to the structure of the self. He finds himself experiencing these feelings fully, completely, in the relationship, so that for the moment he *is* his fear, or his anger, or his tenderness, or his strength. And as he lives these widely varied feelings, in all their degrees of intensity, he discovers that he has experienced *himself*, that he *is* all these feelings. He finds his behavior changing in constructive fashion in accordance with his newly experienced self. He approaches the realization that he no longer needs to fear what experience may hold, but can welcome it freely as a part of his changing and developing self.

This is a thumbnail sketch of what client-centered therapy might be at its optimum. I give it here simply as an introduction to my main concern: What personality characteristics would develop in the client as a result of this kind of experience?

THE CHARACTERISTICS OF THE PERSON AFTER THERAPY

What then is the end-point of optimal psychotherapy, of maximal psychological growth? I shall try to answer this question for myself, basing my thinking upon the knowledge we have gained from clinical experience and research, but pushing this to the limit in order better to see the kind of person who would emerge if therapy were most effective. As I have puzzled over the answer, the description seems to me quite unitary, but for clarity of presentation I shall break it down into three facets.

1.) *This person would be open to his experience.*

This is a phrase which has come to have increasingly definite meaning for me. It is the polar opposite of defensiveness. Defensiveness we have described in the past as being the organism's response to experiences which are perceived or anticipated as incongruent with the structure of the self. In order to maintain the self-structure, such experiences are given a distorted symbolization in awareness, which reduces the incongruity. Thus the individual defends himself against any threat of alteration in the concept of self.

In the person who is open to his experience, however, every stimulus, whether originating within the organism or in the environment, would be freely relayed through the nervous system without being distorted by a defensive mechanism. There would be no need of the mechanism of "subception" whereby the organism is forewarned of any experience threatening to the self. On the contrary, whether the stimulus was the impact of a configuration of form, color, or sound in the environment on the sensory nerves, or a memory trace from the past, or a visceral sensation of fear or pleasure or disgust, the person would be "living it," would have it completely available to awareness.

Perhaps I can give this concept a more vivid meaning if I illustrate it from a recorded interview. A young professional man reports in the 48th interview the way in which he has become more open to some of his bodily sensations, as well as other feelings.

Client: "It doesn't seem to me that it would be possible for anybody to relate all the changes that I feel. But I certainly have felt recently that I have more respect for, more objectivity toward my physical makeup. I mean I don't expect too much of myself. This is how it works out: It feels to me that in the past I used to fight a certain tiredness that I felt after supper. Well now I feel pretty sure that I really am *tired*—that I am not making myself tired—that I am just physiologically lower. It seemed that I was just constantly criticizing my tiredness."

Therapist: "So you can let yourself *be* tired, instead of feeling along with it a kind of criticism of it."

Client: "Yes, that I *shouldn't* be tired or something. And it seems in a way to be pretty profound that I can just not fight this tiredness, and along with it goes a real feeling of *I've* got to slow down, too, so that being tired isn't such an awful thing. I think I can also kind of pick up a thread here of why I should be that way in the way my father is and the way he looks at some of these things. For instance, say that I was sick, and I would report this, and it would seem that overtly he would want to do something about it but he would also communicate, 'Oh, my gosh, more trouble.' You know, something like that."

Therapist: "As though there were something quite annoying, really, about being physically ill."

Client: "Yeah, I am sure that my father has the same disrespect for his own physiology that I have had. Now last summer I twisted my back, I wrenched it, I heard it snap and everything. There was real pain there all the time at first, real sharp. And I had the doctor look at it and he said it wasn't serious, it should heal by itself as long as I didn't bend too much. Well this was months ago—and I have been noticing recently that—hell, this is a real pain and it's still there—and it's not my fault, I mean it's—"

Therapist: "It doesn't prove something bad about you—"

Client: "No—and one of the reasons I seem to get more tired than I should maybe is because of this constant strain and so on. I have already made an appointment with one of the doctors at the hospital that he would look at it and take an X-ray or something. In a way I guess you could say that I am just more accurately sensitive—or objectively sensitive to this kind of thing. I can say with certainty that this has also spread to what I eat and how much I eat. And this is really a profound change, as I say. And of course my relationship with my wife and the two children is —well you just wouldn't recognize it if you could see me inside— as you have—I mean—there just doesn't seem to be anything more wonderful than really and genuinely—really *feeling* love for your own child and at the same time *receiving* it. I don't know how to put this. We have such an increased respect—both of us—for Judy and we've noticed just—as we participated in this—we have noticed such a tremendous change in her—it seems to be a pretty deep kind of thing."

Therapist: "It seems to me you are saying that you can listen more accurately to yourself. If your body says it's tired, you listen to it and believe it, instead of criticizing it; if it's in pain you can listen to that; if the feeling is really loving your wife or child, you can *feel* that, and it seems to show up in the differences in them too."

Here, in a relatively minor but symbolically important excerpt, can be seen much of what I have been trying to say about openness to experience. Formerly he could not freely feel pain or illness, because being ill meant being unacceptable. Neither could he feel tenderness and love for his child, because such feelings meant being weak, and he had to maintain his façade of being strong. But now he can be genuinely open to the experience of his organism—he can be tired when he is tired, he can feel pain when his organism is in pain, he can freely experience the love he feels for his daughter, and he can also feel and express annoyance toward her, as he went on to say in the next portion of the interview. He can fully live the experiences of his total organism, rather than shutting them out of awareness.

I have used this concept of availability to awareness to try to make clear what I mean by openness to experience. This might be misunderstood. I do not mean that this individual would be self-consciously aware of all that was going on within himself, like the centipede who became aware of all of his legs. On the contrary, he would be free to live a feeling subjectively, as well as be aware of it. He might experience love, or pain, or fear, living in this attitude subjectively. Or he might abstract himself from this subjectivity and realize in awareness, "I am in pain," "I am afraid," "I do love." The crucial point is that there would be no barriers, no inhibitions, which would prevent the full experiencing of whatever was organismically present, and availability to awareness is a good measure of this absence of barriers.

2.) *This person would live in an existential fashion.*

I believe it would be evident that for the person who was fully open to his experience, completely without defensiveness, each moment would be new. The complex configuration of inner and outer stimuli which exists in this moment has never existed before in just this fashion. Consequently our hypothetical person would realize that "What I will be in the next moment, and what I will do, grows out of that moment, and cannot be predicted in advance either by me or by others." Not infrequently we find clients expressing this sort of feeling. Thus one, at the end of therapy, says in rather puzzled fashion, "I haven't finished the job of integrating and reorganizing myself, but that's only confusing, not discouraging, now that I realize this is a continuing process. . . . It is exciting, sometimes upsetting, but deeply encouraging to feel yourself in action and apparently knowing where you are going even though you don't always consciously know where that is."

One way of expressing the fluidity which would be present in such existential living is to say that the self and personality would emerge *from* experience, rather than experience being translated or twisted to fit a preconceived self-structure. It means that one becomes a participant in and an observer of the ongoing process of organismic experience, rather than being in control of it. In Chapter 6, I have tried to describe how this type of living seems to me.

This whole train of experiencing, and the meaning that I have thus far discovered in it, seem to have launched me on a process which is both fascinating and at times a little frightening. It seems to mean letting my experience carry me on, in a direction which appears to be forward, toward goals that I can but dimly define, as I try to understand at least the current meaning of that experience. The sensation is that of floating with a complex stream of experience, with the fascinating possibility of trying to comprehend its everchanging complexity.

Such living in the moment, then, means an absence of rigidity, of tight organization, of the imposition of structure on experience. It means instead a maximum of adaptability, a discovery of structure *in* experience, a flowing, changing organization of self and personality.

The personality and the self would be continually in flux, the only stable elements being the physiological capacities and limitations of the organism, the continuing or recurrent organismic needs for survival, enhancement, food, affection, sex, and the like. The most stable personality traits would be openness to experience, and the flexible resolution of the existing needs in the existing environment.

3.) This person would find his organism a trustworthy means of arriving at the most satisfying behavior in each existential situation.

He would do what "felt right" in this immediate moment and he would find this in general to be a competent and trustworthy guide to his behavior.

If this seems strange, let me explain the reasoning behind it. Since he would be open to his experience he would have access to all of the available data in the situation, on which to base his behavior; the social demands, his own complex and possibly conflicting needs; his memories of similar situations, his perception of the uniqueness of this situation, etc., etc. The dynamic aspects of each situation would be very complex indeed. But he could permit his total organism, his consciousness participating, to consider each stimulus, need, and demand, its relative intensity and importance, and out of this complex weighing and balancing, discover that course of action which would come closest to satisfying all his needs in the situation. An analogy which might come close to a description would be to compare this person to a giant electronic computing machine. Since he is open to his experience, all of the data from his sense impressions, from his memory, from previous learning, from his visceral and internal states, is fed into the machine. The machine takes all of these multitudinous pulls and forces which were fed in as data, and quickly computes the course of action which would be the most economical avenue of need satisfaction in this existential situation. This is the behavior of our hypothetical person.

The defects which in most of us make this process untrustworthy are the inclusion of non-existential material, or the absence of data. It is when memories and previous learnings are fed into the computation as if they were *this* reality, and not memories and learnings, that erroneous behavioral answers arise. Or when certain threatening experiences are inhibited from awareness, and hence are withheld from the computation or fed into it in distorted form, this too produces error. But our hypothetical person would find his organism thoroughly trustworthy, because all the available data would be used, and it would be present in accurate rather than distorted form. Hence his behavior would come as close as possible to satisfying all his needs—for enhancement, for affiliation with others, and the like.

In this weighing, balancing, and computation, his organism would not by any means be infallible. It would always give the best possible answer for the available data, but sometimes data would be missing. Because of the element of openness to experience however, any errors, any following of behavior which was not satisfying would be quickly corrected. The computations, as it were, would always be in process of being corrected, because they would be continually checked in behavior.

Perhaps you will not like my analogy of an electronic computing machine. Let me put it in more human terms. The client I previously quoted found himself expressing annoyance to his daughter when he "felt like it," as well as affection. Yet he found himself doing it in a way which not only released tension in himself, but which freed this small girl to voice her annoyances. He describes the differences between communicating his angry annoyance or imposing it on her. He continues, "Because it just doesn't feel like I'm imposing my feelings on her, and it seems to me I must show it on my face. Maybe she sees it as 'Yes, daddy is angry, but I don't have to cower.' Because she never does *cower*. This in itself is a topic for a novel, it just feels that good." In this instance, being open to his experience, he selects, with astonishing intuitive skill, a subtly guided course of behavior which meets his need for the release of his angry tension, but also satisfies his need to be a good father, and his need to find satisfaction in his daughter's healthy development. Yet he achieves all this by simply doing the thing that feels right to him.

On quite another level, it seems to be this same kind of complex organismic selection that determines the behavior of the creative person. He finds himself moving in a certain direction long before he can give any completely conscious and rational basis for it. During this period, whether he is moving toward a new type of artistic expression, a new literary style, a new theory in the field of science, a new approach in his classroom, he is simply trusting his total organismic reaction. He feels an assurance that he is on his way, even though he could not describe the end point of that journey. This is the type of behavior which is, I believe, also characteristic of the person who has gained greatly from therapy, or of the person whose educational experience has enabled him to learn how to learn.

THE FULLY FUNCTIONING PERSON

I should like to pull together these three threads into one more unified descriptive strand. It appears that the person who emerges from a theoretically optimal experience of personal growth, whether through client-centered therapy or some other experience of learning and development, is then a fully functioning person. He is able to live fully in and with each and all of his feelings and reactions. He is making use of all his organic equipment to sense, as accurately as possible, the existential situation within and without. He is using all of the data his nervous system can thus supply, using it in awareness, but recognizing that his total organism may be, and often is, wiser than his awareness. He is able to permit his total organism to function in all its complexity in selecting, from the multitude of possibilities, that behavior which in this moment of time will be most generally and genuinely satisfying. He is able to trust his organism in this functioning, not because it is infallible, but because he can be fully open to the consequences of each of his actions and correct them if they prove to be less than satisfying.

He is able to experience all of his feelings, and is afraid of none of his feelings; he is his own sifter of evidence, but is open to evidence from all sources; he is completely engaged in the process of being and becoming himself, and thus discovers that he is soundly and realistically social; he lives completely in this moment, but learns that this is the soundest living for all time. He is a fully functioning organism, and because of the awareness of himself which flows freely in and through his experiences, he is a fully functioning person.

SOME IMPLICATIONS OF THIS DESCRIPTION

This, then, is my tentative definition of the hypothetical endpoint of therapy, my description of the ultimate picture which our actual clients approach but never fully reach, the picture of the person who is continually learning how to learn. I have come to like this description, both because I believe it is rooted in and is true of my clinical and educational experience, and also because I believe it has significant clinical, scientific, and philosophical implications. I should like to present some of these ramifications and implications as I see them.

A.) APPROPRIATE TO CLINICAL EXPERIENCE

In the first place it appears to contain a basis for the phenomena of clinical experience in successful therapy. We have noted the fact that the client develops a locus of evaluation within himself; this is consistent with the concept of the trustworthiness of the organism. We have commented on the client's satisfaction at being and becoming himself, a satisfaction associated with functioning fully. We find that clients tolerate a much wider range and variety of feelings, including feelings which were formerly anxiety-producing; and that these feelings are usefully integrated into their more flexibly organized personalities. In short, the concepts I have stated appear to be sufficiently broad to contain the positive outcomes of therapy as we know it.

B.) LEADS TOWARD OPERATIONAL HYPOTHESES

While the formulation as given is admittedly speculative, it leads, I believe, in the direction of hypotheses which may be stated in rigorous and operational terms. Such hypotheses would be culture-free or universal, I trust, rather than being different for each culture.

It is obvious that the concepts given are not easily tested or measured, but with our growing research sophistication in this area, their measurability is not an unreasonable hope.

C.) EXPLAINS A PARADOX OF PERSONAL GROWTH

We have found, in some of our research studies in psychotherapy, some perplexing differences in the analyses of before-and-after personality tests, by different outside experts. In clients whose personal gain in therapy is amply supported by other evidence, we have found contradictions among the experts in the interpretation of their personality tests. Briefly, psychologists who are oriented strictly toward personality *diagnosis*, who are comparing the individual with general norms, tend to be concerned over what they see as a lack of personality defenses, or a degree of disorganization, at the conclusion of therapy. They may be concerned that the person is "falling apart." The psychologist who is therapeutically oriented tends to see the same evidence as indicative of fluidity, openness to experience, an existential rather than a rigid personality organization.

To me it seems possible that the "looseness," the openness, of the person who is undergoing marked personal growth may be seen, in terms of population norms, as deviating from those norms, as "not normal." But these same qualities may indicate that all personal growth is marked by a certain degree of disorganization followed by reorganization. The pain of new understandings, of acceptance of new facets of oneself, the feeling of uncertainty, vacillation, and even turmoil within oneself, are all an integral part of the pleasure and satisfaction of being more of oneself, more fully oneself, more fully functioning. This to me is a meaningful explanation of what would otherwise be a puzzling paradox.

D.) CREATIVITY AS AN OUTCOME

One of the elements which pleases me in the theoretical formulation I have given is that this is a creative person. This person at the hypothetical end-point of therapy could well be one of Maslow's "self-actualizing people." With his sensitive openness to the world, his trust of his own ability to form new relationships with his environment, he would be the type of person from whom creative products and creative living emerge. He would not necessarily be "adjusted" to his culture, and he would almost certainly not be a conformist. But at any time and in any culture he would live constructively, in as much harmony with his culture as a balanced satisfaction of needs demanded. In some cultural situations he might in some ways be very unhappy, but he would continue to be himself, and to behave in such a way as to provide the maximum possible satisfaction of his deepest needs.

Such a person would, I believe, be recognized by the student of evolution as the type most likely to adapt and survive under changing environmental conditions. He would be able creatively to make sound adjustments to new as well as old conditions. He would be a fit vanguard of human evolution.

E.) BUILDS ON TRUSTWORTHINESS OF HUMAN NATURE.

It will have been evident that one implication of the view I have been presenting is that the basic nature of the human being, when functioning freely, is constructive and trustworthy. For me this is an inescapable conclusion from more than thirty years of experience in psychotherapy. When we are able to free the individual from defensiveness, so that he is open to the wide range of his own needs, as well as the wide range of environmental and social demands, his reactions may be trusted to be positive, forward-moving, constructive. We do not need to ask who will socialize him, for one of his own deepest needs is for affiliation with and communication with others. When he is fully himself, he cannot help but be realistically socialized. We do not need to ask who will control his aggressive impulses, for when he is open to all of his impulses, his need to be liked by others and his tendency to give affection are as strong as his impulses to strike out or to seize for himself. He will be aggressive in situations in which aggression is realistically appropriate, but there will be no runaway need for aggression. His total behavior, in these and other areas, when he is open to all his experience, is balanced and realistic, behavior which is appropriate to the survival and enhancement of a highly social animal.

I have little sympathy with the rather prevalent concept that man is basically irrational, and thus his impulses, if not controlled, would lead to destruction of others and self. Man's behavior is exquisitely rational, moving with subtle and ordered complexity toward the goals his organism is endeavoring to achieve. The tragedy for most of us is that our defenses keep us from being aware of this rationality, so that consciously we are moving in one direction, while organismically we are moving in another. But in our hypothetical person there would be no such barriers, and he would be a participant in the rationality of his organism. The only control of impulses which would exist or which would prove necessary, is the natural and internal balancing of one need against another, and the discovery of behaviors which follow the avenue most closely approximating the satisfaction of all needs. The experience of extreme satisfaction of one need (for aggression, or sex, etc.) in such a way as to do violence to the satisfaction of other needs (for companionship, tender relationship, etc.)—an experience very common in the defensively organized person—would simply be unknown in our hypothetical individual. He would participate in the vastly complex self-regulatory activities of his organism—the psychological as well as physiological thermostatic controls—in such a fashion as to live harmoniously, with himself and with others.

F.) BEHAVIOR DEPENDABLE BUT NOT PREDICTABLE

There are certain implications of this view of the optimum human being which have to do with predictability, which I find fascinating to contemplate. It should be clear from the theoretical picture I have sketched that the particular configuration of inner and outer stimuli in which the person lives at this moment has never existed in precisely this fashion before; and also that his behavior is a realistic reaction to an accurate apprehension of all this internalized evidence. It should therefore be clear that this person will seem to himself to be dependable but not specifically predictable. If he is entering a new situation with an authority figure, for example, he cannot predict what his behavior will be. It is contingent upon the behavior of this authority figure, and his own immediate internal reactions, desires, etc., etc. He can feel confident that he will behave appropriately, but he has no knowledge in advance of what he will do. I find this point of view often expressed by clients, and I believe it is profoundly important.

But what I have been saying about the client himself, would be equally true of the scientist studying his behavior. The scientist would find this person's behavior lawful, and would find it possible to postdict it, but could not forecast or predict the specific behavior of this individual. The reasons are these. If the behavior of our hypothetical person is determined by the accurate sensing of all of the complex evidence which exists in this moment of time, and by that evidence only, then the data necessary for prediction is clear. It would be necessary to have instruments available to measure every one of the multitudinous stimuli of the input, and a mechanical computer of great size to calculate the most economical vector of reaction. While this computation is going on, our hypothetical person has already made this complex summation and appraisal within his own organism and has acted. Science, if it can eventually collect all this data with sufficient accuracy, should theoretically be able to analyze it and come to the same conclusion and thus postdict his behavior. It is doubtful that it could ever collect and analyze the data instantaneously, and this would be necessary if it were to predict the behavior before it occurred.

It may clarify this if I point out that it is the maladjusted person whose behavior can be specifically predicted, and some loss of predictability should be evident in every increase in openness to experience and existential living. In the maladjusted person, behavior is predictable precisely because it is rigidly patterned. If such a person has learned a pattern of hostile reaction to authority, and if this "badness of authority" is a part of his conception of himself-in-relation-to-authority, and if because of this he denies or distorts any experience which should supply contradictory evidence, *then* his behavior is specifically predictable. It can be said with assurance that when he enters a new situation with an authority figure, he will be hostile to him. But the more that therapy, or any growth-promoting relationship, increases the openness to experience of this individual, the less predictable his behavior will be. This receives some crude confirmation from the Michigan study (Kelly & Fiske, 1951) attempting to predict success in clinical psychology. The predictions for the men who were in therapy during the period of investigation were definitely less accurate than for the group as a whole.

What I am saying here has a bearing on the common statement that the long range purpose of psychology as a science is "the prediction and control of human behavior" a phrase which for me has had disturbing philosophical implications. I am suggesting that as the individual approaches this optimum of complete functioning his behavior, though always lawful and determined, becomes more difficult to predict; and though always dependable and appropriate, more difficult to control. This would mean that the science of psychology, at its highest levels, would perhaps be more of a science of understanding than a science of prediction, an analysis of the lawfulness of that which has occurred, rather than primarily a control of what is about to occur.

In general this line of thought is confirmed by our clients, who feel confident that what they will do in a situation will be appropriate and comprehensible and sound, but who cannot predict in advance how they will behave. It is also confirmed by our experience as therapists, where we form a relationship in which we can be sure the person will discover himself, become himself, learn to function more freely, but where we cannot forecast the specific content of the next statement, of the next phase of therapy, or of the behavioral solution the client will find to a given problem. The general direction is dependable, and we can rest assured it will be appropriate; but its specific content is unpredictable.

G.) RELATES FREEDOM AND DETERMINISM

I should like to give one final philosophical implication which has meaning for me. For some time I have been perplexed over the living paradox which exists in psychotherapy between freedom and determinism, as I have indicated in the preceding chapter.

I would like to add one more thought on that topic. In the therapeutic relationship some of the most compelling subjective experiences are those in which the client feels within himself the power of naked choice. He is *free*—to become himself or to hide behind a façade; to move forward or to retrogress; to behave in ways which are destructive of self and others, or in ways which are enhancing; quite literally free to live or die, in both the physiological and psychological meaning of those terms. Yet as we enter this field of psychotherapy with objective research methods, we are, like any other scientist, committed to a complete determinism. From this point of view every thought, feeling, and action of the client is determined by what precedes it. The dilemma I am trying to describe is no different than that found in other fields—it is simply brought to sharper focus. I tried to bring this out in a paper written some time ago contrasting these two views. In the field of psychotherapy,

> Here is the maximizing of all that is subjective, inward, personal; here a relationship is lived, not examined, and a person, not an object, emerges, a person who feels, chooses, believes, acts, not as an automaton, but as a person. And here too is the ultimate in science—the objective exploration of the most subjective aspects of life; the reduction to hypotheses, and eventually to theorems, of all that has been regarded as most personal, most completely inward, most thoroughly a private world (Rogers, 1955).

In terms of the definition I have given of the fully functioning person, the relationship between freedom and determinism can, I believe, be seen in a fresh perspective. We could say that in the optimum of therapy the person rightfully experiences the most complete and absolute freedom. He wills or chooses to follow the course of action which is the most economical vector in relation to all the internal and external stimuli, because it is that behavior which will be most deeply satisfying. But this is the same course of action which from another vantage point may be said to be determined by all the factors in the existential situation. Let us contrast this with the picture of the person who is defensively organized. He wills or chooses to follow a given course of action, but finds that he *cannot* behave in the fashion that he chooses. He is determined by the factors in the existential situation, but these factors include his defensiveness, his denial or distortion of some of the relevant data. Hence it is certain that his behavior will be less than fully satisfying. His behavior is determined, but he is not free to make an effective choice. The fully functioning person, on the other hand, not only experiences, but utilizes, the most absolute freedom when he spontaneously, freely, and voluntarily chooses and wills that which is absolutely determined.

I am quite aware that this is not a new idea to the philosopher, but it has been refreshing to come upon it from a totally unexpected angle, in analyzing a concept in personality theory. For me it provides the rationale for the subjective reality of absolute freedom of choice, which is so profoundly important in therapy, and at the same time the rationale for the complete determinism which is the very foundation stone of science. With this framework I can enter subjectively the experience of naked choice which the client is experiencing; I can also as a scientist, study his behavior as being absolutely determined.

CONCLUSION

Here then is my theoretical model of the person who emerges from therapy or from the best of education, the individual who has experienced optimal psychological growth—a person functioning freely in all the fullness of his organismic potentialities; a person who is dependable in being realistic, self-enhancing, socialized, and appropriate in his behavior; a creative person, whose specific formings of behavior are not easily predictable; a person who is ever-changing, ever developing, always discovering himself and the newness in himself in each succeeding moment of time.

Let me stress, however, that what I have described is a person who does not exist. He is the theoretical goal, the end-point of personal growth. We see persons moving *in this direction* from the best of experiences in education, from the best of experiences in therapy, from the best of family and group relationships. But what we observe is the imperfect person moving *toward* this goal. What I have described is my version of the goal in its "pure" form.

I have written this chapter partly to clarify my own ideas. What sort of persons tend to come from my classes, from my groups, from my therapy? But much more important, I have written it to try to force educators to think much more deeply about their *own* goals. The assumption has been prevalent for so long that we all know what constitutes an "educated man," that the fact that this comfortable definition is now *completely irrelevant* to modern society is almost never faced. So this chapter constitutes a challenge to educators at all levels. If my concept of the fully functioning person is abhorrent to you as the goal of education, then give *your* definition of the person who should emerge from modern day education, and publish it for all to see. We need many such definitions so that there can be a really significant *modern* dialogue as to what constitutes our optimum, our ideal citizen of *today*. I hope this chapter makes a small contribution toward that dialogue.

References

Kelley, E. L. & Fiske, Donald W. *The prediction of performance in clinical psychology*. Ann Arbor: University of Michigan Press, 1951.

Rogers, C. R. Persons or science: A philosophical question. *American Psychologist*, 1955, *10*, 267-278.

part V

A Model for Revolution

Introduction to Part V

We are approaching the end of the volume. Part III took us somewhat out of the classroom into areas of assumptions, principles, and general plans. Part IV left the educational system entirely, dealing with value and philosophical questions about which the educator *should* be thinking deeply, but in my opinion, rarely does.

Now in Part V, we come back to the *real everyday* world of education. Here is a *practical* plan for change—a plan which could be put into operation by any educational organization which has *courage* and is either willing to channel some of its ordinary funds into a process of change, or has ability to obtain funds for such a purpose.

Thus, with this chapter, we come full circle. Here is a way—not necessarily *the* way—in which a whole system might move toward the kinds of classroom approaches described in Part I, and the administrative approach described in Chapter 10. Better yet, such an educational system might devise even more imaginative ways for providing *freedom to learn*—for students, for faculty, for parents, for administrative staff. They might find themselves moving boldly into the future of what education might become. What a refreshing *experience* this would be for them, and what an exciting sight it would be for all of us!

15

A Plan for Self-Directed Change
in an Educational System

I have endeavored to make this chapter as fully realistic as I am able—a practical workable plan for change. It is not theory nor philosophy (though both are implicit). It is a "how-to-do-it" chapter in which I have tried to face both the exciting potentialities, as well as the risks and pitfalls, involved in a process of personal and organizational change.[1]

I should confess at the outset that the title which I first chose for this chapter was "A Practical Plan for Educational Revolution." I felt that this might offend and antagonize too many people. Why is there need for a revolution in education? After all, tens upon tens of thousands of dedicated student-teachers, teachers, instructors, and professors—over the whole spectrum from nursery school to graduate school—are working wholeheartedly in our educational system, trying to improve it in a multitude of ways. Why then any talk of revolution? I should like to make clear my reasons for believing that only a tremendous change in the basic *direction* of education can meet the needs of today's culture.

A NEW GOAL FOR EDUCATION: A CLIMATE FOR CHANGE

The world is changing at an exponential rate. If our society is to meet the challenge of the dizzying changes in science, technology, communications, and social relationships, we cannot rest on the *answers* provided in the past, but must put our trust in the *processes* by which new problems are met. For so quickly does change overtake us that answers, "knowledge," methods, skills, become obsolete almost at the moment of their achievement.

---

[1] This chapter is a revised version of a paper first published in *Educational Leadership*, May, 1967, Vol. 24, 717-731. Copyright © by the Association for Supervision and Curriculum Development, NEA.

This implies not only new techniques for education but, as I have indicated previously, a new goal. In the world which is already upon us, the aim of education must be to develop individuals who are open to change. Only such persons can constructively meet the perplexities of a world in which problems spawn much faster than their answers. The goal of education must be to develop a society in which people can live more comfortably with *change* than with *rigidity*. In the coming world the capacity to face the new appropriately is more important than the ability to know and repeat the old.

But such a goal implies, in turn, that educators themselves must be open and flexible, effectively involved in the processes of change. They must be able both to conserve and convey the essential knowledge and values of the past, and to welcome eagerly the innovations which are necessary to prepare for the unknown future.

A way must be found to develop, within the educational system as a whole, and in each component, a climate conducive to personal growth, a climate in which innovation is not frightening, in which the creative capacities of administrators, teachers, and students are nourished and expressed rather than stifled. A way must be found to develop a climate in the *system* in which the focus is not upon *teaching*, but on the facilitation of self-directed *learning*. Only thus can we develop the creative individual who is open to all of his experience; aware of it and accepting it, and continually in the process of changing. And only in this way, I believe, can we bring about the creative educational organization, which will also be continually in the process of changing.

A TOOL FOR EDUCATIONAL CHANGE

One of the most effective means yet discovered for facilitating constructive learning, growth, and change—in individuals or in the organizations they compose—is the intensive group experience. Known by a variety of names ("T" group, laboratory training, sensitivity training, basic encounter group, workshop), it has a common underlying theme and quality of experience.

The intensive group or "workshop" group usually consists of ten to fifteen persons and a facilitator or leader. It is relatively unstructured, providing a climate of maximum freedom for personal expression, exploration of feelings, and interpersonal communication. Emphasis is upon the interactions among the group members, in an atmosphere which encourages each to drop his defenses and façades and thus enables him to relate directly and openly to other members of the group—the "basic encounter." Individuals come to know themselves and each other more fully than is possible in the usual social or working relationships; the climate of openness, risk-taking, and honesty generates trust, which enables the person to recognize and change self-defeating attitudes, test out and adopt more innovative and constructive behaviors, and subsequently to relate more adequately and effectively to others in his everyday life situation.

Since the mid-1940's, such workshop groups have been used extensively with industrial executives, government administrators, professional groups, and laymen—groups considered to be normal and well-functioning—under a wide variety of auspices, of which the National Training Laboratory is perhaps the best known (Benne, Bradford, & Lippitt, 1964).

Generally speaking, the aim of these intensive group experiences is to improve the learnings and abilities of the participants in such areas as leadership and interpersonal communication. Another aim is to bring about change in the organizational climates and structures in which the members work. These group experiences are characteristically conducted as an intensive residential experience in which the participants live and meet together for periods ranging from three days to two or three weeks. (A widely used variant is the sensitivity-training course offered by university departments in which groups meet once a week throughout a semester or more.)

Within the past several years, educators have begun to make use of the intensive group experience, though only to a small extent. Groups involving educational administrators (Clark, T. C. & Miles, M. B., 1954), teachers (Bowers & Soar, 1961), student-faculty groups from the same institution (Boyer, 1964), and occasionally intensive groups within the classroom (Miles, 1964; Clark, J. V. & Culbert, 1965) have been used. In the educational setting, the aims have been to release the capacity of the participants for better educational leadership through improved interpersonal relationships, or to foster learning by the whole person—student, teacher, or administrator.

The workshop group has also been used on an experimental basis with school dropouts, unemployed youth, and pre-delinquents, as a means of helping them achieve greater personal maturity and effectiveness through improved personal and interpersonal competence in coping with a variety of life situations.

Although these several uses in educational settings have had satisfying and promising results, there has been almost no attempt to utilize the intensive group experience in a coherent approach to change in a total public educational system. Hence, an all too common consequence has been that a teacher or faculty member returns from such an experience ready to behave in new and changing ways, only to discover that his attitudes are not welcomed in a "stable and well-regulated" educational organization. Two alternatives are open: he returns disappointedly to his previous conventional behavior, or he becomes a puzzling and disruptive influence in his institution, neither understood nor approved.

It seems quite clear that this new tool for change cannot be used in the most effective manner unless the *whole system* is moving toward changingness in a way which accommodates change in its own personnel and its own units. Industry is already learning this. It is this principle of opening up the possibilities for change in the *whole system* during a *relatively short period of time* which is the essence of the plan which will be presented.

THE HYPOTHESES OF THE INTENSIVE GROUP EXPERIENCE

Before proceeding further, it seems advisable to state, somewhat more fully and more precisely, the hypotheses which underlie the process of the basic encounter group (see Rogers, 1967, for a more complete description of this process). This whole area is one in which practice has far outrun both theory and research. Consequently, the hypotheses stated below have been often validated in practice, but there has been only a modest amount of research on these points.

Here then are the practical hypotheses:

A facilitator can develop, in a group which meets intensively, a psychological climate of safety in which freedom of expression and reduction of defensiveness gradually occur.

In such a psychological climate, many of the immediate feeling reactions of each member toward others, and toward himself, tend to be expressed.

A climate of mutual trust develops out of this mutual freedom to express real feelings, positive and negative. Each member moves toward greater acceptance of his total being—his emotional, intellectual, and physical being, as it *is*.

With individuals less inhibited by defensive rigidity, the possibility of change—in personal attitudes and behavior, in teaching methods, in administrative methods—becomes less threatening.

With a reduction of defensive rigidity, individuals can hear each other, can learn from each other, to a greater extent.

There is a development of feedback from one person to another, such that each individual learns how he appears to others, and what impact he has in interpersonal relationships.

As individuals hear each other more accurately, an organization tends to become a relationship of persons with common goals, rather than a formal hierarchical structure.

With this greater freedom and improved communication, new ideas, new concepts, new directions, emerge. Innovation becomes a desirable rather than a threatening possibility.

These learnings in the group experience tend to carry over, temporarily or more permanently, into the relationships with peers, students, subordinates, and even to superiors, following the group experience.

A PLAN

Having described the need for educational change, and the intensive group experience as the tool or process by which it might be brought about, I would like now to present a specific plan for implementing this purpose. I would stress that every element of this plan has been tried and found to be effective either in industry, in education, or with other groups. Experienced personnel are available throughout the country who have the attitudes and "know-how" for carrying out these activities. It is the weaving of these elements into a comprehensively integrated plan which constitutes its novelty.

THE SELECTION OF A TARGET EDUCATIONAL SYSTEM

The plan is such that it could be applied to any educational organization, or to a number of such organizations simultaneously. It is believed the plan would be equally effective in an elementary school system, an elementary-secondary system, a junior college, a college or university, or a graduate school. One might find some increase in the degree of rigidity as one goes up this progression, but the same principles would apply, with some commonsense modification of specifics to meet each situation.

The first step in the inauguration of the plan is the selection of an educational system at one of these levels. There is only one criterion for this selection. It is that one or more individuals in positions of power—preferably the chief administrator and one or two of his associates or board members—have the desire and the willingness to involve themselves in a basic encounter group. If they are willing themselves to *experience* the changes which come about in such an intensive group experience, then they could make a reasonable and experientially informed judgment about the remainder of the plan. This is a very simple but also extremely important base for the whole plan which follows. A number of educational administrators and systems have already indicated their interest in involving themselves in such an experience.

AN INTENSIVE GROUP EXPERIENCE FOR ADMINISTRATORS: THE FIRST STEP

The opportunity would be given for administrators and board members in the system to participate in a one-week intensive workshop (or encounter group, or "T" group) to be held away from their offices, preferably in a relatively secluded resort where they would be free from the usual interruptions and distractions of an administrator's life. This would doubtless have to be in the late summer, before school is underway. The cost would be largely subsidized, as discussed later in this chapter, but the individual would pay a portion of the cost as evidence of his commitment. It seems preferable that this group experience should be voluntary, though if the administration decided that all staff above a certain level must attend, this will be acceptable.

An experienced facilitator from outside (and there is an ample pool from which to draw) will serve as a catalyst and participant in each group of ten to fifteen administrators. Organizations such as the Center for Studies of the Person, the National Training Laboratory, or the Western Training Laboratory can be the source of facilitators for each group and could constitute the professional planning staff.

The group (or groups) will be relatively unstructured, and if past experience is any guide, exploration of current interpersonal feelings and relationships will become a major focus. Often gripes and feuds which have for years prevented real communication come to the surface and are resolved in the eight or ten hours per day of intensive group meetings. The encounter group provides the administrator with a microcosm for studying the problems he faces, and the problems he *creates*, in his own organization. Through confrontation he discovers how he appears to others. He also has the opportunity for experimenting with and trying out new modes of behavior, in a relatively safe situation.

Although the small encounter groups will constitute the core of the experience, there will be substantive general sessions in which the groups will be exposed to stimulating educational topics presented either by members of their own staff, or by members of the facilitative staff. This can provide cognitive data to be added to the interpersonal data with which each small group deals.

What will happen in such an intensive week? It is almost impossible to convey intellectually the quality of the relationships which develop. Drawing upon past experience, I think of administrators who have worked together for twenty years, and discover they have never known each other at all as persons; of negative feelings which have "loused up" planning and work for years, which can now safely be brought into the open, understood, and dissolved; of positive feelings which have always seemed too risky to voice; of ideals and hopes which have seemed too fantastic to share with others; of quick angers which arise in the group, are expressed, and strengthen rather than destroy relationships, in the context of trust and openness which has been built; of personal tragedies and problems which make understandable the armor plate behind which some individuals have hidden, and from behind which they begin to emerge; the intense sense of community which develops, in place of the alienation each has felt; the willingness to risk new behaviors, new directions, new purposes; determinations to rebuild family relationships and organizational procedures. These are only a few of the manifestations of the occurrences in an intensive group experience in which individuals who have interacted as roles—superintendent, board member, supervisor—begin to interact as persons, whole persons with feelings as well as thoughts, capable of being hurt as well as being actualized. Again reference is made to a recent paper in which recorded excerpts of group experiences bring some of these descriptions to life (Rogers, 1967).

What may we expect as outcomes of such an experience for the trustee, the superintendent or president, the deans, supervisors, or administrative specialists in various fields? It has been our experience that some of the outcomes can be described in a somewhat schematic form, as in the following statements.

The Administrator

- will be less protective of his own constructs and beliefs, and hence can listen more accurately to other administrators and to faculty members;

- will find it easier and less threatening to accept innovative ideas;

- will have less need for the protection of bureaucratic rules, and hence will decide issues more on the basis of merit;

- will communicate more clearly to superiors, peers, and sub-ordinates, because his communications will be more oriented toward an openly declared purpose, and less toward covert self-protection;

- will be more person-oriented and democratic in staff or faculty meetings; hence

- will draw more widely and deeply on the resource potential of his faculty and staff;

- will be more likely to face and openly confront personal emotional frictions which develop between himself and his colleagues, rather than burying the conflict under new "reg-ulations" or avoiding it in other ways;

- will be more able to accept feedback from his staff, both positive and negative, and to use it as constructive insight into himself and his behavior;

- will be more able to communicate realistically with his board of trustees, and thus possibly lay the groundwork for altering the organizational *structure* of the educational system (this will be especially true if the trustees themselves have been involved in an intensive group experience).

I have gone into some detail in describing this initial group experience for the administrators. I will be much more brief in describing the following workshops or encounter groups, since the nature of the process, and the context for it, will be very similar.

Judging from my own experience in working with educators and educational systems, there is little reason to believe that the plan would stop with the workshop just described. With a number of influential members of the system now involved, they are likely to come to the decision to go ahead with making this experience more widely available throughout the system. From this point on, the steps I describe are only one possible program and plan, since the professional staff and the administrators will now become collaborators in planning the ways in which to proceed. Nevertheless, I will describe some of the possible and probable elements which will follow.

INTENSIVE GROUP EXPERIENCES FOR TEACHERS

Following much the same pattern, those teachers or faculty members who wish to become involved in basic encounter groups will be given the opportunity. Depending on the size of the system, this number might be quite small or it might be large. Experience has shown that 80 to 120 individuals can be involved at one time, with six to ten small groups as the core of the experience. Again the aim would be to get them off campus in some appropriately secluded setting, for a period of a week if possible, during a vacation time, or a long weekend of four days if the full week were not feasible. The question of whether to include spouses should certainly be discussed, since an initial impact on home and family is a common occurrence, and if both spouses are included (perhaps in separate groups), it gives a common basis for sharing significant experiences.

Perhaps a word should be said about the voluntary aspect of these groups. Some individuals, in industry as well as education, have heard stories about "T" groups which frighten them—they are "group therapy," they *force* individuals to reveal their feelings, etc. Or they are completely ignorant of such developments and are full of such questions as, "What could you *possibly* talk about for a whole week?" It seems that such situations are best handled by first dealing with those who are ready to risk themselves in a group, and letting reports of the experience permeate the total group, creating further readiness. (In a recent group of nurses, I found that the most important single reason for registering for the group was that individuals had seen significant and compelling changes in behavior and personal relationships in nurses who had been previous participants, and now these individuals wanted to experience the process for themselves.)

Another point which should be mentioned is that there is no expectation, at this stage, of reaching every teacher or faculty member. It is quite sufficient that any participant will have peers with whom he or she can share experiences growing out of the intensive workshop. Since many of the teachers' superiors will also have had such growing experiences, the faculty member will be going back into a school environment which will be essentially responsive to any changes in his behavior, attitudes, purposes, and relationships.

Another point worth stressing is that changes and innovations which are decided upon (in this or the other groups) are likely to be implemented in practice, because they are self-chosen. It has been a familiar complaint that new ideas in teaching, in curriculum, in methods, are literally "a dime a dozen," but that they tend to be resisted by teachers and administrators. But when individuals have *chosen* to try some of these new ideas, the outcome is quite different.

If we ask what the personal outcomes might be for the teacher or faculty member, we may again try to list some which seem supported by experience.

The Teacher

- will show many of the characteristic changes listed for the administrator, and in addition
- will be more able to listen to students, especially to the feelings of students;
- will be able better to accept the innovative, challenging, "troublesome," creative ideas which emerge in students, rather than reacting to these threats by insisting on conformity;
- will tend to pay as much attention to his relationship with his students, as to the content material of the course;
- will be more likely to work out interpersonal frictions and problems *with* students, rather than dealing with such issues in a disciplinary or punitive manner;
- will develop a more equalitarian atmosphere in the classroom, conducive to spontaneity, to creative thinking, to independent and self-directed work.

ENCOUNTER GROUPS FOR CLASS UNITS

The next phase will be an intensive group experience for a class or course unit. This may very possibly be desired by a teacher who finds, from his own intensive group experience, that he would like to implement new directions in his relationship with his class, but is somewhat at a loss to know how to do so.

For a group involving such a class or course unit, everyone in any way related to the class will be included—assistants, student teachers, supervisors, even the janitor if he has a real relationship with the class. Since a residential off-campus experience will probably be impossible, except at the college level, a different format will often be necessary. It may be that five full school days will be devoted to the intensive group experience, with an outside facilitator again helping to provide the climate of freedom for expression and freedom for responsible choice. Students and teachers will be permitted and encouraged to discuss problems the class has had. These may start with problems of too great difficulty or too little difficulty in the content matter, but soon the context of feelings will begin to be expressed. Perhaps for the first time in his life the student will find that his attitudes, his feelings, his opinions, will be *heard*, will be listened to, first perhaps by the facilitator only, but gradually by the other students and the teaching faculty. Often for the first time he will find himself a *participant* in classroom choices and policies, not merely a passive recipient. In one school where something of this sort has been tried, it has been found that nearly always the solution to a classroom problem or impasse, as reached by the total group, is that students choose to take a *larger* responsibility for themselves and their work and actions.

While it is not expected that more than a small fraction of classes will, at this stage, have this type of intensive group experience, the effect upon the students in these classes can be reasonably well predicted.

The Student

- will feel more free to express both positive and negative feelings in class—toward other students, toward the teacher, toward content material;
- will tend to work through these feelings toward a realistic relationship, instead of burying them until they are explosive;

- will have more energy to devote to learning, because he will have less fear of continual evaluation and punishment;

- will discover he has a responsibility for his own learning, as he becomes more of a participant in the group learning process;

- will feel free to take off on exciting avenues of learning, with more assurance that his teacher will understand;

- will find that both his awe of authority and his rebellion against authority diminish, as he discovers teachers and administrators to be fallible human beings, relating in imperfect ways to students;

- will find that the learning process enables him to grapple directly and personally with the problem of the meaning of his life.

INTENSIVE GROUPS FOR PARENTS

If the groups described above are at all effective in achieving their aims, the ferment will attract attention in the community. Consequently, it will be helpful if concurrently with some of the above, an intensive group experience is offered to parents (assuming we are dealing with an elementary or elementary-secondary system). A group might be offered for officers and chairmen of the PTA, or for parents of students who have been involved in a classroom group experience. The pattern will doubtless have to be different. A weekend group experience might be offered—and these have been shown to be effective—or a three-hour evening session once a week, or a twenty-four hour "marathon" session. Both parents of a student might well be included, if both are interested.

The purpose of such groups is to enrich the parents' relationship with each other, the child, and the school, as well as to make clear the significance of the program being carried on in the school system. Certainly only the smallest fraction of parents can be reached in this way, but these may serve as interpreters of the program to other members of the community.

"VERTICAL" GROUPS

Up to this point almost all of the groups planned are groups of peers or near peers. It is usually easier for people to relate significantly to each other when there is not too frightening a difference in status. But at some point the "vertical" group will be attempted. This should probably be on an invitation basis at the outset, and include individuals who have been involved in some previous encounter group. If at all possible, it should be residential and off-campus. Let me sketch such a group and its probable consequences.

Invited would be two members of the board of trustees, two administrative officials, two parents, two teachers, two excellent students, and two failing students or school dropouts. Since such a group might have difficulty getting under way, it could be brought together under some such theme as "The———Schools: What I like and don't like about them, and what I want them to be."

The person who has never been involved in a group experience may believe it impossible for such a diverse group of individuals truly to communicate. Yet, very similar groups have been conducted, with extremely rewarding results. When a board member reaches the point where he can *hear* the hatred and contempt of the dropout for the schools, and the reasons for those negative feelings; when the teacher discovers that the board member is not "the big stick," but a human being, often with mixed and insecure feelings about the role he is attempting to play; when the "A" student learns that others less brilliant are sometimes more perceptive in the feeling realm than he; when a parent finds he can truly learn from an adolescent, and vice-versa; when widely divergent criticisms of and hopes for the schools are brought fully into the open, and examined and challenged in the feeling context in which they exist; when mutual trust grows in a climate which includes mutual differences; then we can say with considerable assurance that no person in the group will remain unchanged. Each will have incorporated broader understandings of self and of the others. Each will to some degree have become more flexible. Each will find that he is involved in changingness.

I think it scarcely need be added that even a very few such vertical groups would drastically change the climate and the flavor of any educational system. Though it has been described in terms most appropriate to a secondary school, it can be utilized at any level from nursery school (yes, nursery school children have feelings too) to graduate school. At any level, it contains the yeast of a revolution in the educational climate.

THE TIME TABLE

In carrying out the plan as outlined thus far, it is essential that the various group experiences should be held within a reasonably short period of time, so that the impact will not be dissipated. It is impossible to be specific, since much depends on whether we are dealing with an elementary school system of six schools, or a university with tens of thousands of students and a faculty of thousands. Nevertheless, the aim will be to hold at least nine workshops during the first academic year of the program, with from one to ten encounter groups in each of these workshops. Thus, at a minimum, the number of people involved in the intensive group experience will run into the hundreds, a sufficient fraction of the total administrative, faculty, and student body so that the effects will not be lost.

A PLAN FOR CONTINUING CHANGE

It is a very important part of the plan that a capability for continuing change be built into the system, so that a larger and larger fraction of its members may have the opportunity for one or more intensive group experiences. It is also important that the initial staff of outside facilitators be able to withdraw, retaining only a consultant function, if that is desired. Both these aims are served in the fashion described below.

THE TRAINING OF FACILITATORS

Those who have participated in the preceding workshops will be given opportunity to apply for further training as group facilitators. From these applicants a number will be selected, not so much on the basis of academic background, but on the basis of attitudes. The person who is relatively non-defensive, who relates in a real and genuine way to others, who is aware of and can express his feelings, who is capable of a sensitive empathy with the feelings of others, who has shown that he cares for others in a non-possessive way, will be the type of person selected.

Such individuals will be given a three-week residential training workshop, during a summer vacation period, in which there will be ample opportunity for reading, listening to recordings of groups with a variety of leaders, for seeing movies of group experience and interpersonal relationships, as well as for further participation in basic encounter groups. The various procedures advocated by different leaders will be tried out. The participants will be given the opportunity to serve as "co-facilitators" in leading groups.

As a supplement to, or an alternative to this workshop, these trainees would be encouraged to apply for the internship training program or the workshop for educators offered by the National Training Laboratories.

With this amount of preparation, each trainee can work as a co-facilitator with a member of the outside staff in conducting groups during the ensuing year. When it is mutually agreed that he is competent to handle groups on his own, he will do so, with one or more outside staff members serving as consultants.

In this way, a foundation has been laid for an ongoing change and ferment in the system. Further group experiences for faculty members, for parents, for administrators, can be held. New vertical groups can be formed. By this time, too, new ways of working, impossible now to foresee, will have developed and can be tried out. Thus, as the original professional group withdraws to a less active role, the educational system will have incorporated into itself a facilitative function which will mean continuous openness to innovation, continuous change.

It is quite possible that other systems will wish to utilize the services of these facilitators in inaugurating a program of change in their own organizations. This will only make the process more pervasive.

RISKS AND OBJECTIONS

Thus far the plan has been presented in positive terms. What are its dangers? What criticisms may be made of it? In what ways may it go wrong?

THE POSSIBILITY OF DAMAGE TO INDIVIDUALS

There is often fear that the openness of a group experience, the revealing of heretofore hidden feelings, may result in damage to person. This risk exists, but it is very small. In followup questionnaires of nearly 500 persons who had been members of groups for which I had been responsible, two felt that the experience had been damaging rather than helpful. This is a serious matter, and needs further study, but it indicates that the fear is almost entirely un-justified. Other responses were mostly very favorable, to "the most meaningful experience of my life."

THE POSSIBILITY OF TOO RAPID A CHANGE

Administrators—particularly those who have prided themselves on the "smooth-running" quality of their organization—may fear that the plan as out-lined would produce *too much* change. It cannot be denied that when problems, especially interpersonal problems, are faced openly rather than being swept under the rug, when interpersonal relationships are substituted in place of roles and rules, when learning and its facilitation becomes the focus rather than teaching, a certain amount of constructive turbu-lence is inevitable. It should be stressed that the proposed plan does not pretend to solve all problems—instead it substitutes the problems of a *process*-centered organization for those of an organization aimed toward a static stability.

THE POSSIBILITY OF REJECTION BY THE COMMUNITY

The plan outlined would set the educational system on a path, a direction, rather sharply different from that of the ordinary school or university. This involves the risk of too great a discrepancy between the directions approved by the community, and the direc-tions being taken. This risk has been partially decreased by the involvement of board members and parents in the intensive group experience. Yet it cannot be denied that in every community there are individuals and groups who are devoted to a return to the past, to rigid views of what a school or university should be, and who are deeply frightened by freedom of thought, choice and action, and by the rapid change which characterizes the modern world. Since these individuals and groups would be unlikely to avail themselves of opportunities for an intensive group experience precisely because it might involve change, they represent a difficult problem to which no easy or pat answer seems possible. Much depends on the context within which the individual system exists. (Some right wing groups now see encounter groups as Commu-nist-inspired brainwashing!)

THE POSSIBILITY OF CRITICISM BY PROFESSIONAL GROUPS

One element of the plan which is likely to arouse criticism and even indignation on the part of psychologists, psychiatrists, and others professionally involved in the field of interpersonal relationships, is the training of faculty members and administrators as group facilitators. The argument is that a full professional training with a Ph.D. or an M.D. is a necessity if an individual is to undertake such a function. There is solid evidence that this is a mistaken view. An outstanding example is the work of Rioch (1963) showing that selected housewives can be given training in a year's time which enables them to carry on therapy with disturbed individuals—therapy which in its quality is indistinguishable from the work of experienced professionals. Thus, the goal and procedure outlined has good precedent. This does not guarantee that it will be free from attack by professional groups.

THE FINANCIAL ASPECTS

Though there are several reasons why the intensive group experience has been much more heavily used in industry and in government (State Department, Internal Revenue Service, etc.) than in education, one of the most important reasons has been financial. The costs are considerable, and involve primarily two items. The first is the cost of the facilitative professional staff to inaugurate the program, a cost which decreases as the newly trained facilitators from the system take over. The second is the cost of the residential workshops, which amount to approximately $15 per day per person and up, depending on accommodations. The usual public educational institution is not prepared to put this kind of money into its own self-improvement, where industry is willing, able, and eager to do this.

Hence, funds should be sought—either by the educational system or by the organization which has been called upon for professional help (CSP, NTL, WTL, etc.) to finance these extra costs. The U.S. Office of Education would seem to be a natural source, or a foundation. One should not proceed with too easy an optimism, because all fund-granting agencies tend to be both conservative and bureaucratic and a plan for producing significant and pervasive change in education may be looked upon with suspicion. Clearly, what is needed is an organization which not only has funds to grant but is imaginative and forward looking in its policies. Such organizations are not numerous.

Naturally, the exact amounts needed will depend on the size of the educational system. Hence, no estimates of any kind are attempted here.

ASSESSMENT OF CHANGE

What has been described is a program of action rather than research. Yet one could hardly undertake such a series of steps responsibly without making some provision for assessment of the change, or lack of change, which occurs. There are a variety of ways in which such assessment could be made. One possible procedure is as follows.

The assessment before any of the program begins, made by well-qualified observers, can be compared with the assessment at intervals after the program has begun. Since it is possible that the observers may themselves become biased by continuing association with the system, additional observers should make an assessment at one given followup point. Their assessment can be compared with that of the original team, both at the beginning and at the same followup point.

It is suggested that each assessment team observe and interview a representative sample of administrative, supervisory, and teaching staff and students at each assessment point. They will make descriptive assessments and ratings on at least the following dimensions of implicit assumptions, attitudes and behaviors, educational methods and innovations:

a.) The organizational theory implicit in the operation of the educational system;

b.) The educational assumptions or implicit educational philosophy;

c.) The implicit assumptions as to personality development and human growth;

d.) The attitudes of superiors and subordinates to each other; the attitudes of teachers and students to each other;

e.) The level of morale among all levels of the system;

f.) The major educational methods in use;

g.) The degree to which self-initiated learning is encouraged;

h.) The degree to which constructive educational innovations are being developed and employed;

i.) The degree to which constructive interpersonal behaviors—open communication, trust, openness to new ideas, flexibility of organizational structure—exist in the system.

For the widest possible range of assessment information, it is suggested that such teams as the following be involved to make these observations and ratings:

1.) A team composed of an educator, an organization consultant, and a social psychologist. This team would make repeated assessments, every six months for two or three years.

2.) A similar team which would make only one assessment during the second year of the program, its judgments to be compared with the judgments of the first group, with the aim of discounting possible bias.

3.) A team composed of an administrator, a faculty member, and a student from the educational system. The information obtained by this team might be somewhat less objective, but it is likely that it would be much richer in detail. At least two assessments, one at the beginning, and one at the end of two years, would be made by this team.

A RESEARCH PROGRAM

The plan which has been described would also provide the possibility for a rigorous research program, studying one or more of the basic encounter groups proposed, in order to determine whether measurable changes in the specified dimensions of attitude and behavior do in fact occur. Such a research would make use of instruments of known reliability, administered to the experimental group and to a matched control group which did not undergo the group experience. These instruments would be administered before and after the group experience, and after a followup period of six months or one year.

Suffice it to say that such a research proposal has been carefully developed, and could be included in the program if desired.

CONCLUDING REMARKS

In drawing this chapter to a conclusion, I would like to say that I have tried to draw up a practical plan for self-directed change in an educational organization. Every element in the proposal has been tried out and found to be effective. What is new is the weaving of all these elements into a comprehensive plan which could be used as a pattern not only in one system, but in many.

The only requirements for putting the proposal into action would be the willingness of one educational system (this would not be difficult) and the financial support of some agency or foundation (and this might be more difficult).

Why have I wished to present such a plan? Because I believe that:

Here is a procedure which is appropriate to the educational needs of our present-day culture;

Here is a plan which is capable of being reproduced in many educational systems at all levels;

This plan draws on the natural, built-in motivation for growth and change which exists in every individual and is latent in every organization;

It does not depend on a submissive acceptance of changes suggested from the outside;

This plan could result in the kind of educational revolution which is needed to bring about confidence in the *process* of learning, the *process* of change, rather than in static knowledge.

References

Benne, K., Bradford, L., & Lippitt, R. The laboratory method. In L. Bradford, J. R. Gibb, & K. D. Benne (Ed.), *T-group theory and laboratory method*. New York: Wiley, 1964. Pp. 15-45.

Bowers, N. D. & Soar, R. S. Evaluation of laboratory human relations training for classroom teachers. Studies of human relations in the teaching-learning process: V. Final report. 1961, Columbia: University of South Carolina, Contract No. 8143, U. S. Office of Education.

Boyer, R. K. A laboratory approach to the improvement of student-faculty relations and educational systems in engineering. *National Training Laboratories Human Relations Training News*, 1964, *8* (2), 1-2.

Clark, J. V. & Culbert, S. A. Mutually therapeutic perception and self-awareness in a T-group. *Journal of Applied Behavioral Science*, 1965, *1*, 180-194.

Clark, T. C. & Miles, M. B. Part II: The Teachers College studies, human relations training for school administrators. *Journal of Social Issues*, *1954, 10* (2), 25-39.

Miles, M. B. The T-group and the classroom. In L. Bradford, J. R. Gibb, & K. D. Benne (Ed.), *T-group theory and laboratory method*. New York: Wiley, 1964.

Rioch, Margaret J., Elkes, E., Flint, A. A., Usdansky, B. S., Newman, R. G., & Sibler, E. NIMH pilot study in training mental health counselors. *American Journal of Orthopsychiatry*, 1963, *33*, 678-689.

Rogers, C. R. The process of the basic encounter group. In J. F. T. Bugental (Ed.), *The challenges of humanistic psychology*. New York: McGraw-Hill, 1967. Pp. 261-276.

Epilogue

Self-Directed Educational
Change in Action

The plan described in the preceding Part, to be applied to a complete educational system, was until recently nothing but a dream. Though attempts had been made to find support for it, two government agencies, including the U. S. Office of Education, and two of the major foundations, had found it to be impractical, unwise, unsound, too "far out" to win approval. At the same time that the officials and bureaucrats were finding it unacceptable, word of the plan spread and a number of school systems were clamoring to have the plan carried out in their own system.

At last, however, the plan was funded[1] and what was a fantasy is now a plan which is in the midst of being translated into the hard area of reality, with all the attendant problems of that metamorphosis.

SELECTION OF A SYSTEM

From among the various educational systems which had expressed a wish to be the target system for the enterprise, we chose one because of several advantages.

It included a women's college which was heavily invested in the training of teachers, several high schools, and a large number of elementary schools;

It was a system in which the two top administrators and many of the influential leaders were enthusiastically in favor of trying the experiment;

It was geographically close to the professional staff;

It had good facilities for holding off-campus workshops.

[1] The funds which have made this project possible were a generous grant from the Babcock Foundation and a personal gift from Charles F. Kettering II, both made to the staff group which has become the Center for Studies of the Person; a grant from the Merrill Foundation; and a gift from Everett Baggerly, made to the Immaculate Heart College.

It was the Immaculate Heart system in the Los Angeles area, which included the Immaculate Heart College, several high schools, and many elementary schools which the Order staffed and supervised.

The program is only a few months underway at the time of this writing. It is much too soon to give any more than a tentative report on it. The joint planning committee of the two institutions has already introduced many significant modifications in the original plan, as would be expected, but the plan is definitely in operation.

SOME FIRST STEPS

Forty-five administrators and faculty members of the College volunteered for the first encounter sessions. They were divided into four groups, met for one intensive weekend and then these same four groups met for a second weekend.

Thirty-six high school administrators and faculty members from three high schools met in small groups for two weekends. (These and all the other groups described were voluntary.)

Forty student leaders from a high school met in three groups for one weekend. When, a month or more later, they met for a second weekend their faculty (counted in the preceding paragraph) were now willing to meet in groups composed of both faculty and students, a mingling which they had at first avoided. They soon found themselves communicating across generations.

One hundred and eighty teachers, administrative staff, and principals from twenty-two elementary schools have met in many small groups at different times for two weekend encounter groups, often separated by a month or more. In each case individuals continued in the same group in which they had started.

Members of the CSP staff met twice in meetings with the faculty of the College. One session was on innovation in education and the other was on the encounter group program itself with all of the questions and criticisms which had arisen in regard to it.

Members of the CSP staff were invited to participate in an assembly with the Immaculate Heart students. A sizeable number of the college faculty attended also. Questions raised helped us to realize that the students had much less of a picture of the project than the faculty and this naturally led to fear and apprehension on their part. The most dramatically fearful and critical questions came from those who had had no group experience at all.

Perhaps the listing of these steps all taken within a period of ninety days from the start of the project will indicate something of the intensity of the program as it is being carried on.

SOME CRITICISMS

While it would be inappropriate and unwise to discuss the significant events which have taken place in any of the encounter group sessions, there are a number of reactions, critical and positive, which will be given in the following sections, which appear as straws in the wind, both positive and negative, to the planning groups from CSP and Immaculate Heart College. The criticisms will be mentioned first.

There has been criticism of some of the facilitators, some members of certain groups feeling that their facilitators were not as competent as they should be and that some were too "pushy," having goals for the group instead of permitting the group to move toward its own goals.

There have been some individuals who have not returned for the second weekend, feeling either that the experience was not useful to them or that their feelings had been hurt in the group sessions or that they had not yet assimilated all of the experiences of the first weekend.

Although all groups have been voluntary, there are a few individuals who have felt a subtle coercion to attend, the social pressure coming either from their peers or from their superiors.

Some of the College faculty members particularly have been critical of the emphasis they feel is placed on the person in the encounter groups. They feel that an individual is as much a biologist or a teacher or an English instructor as he is a person and that it is unreasonable to demand, even by implication, that they be separated from their roles. So far as possible, they have been reassured that every facet of the person, including his work and his career interests, as well as his most private feelings, are welcome in an encounter group.

SOME POSITIVE REACTIONS

Some of the immediate reactions to the initial workshops seemed noteworthy to the planning staff.

There are a considerable number of faculty at all levels who did not attend the first weekend group but who attended, at the very next opportunity, a second weekend group.

There were almost immediately two requests to hold encounter groups for the faculty of given departments of the College.

The regular faculty meeting following the College encounter groups was said to be the liveliest, most participative meeting in memory.

Some of the College department meetings since the workshops have been described as more communicative than previously with problems being brought more expressively into the open.

A faculty member embarking on a new course about which she admittedly felt very insecure—an insecurity which she expressed to her encounter group—decided to enlist the students in planning and carrying on the course and reports this is a very exciting venture.

There have been several invitations to meet with a faculty member in his or her class for a brief encounter group.

An almost immediate reaction was that, in two instances, there was an invitation to conduct a brief session of an encounter group type including all students majoring in a given department together with the faculty of that department.

In the faculty groups, progress was made in resolving some interpersonal feuds which had hampered the work of a particular school or department for years.

In other instances such feelings have been expressed and opened up but have not yet been resolved.

The request was made almost immediately that a training program be inaugurated next summer for at least twenty of those faculty, administrators, and students who wish to become facilitators of groups.

RESPONSE TO INVITATIONS

After the first series of encounter groups, practically all of the groups have been self-initiated and CSP has been *invited* to send a facilitator. This we have been able to do. In my judgment, this is the best indication we have thus far that the program is achieving its aims.

It would be impossible to describe all the invitations we have received, but some of those that have had particular meaning are listed here.

> The Student Council of the College asked to turn their weekly meetings into sensitivity sessions for a time, and they spent five such sessions as an encounter group.
>
> The staff of the College student newspaper decided to hold a twelve-hour encounter group, with an invited CSP facilitator, and their faculty sponsor. This was a very constructive session. Some members of the staff had been most skeptical, and they tend, in general, to be a "rebellious" group. At the end they felt that encounter groups were not only compatible with but one way of helping in their aim to achieve a more humane world.
>
> Some of the black students initiated and organized a Negro-white seminar, and invited a facilitator to be present for the first three sessions only, sitting on the sidelines and only participating if it seemed clearly necessary. Later this invitation was extended to apply to all sessions. This has been one of the deepest, most moving, and most heated encounters of the year. This dialogue still continues.
>
> Due to initiative from students of both institutions, a co-educational weekend encounter group of IHC women students and Cal Tech men students was held. Great progress was made in helping young men and women relate as *persons*, not simply as "dates." It was regarded as a great success, and has continued to have far-reaching ramifications in other activities. Plans have been made for more of such experiences.

SELF-DIRECTED CHANGE IN CLASSES

It has been something of a surprise to the joint planning committee to find so many changes taking place in so-called class-

room instruction. This can be illustrated from some of the feedback letters we have had. Here is one from an elementary school
teacher:

> You asked what happened to me . . . pure and simple someone
> got to me—the inside "new" me . . . I listened. And I heard, have
> heard and am hearing things I have never listened to before . . .
> and love it. Results? All I know is it's fun. I've *listened* to my
> students. I asked them if I had previously turned any off or not
> listened—the biggest *thugs* all raised their hands. Also—they are
> the most sensitive . . . I've had the busiest, most arousing, sapping,
> exciting, fun-filled, fulfilling, and happiest month since I started
> teaching, and it hasn't stopped yet.

One of the teachers at the College has conducted her courses
in a completely different fashion since being in an encounter group.
She sends with some pleasure the announcement which she gave out
in advance and three full pages of student reactions. This is
obviously much too lengthy to quote, but a couple of sentences
from her announcement to the students will give the spirit in which
she is conducting the course:

> My own personal goal in this course is to permit you all possible
> freedom in pursuing the study of_____. I in no way consider
> you as empty recipients into which I will pour a stream of facts
> about this course. On the contrary, I hope to discover with you
> new insights which will be most meaningful for all of us in
> individual ways because education which does not dynamically
> involve the whole person does not involve real learning.
>
> . . . You are the best critic of any work you read because only
> you can make the important and relevant applications to yourself
> as a person. . . . Some of you might be frightened by this type of
> course. Please feel free to express this or any other reaction you
> may have enroute. I myself am apprehensive on many scores
> but I feel the risk is worth taking. How about you?

The student reactions are so favorable it would seem almost
like a repetition of the material in Chapter 3 and, thus, they are
not given here.

An elementary school teacher says:

> When I got back from the first weekend, I simply could not
> teach. There were too many things going on in me. So I told

my children about my experience and tried to convey something of the spirit of the thing. They were fascinated and some of them even wept as I told them about it. Since then the class relationships have been *so much* better. They see me as a person and I see them as persons. They come to me much more often individually. They come to me for hugs and love. It is just fabulous what has happened in our class.

From a college faculty member:

My classroom behavior is radically different. I have been able to confess anxiety to my classes, and consequently feel more comfortable in the classroom than I have ever felt before. I invited the girls to call me by my first name, and after a couple of weeks, they are doing so. This allows for a lot of free exchange. I am not giving grades, and am not even giving exams. They are writing their own questions—the ones that are meaningful to them in terms of the material, and then discussing them.

RESEARCH PLANS

Should it be thought that we have been relying entirely on such spontaneous feedback, which obviously tends to come from the more favorable sources, here are some of the steps we have been taking to gain more empirical data:

Plans have been made for a rigorous empirical investigation of the outcomes of some of the groups, using before and after measures, either in the Immaculate Heart system or in some of the public school systems which have been eager to cooperate. This rigorous study is to be carried on during the second year of the project. Various instruments are being tried out in pilot fashion during the first year.

An assessment of the teaching and administrative procedures of the College, of the faculty-student relationships in the College, of faculty and student morale, as well as a number of other dimensions, has been undertaken by an experienced, outside team of educators and this assessment will be repeated at intervals throughout the program which is intended to last two to three years. These assessments will not be made known to the research staff nor to the College until the program is completed.

Several graduate students from universities in the area are planning to carry out, or are carrying out, research investigations of dif-

ferent aspects of the program, as a basis for their doctoral disser-
tations.

Students in the sociology and psychology departments of the
College have responded enthusiastically to an invitation to participate in a research evaluation of the total program and they are
working very hard at this. They have sent out to all participants
a much longer questionnaire than the research staff would ever
have dared to impose on the students or faculty.

Perhaps this listing of some of the items that have thus far
been accomplished will convey something of the problems being
encountered and the excitement being generated by the program,
even in its initial phases.

FEEDBACK

Although it is too soon to have a great deal in the way of feedback from the participants in the various groups, here are some
from members of the various groups who have participated.

From Administrators:

It is amazing to realize the bond that is engendered from being
together in a session.

*   *   *

The more I think about it, the more I realize how unbelievably
fortunate we Sisters are to be working with you. If there is
anything needed today, it is the beautiful openness and responsiveness that makes the potential of young (and old!) flower.

*   *   *

Many thanks for the days at IHC spent in your group. I find
after the session I got more out of the group than I realized at
the time.

From Faculty:

Faculty members at all levels have responded freely. Only two
examples will be given. The first comes from a newly appointed
lay faculty member:

I personally feel fully integrated into the College community,
not at all alienated. I'm sure that this is a result of the group.

For one thing, it allowed me to experience nuns as human beings. Since I have never known a nun before, I was somewhat apprehensive—over polite—as I tend to be with someone with whose opinion I don't agree. The group allowed me to break through the "Sister" hangup.

An elementary school principal writes:

It has taken me a while to be able to respond in writing to our sensitivity workshop. When we returned to school that following morning everyone really seemed "shot"—yet I wonder if it wasn't one of our best teaching days—teachers seemed so aware of their children as people.

Some other very subjective remarks—faculty members mentioned more than once their concern for _____ [a teacher in the school]. Yet I really feel that she wasn't acting any differently. We were just more aware of her reactions and responses. I think socially the faculty has become much more aware of each other. Everyone seems to be trying to get to know each other more, not as fellow workers but as human beings.

Oh, another reaction just zoomed up. I remember that Monday morning—I must have had 25 different feelings within an hour, but most of all I was *scared*—for the first time I was going to school as _____ [her name] the person instead of _____ the principal. It was a "freeing" feeling too! And I survived!

. . . the strength that you gave me is still very vivid in my feelings and again I want to say "thank you" and I am also trying to "soak up" the idea that _____ *is* a lovable and loving person.

From College Students:

A serious young student who had been in a three and one-half hour session with her class and its instructor wrote the facilitator several months later:

I still can't believe how happy and peaceful I was that night. I felt I had conquered something within myself. Since then I've felt like a new person. I've tried to be more open, and though serious-minded, show a smile more often. I feel more at ease with my college classmates, and I feel there has been an air of friendliness since our session. This will be one college class that I can truly say I had enjoyed.

. . . this may seem strange but I really want to say "thank you" for asking me the pointed question and getting me to talk. Otherwise I think I would have come away from our session dissatisfied and not willing to try again.

Another student writes:

I think having CSP on campus is fantastic. I've noticed results of these encounter groups in class, dorm, and other areas. I only hope I can participate in more groups.

Not all feedback is entirely positive. A group of nineteen students had asked to have a "marathon" experience in which they met with two facilitators for nearly 24 hours without a break. This was just before examination time and it is probable that the experience was too change-producing, too moving, and too deep for some students to assimilate and still return at once to cramming for examinations. One student who had written some very positive things about the effects of her marathon experience also includes this paragraph:

. . . for a while I thought our weekend group was really a disaster and it had destroyed a couple of people, but I think things are looking up. No kidding, though, for a couple of days that campus was like a disaster area—everybody was really racked up. It was like they were all cut up in little pieces and they didn't know how to get back together again. [To relieve the reader it should be remarked that no lasting damage appears to have been done to any of the students and much that was highly constructive was achieved.]

A very common reaction, but very succinctly put, is as follows:

Oh man! I care to learn as much as is humanly possible. This is an exercise in patient listening. I want to be a part of this.

From High School Students:

It would seem as though the less status the person has to protect, the more he gets out of and the more enthusiastic he is about the encounter group experience. Pages could be filled with reactions from the high school girls who participated. Only a few will be quoted here. Particular attention might be paid to the second quotation. It sounds as though here a student was rescued from really serious alienation and psychological disturbance:

I should state clearly right now that the workshop was one of the most important and beautiful experiences of my (relatively short) lifetime. I find personally that I am very much changed in my attitude toward teachers, fellow students, and just plain everybody. I am far more open now (or at least I try very hard to be) than I have ever been.

*   *   *

The workshop gave me a deeper insight into the art of listening . . . already I have found a value in this "art" because many new friendships have opened up to me and old ones have become stronger and more important than ever. For quite a while I had been feeling very distant from people to the point where I was actually very worried about myself. Ever since the workshop, however, this feeling has been abolished and again I feel a real union between people and myself.

*   *   *

. . . faculty student-body relationships have absolutely *zoomed*.

*   *   *

I feel that already there is a sense of cooperation circulating throughout the school. This has been made possible by the attitudes of our own student council.

*   *   *

. . . I felt a real depression during the workshop itself but it faded a few days later. I feel it was a really good thing for me.

*   *   *

I haven't noticed any change in the teaching methods in my classes except my religion class is remarkably different from previous years. We discuss subjects of interest freely. We are encouraged to question, to challenge, and to say exactly what we feel without worrying about grades.

*   *   *

All I can really say is that you gave me the chance to learn how to look, to listen, to love. I say thank you.

*   *   *

Not only have I learned to listen but to act, and to speak out what I feel.

SOME LEARNINGS

We certainly have no conclusions from our study at this point and it may seem even absurd to jot down some of our very tentative learnings. Yet, learnings there have been and some of them quite profound ones, so far as we are concerned.

1.) *We have learned all over again the great importance of the quality of the facilitator.* This has nothing to do with his training. What makes a leader less than an adequate facilitator? We believe the list would include such things as these: When the facilitator is to any degree "phony" or ingenuine, presenting himself as something different than the real person he is; when the facilitator has an unspoken goal for the group to reach; when he is over-eager for progress in the group; when he pushes or probes an individual, unless that individual is clearly desirous of being brought more fully into the open; when he acts in terms of some formula rather than in terms of the immediate group situation; when he consciously uses a "technique"; when he is overly concerned with his own problems and takes more than his share of time with the group. On the other hand, a facilitator seems to be most effective when he is able openly to be himself; is able to accept the group exactly where it is, even though it may be highly defensive and rigid; who feels trust in the group process; who spontaneously uses different approaches as they seem natural to him in the situation; who is an empathic listener; who becomes a participant in the group when he feels like it and who serves a facilitating function when that appears to be needed.

2.) *We have learned that there is a distinct gradation of difficulty in initiating the process of encounter groups.* Administrators tend to find it most difficult to reveal their feelings and attitudes and persons; college faculty come a close second. High school faculty are more open; elementary teachers and principals, who are in daily contact with many, many instances of feelings, tend to be more open to their own; college students would rank next, high school students next, and then elementary students (we have had very little opportunity for contact with the latter but what we have had is exciting indeed!). In general, then, it would seem that the hypothesis holds that the more prestige and status and intellectual expertise the person has to defend, the more difficult it is for him to come into a real basic encounter with other persons.

3.) *We have learned to expect a gradation of change.* The encounter group experience seems to effect its first and most easily noticeable change in the close personal relationships of the individual—his spouse, his children, his friends, or among nuns, their living group; the next effect is upon those areas of his life where he feels himself to be potent—for example, the classroom teacher is potent when he closes the door of his room and feels that he can relate in any way he wishes to his students, the principal is potent in dealing with his teachers. Change is slower in relation to one's peer group: they are a little more threatening; it is easier to hold to the old habits. Change seems to come last in organizational structure and organizational procedures. We are hard at work to try to determine how to have more effect on this last facet of the educational system.

4.) *We have learned the importance of immediate and available follow-up help.* Many people who have a splendid experience in the encounter group itself, or a poor experience, wish very much in the days and weeks which follow for someone to whom they could talk out certain of the things that are happening to them. This can partly be done with other members of the group, but an individual whom they could look upon as a facilitator would be even more helpful. This is why we are planning definitely to train many facilitators from the system to be of assistance. In one way or another, we wish to make a helping person available to each group and each member of the group very soon after any encounter experience.

5.) *We have relearned the fact, which we thought we knew before, that all significant learning is to some degree painful and involves turbulence, within the individual and within the system.* One of the most marked indications of this is that while some of the schools we have worked with have been literally transformed, in other schools we have learned that we have been a divisive influence —dividing members into those who favor more open communication and more innovative change and more utilization of feelings in the communication of faculty and students, and those who see all these elements as a troublesome or even destructive influence in the life of the school. Whatever the long range effect of this divisiveness, there is no doubt that it is unhelpful to the administrator from a *short* range point of view.

6.) *We have come to restate quite completely the purpose of the plan, which was outlined so clearly in advance form in the preceding chapter.* We have come to recognize that we are not simply studying the impact of encounter groups on an educational system. A more truthful statement would be that

> *we are studying the impact of a dedicated group of individuals who are interested in persons, who want to communicate with persons, and who are interested in facilitating communication between persons, upon an educational system.*

We have come to recognize that where we have seemed to facilitate constructive change it may have been through the joint planning sessions, through countless individual contacts after encounter sessions and elsewhere, through talks to faculty and student groups, through correspondence with people in our groups, through follow-up visits, and through many other relationships— as well as through the encounter groups themselves. In short, we have come to see that encounter groups used as a "technique" could be as futile in an educational system as any other approach. The success or failure will all depend upon the dedication, genuineness, realness, of the staff which is implementing that plan. We have also realized the "wisdom of the group" in initiating things for themselves in which they use facilitators in ways we would never have dreamed of in advance.

7.) *We are delighted that we put off our serious research efforts until the second year because it has made us raise far more profound questions.* How can we measure the variable which we have introduced into an educational system? We can no longer say that it is simply the encounter group but, as indicated above, there is a much broader variable. How can we measure outcomes? It would have some meaning to know that the morale of a school faculty has gone up or down or that a certain percentage of teachers have tried innovative methods in their classrooms. But this is definitely not enough. How can we measure the fact that the teacher now talks to the students as a person, or relates to the principal as a person? Because of questions of this sort we realize that we are groping toward some new science of the person which we can but dimly see. It is for this reason that we have come to lean more and more on phenomenological data where we are trying to get inside the experience of the individual in order to estimate the impact which he or she has felt in the many different aspects of the project. Some will scoff at this data as being merely "self reports." Some will begin to recognize that such self reports, taken over extensive periods of time, may be the very best of "objective" evidence. At any rate, our project has raised for us many profound questions in relation to the meaning of the term "science" when it is applied to the science of man, and when we are trying to study the incredibly complex variables which enter into a human system. We have almost come to the point where we desire "knowledge" rather than "science."

WHERE ARE WE?

I trust it will be evident from the varied and occasionally conflicting reports which have come in to us that we are less than halfway into a most exciting project involving hundreds of adults and thousands of students. We have no definitive answers. The project staff itself is in the midst of the most intense learning process it has ever undergone. For this reason, this chapter will end with no neat conclusion.

COMMENCEMENT

To me it seems very appropriate that this volume should end with a beginning, a commencement. In trying to help an educational system change itself in the direction of becoming more free, more communicative, with more self-reliant and self-directed participation on the part of both students and faculty, we are engaged in a process, the outcome of which we cannot clearly predict. Will it succeed? Will it fail? Even these questions are meaningless unless the terms are defined, and the individual members of the system will have to provide their own definitions. So we can only say that a significant process has been inaugurated.

We have no illusions that the program will avoid problems—it merely substitutes the problems of a process-oriented organization for those of a static organization. Many of the initial events give us reason to hope that we are affecting the human climate, and perhaps the procedures, of an educational system which was already experiencing ferment. It does not seem unreasonable to hope that this change in the psychological climate will give to students, to faculty, to administrators, a greater freedom to learn.

BIBLIOGRAPHY
by Alice Elliott

I. THE NEED FOR ACADEMIC REVISION

II. MAN AND HIS VALUES

His search for meaning and self-awareness.

III. VIEWS AND REVIEWS OF SCIENCE

The growing edges of research which bring a holistic approach to man and his understanding of himself as he examines the polarities of the scientific dilemma in which he finds himself.

I am very grateful to Alice Elliott for preparing this Bibliography to tempt the reader to go further in his explorations.

Miss Elliott is a teacher in high school, and also a teacher of teachers in graduate courses in communication. She is, therefore, particularly well equipped, both at the "grass roots" and at the teacher education level, to make suggestions. She is one of the most widely read persons I know and has truly "made friends" with the great minds of our age through her reading. She is not simply a scholar in the pedantic sense, but a person who has considered, digested, and thought deeply about many of the contradictory viewpoints in education, educational philosophy, and the modern concepts of science.

For these reasons I believe that her selection—from among hundreds of volumes—of highly relevant readings will give educators and laymen the chance to pursue their interests far beyond the confines of this book.

A book ends. One's interest in the subject does not. This reading list has been planned to assist those wishing further study in modes of creating educational environments, in practical analyses of our educational system, and in the philosophy of change and ways of changing one's own attitudes.

This Bibliography has been compiled to include books of various degrees of conceptual difficulty. Both laymen and educators at all instructional levels will find something of interest here. Areas include science, philosophy, religion, values, self-awareness, freedom to teach and learn, and revolutionary suggestions of future planning.

Recent proliferation of books dealing with problems of urban schools and minority groups makes it advisable for the interested reader to choose his own.

I. THE NEED FOR ACADEMIC REVISION

Bennis, W. G., K. D. Benne, and R. Chin, eds., *The Planning of Change*. New York: Holt, Rinehart and Winston, 1961. An excellent collection of papers on interpersonal relationships and the group process. Also included are valuable suggestions regarding values and social change.

Berman, Louise M., *New Priorities in the Curriculum*. Columbus, Ohio: Charles E. Merrill Publishing Company, 1968. The purpose of *New Priorities* is to revitalize the curriculum through human process skills rather than traditional methods. Excellent suggestions for teachers.

Combs, Arthur W., Chairman A.S.C.D. Year Book Committee, *Perceiving Behaving Becoming*. Washington, D.C.: National Education Association, 1962. A timely new focus in a technologically oriented world. All educators interested in contributing to the self-actualizing process toward more fully functioning behavior of their students will find this profitable reading.

Doll, Ronald C., and Robert S. Fleming, *Children Under Pressure.* Columbus, Ohio: Charles E. Merrill Publishing Company, 1966. Anyone who loves children will find food for thought in this book. The medical and psychological implications of "Force-Fed Erudition" and the "Academic Rat Race" are well stated.

Farber, Seymour M., and R. H. L. Wilson, eds., *Creativity and Conflict: Control of the Mind*, Part II. New York: McGraw-Hill Book Company, 1963. An interdisciplinary discussion of the forces in our world which act on the mind. Twenty-eight contributors from the fields of medicine, psychology, philosophy, religion, and the social sciences discuss freedom and creative expression—constraint and control of man.

Friedenberg, Edgar Z., *The Vanishing Adolescent.* Boston, Mass.: Beacon Press, 1964. Adolescence and its pressures can be devastating. The author, a keen observer, sees these young people as victims of hostile social pressures which often goad them toward hostile behavior. Written with wit and understanding.

Friedman, Maurice, *Problematic Rebel.* New York: Random House, Inc., 1963. Presents an image of modern man through an intensive study of three writers, Melville, Dostoievsky, and Kafka, and the novels of Albert Camus. The chapter "The Problematic Rebel and the Modern Job" is an excellent summary.

Goodman, Paul, *Compulsory Mis-Education and the Community of Scholars.* New York: Random House, Inc. (Vintage Books), 1966. Sensitive to children and adolescents, the author feels that long schooling is not only unnecessary and inept—it is damaging, and that schools compound the social ills by catering to false values. In this critique of the structure of the U.S. college system, the author of *Growing Up Absurd* advocates secession by faculty members, and re-settling where they can teach and learn as was done in medieval universities without bureaucratic administrative control.

Goulet, Richard R., ed., *Educational Change: The Reality and the Promise.* New York: Citation Press, 1968. Teachers committed to creative change in education know that sharing ideas is necessary. The report on this Seminar on Innovations is a sharing of the many ideas discussed.

Greene, Maxine, ed., *Existential Encounters for Teachers.* New York: Random House, Inc., 1967. Excellent help for teachers interested in

understanding the ideas of the great existential thinkers. Various selections are presented with comments on each by the author.

Hutchins, Robert M., *The Learning Society*. New York: Frederick A.
Praeger, Inc., 1968. Expresses hope that education will be considered "an investment in man" and that a more humanistic society
will result. The author, widely known for his championship of the
liberal arts, feels that cultural influences besides education will have
wide effect in the decades ahead.

Jencks, Christopher, and David Riesman, *The Academic Revolution*.
New York: Doubleday & Company, Inc., 1968. Lucid discussion of
the crisis of the inflexibility in requirements, training, and attitudes
in U.S. graduate schools and the need for revolutionary thinking
on the part of the major shapers of our culture.

Keats, John, *Schools Without Scholars*. Cambridge, Mass.: The River-
side Press, 1958. A layman's "report card" on public education. Effective, devastating critique written with humor. Could be helpful
to scholars and laymen who wish school improvement.

Keppel, Francis, *The Necessary Revolution in American Education*.
New York: Harper & Row, Publishers, 1966. Concerned educators
and especially laymen can find here focus on the national concerns
of American education. This presentation shows a greater national
commitment to the crucial need for education's role in the transformation of society.

Leonard, George B., *Education and Ecstasy*. New York: The Dela-
corte Press, 1968. A creative, compassionate, thought-provoking
book written for those who see the need for revolutionary thinking
about our schools and the curriculum. A look at the potential school
of tomorrow where the ecstasy of learning could be enjoyed.

Neill, Alexander S., *Freedom Not License*. New York: Hart Publishing Co., Inc., 1966. Addressing himself primarily to parents, the
English headmaster of controversial Summerhill School stresses the
need for certain balance in the child-parent relationship. The words
"love, approval, freedom, force" are provided new meanings.

Neill, Alexander S., *Summerhill*. New York: Hart Publishing Co., Inc.,
1960. Subtitled *A Radical Approach to Child-Rearing*, this advocates in a vivid and persuasive style extreme permissiveness and describes the English boarding school founded in 1921.

Roszak, Theodore, ed., *The Dissenting Academy*. New York: Random
House, Inc., 1967. Scholars and teachers state their opinions on what

is wrong in academia. Concern for the deep penetration into the curriculum of the military via the federal government and big business.

Skinner, B. F., *Walden Two*. New York: The Macmillan Company, 1948. A model Utopia where human beings are conditioned to behave in planned ways. A behaviorist's dream.

Taylor, Harold, ed., *The Humanities in the Schools*. New York: Citation Press, 1968. A search by distinguished people in the fields of education, criticism, music and literature for ways to incorporate the humanities into the curriculum.

Whitehead, Alfred North, *The Aims of Education*. New York: Mentor Books, 1964. This great philosopher's ideas for education and the need to understand the interdependence among various disciplines, his insistence on openness and his distrust of closed systems in an illimitable world have great significance for today.

Wiener, Norbert, *The Human Use of Human Beings. Cybernetics and Society*. Garden City, N.Y.: Doubleday & Company, Inc. (Anchor Books), 1954. Cybernetics has had a profound effect on science. In this book a great scientist, father of cybernetic thought, shows the marked influence it has on our theories of man as a feed-back organism.

II. MAN AND HIS VALUES

Allport, Gordon, *Becoming*. New Haven, Conn.: Yale University Press, 1955. The author develops a consistent position of considerations for studying personality development. Current theories are examined avoiding polarized views.

Barnes, Hazel E., *An Existentialist Ethics*. New York: Alfred A. Knopf, Inc., 1967. A refutation of the idea that humanistic existentialism leaves no room for ethics. The need for ethical commitment and avoidance of complete despair is stressed, with implications for responsibility and our attitude in education and human relationships.

Barrett, William, *Irrational Man*. Garden City, N.Y.: Doubleday & Company, Inc. (Anchor Books), 1962. Excellent definition of existentialism. Describes its roots and traces its history. Kierkegaard, Nietzsche, Heidegger, and Sartre discussed in detail.

Bois, J. Samuel, *The Art of Awareness*. Dubuque, Iowa: William C. Brown Company, Publishers, 1966. A humanistic approach to man. Excellent techniques for self awareness through examination of epistemology and man's conceptual revolutions. Examines our semantic reactions to our perceptions and awareness of the process world we live in.

Bonner, Hubert, *On Being Mindful of Man*. Boston, Mass.: Houghton Mifflin Company, 1965. An indictment of much of contemporary psychology. A view of man as an open system capable of unique, unpredictable behavior, yet responsible for becoming his choices.

Berne, Eric, *Games People Play*. New York: Grove Press, Inc., 1964. People play games for a variety of reasons; to help us become aware the author analyzes 36 games. Becoming conscious of these may enlighten those who are seeking insight into behavior—their own and others'.

Bugental, James F., *The Search for Authenticity*. New York: Holt, Rinehart and Winston, 1965. In man's search for "self," authenticity becomes a must. This book by a psychotherapist adds to the ever-growing movement toward a humanistic psychology.

Buber, Martin, *The Knowledge of Man*. New York: Harper & Row, Publishers, 1965. Translated by Maurice Friedman and Ronald Gregor Smith. Includes an introductory essay by Maurice Friedman. For those who wish to understand Martin Buber and dialogue. A 1957 dialogue between Martin Buber and Carl Rogers is included in the appendix.

Fingarette, Herbert, *The Self in Transformation*. New York: Basic Books, Inc., Publishers, 1963. Anyone interested in the interrelatedness of the psychological, spiritual, and moral concepts of man will find this existential approach of value.

Fletcher, J. H., *Situation Ethics*. Philadelphia, Pa.: The Westminster Press, 1966. A modern, controversial view of a relativistic morality based on *agape*.

Frankl, Victor E., *Man's Search for Meaning*. New York: Washington Square Press, 1963. Translated by Ilse Lasche. Originally published as *From Death Camp to Existentialism*. Dr. Frankl describes life in a concentration camp, and the effect on him and his subsequent development of Logotherapy.

Gardner, John W., *Self-Renewal*. New York: Harper & Row, Publishers, 1964. Shows the pressing need to renew ourselves and society through a shared vision of having something worth saving. This can be done by an innovative society.

Maslow, Abraham H., *Toward a Psychology of Being.* New York: D. Van Nostrand Co., Inc., 1962. A humanistic psychologist looks at the behavioral sciences.

Matson, Floyd W., ed., *Being, Becoming and Behavior.* New York: George Braziller, Inc., 1967. The major themes and issues of psychology since Socrates which have brought man to a dichotomous culture of science and the humanities. Excellent coverage of the scope of psychology and the debated questions of the day.

May, Rollo, ed., *Existence.* New York: Basic Books, Inc., Publishers, 1958. Chapters by Rollo May are an excellent description of existentialism. Existential analysis and psychiatric phenomenology are also discussed. Several case studies are included.

Morris, Charles, *Varieties of Human Value.* Chicago, Ill.: University of Chicago Press, 1956. A cross-cultural examination of man's valuation of the good life. Investigation in human values covering a 10 year period. His discovery of five common value dimensions in six different cultures is illuminating. An orderly analytic approach.

Moustakas, Clark, *Individuality and Encounter.* Cambridge, Mass.: Howard A. Doyle Publishing Co., 1968. Exploration of individual life, the problems of identity, loneliness, spontaneity, openness, and love. Sensitive personal sharing by the author.

Murphy, Gardner, *Human Potentialities.* New York: Basic Books, Inc., Publishers, 1958. An excellent presentation of what the author calls three kinds of human nature. "Creative Eras," the "Yen to Discovery," and the "Human Natures of the Future" will interest those who are concerned with man's reaching his *human* potentialities.

Rogers, Carl R., *On Becoming a Person.* Boston, Mass.: Houghton Mifflin Company, 1961. A great humanist shares his personal experience as a man, a father, a husband, and a psychotherapist in terms of what he sees as their relevance for personal living in a perplexing world.

Sorokin, Pitirim A., *Ways and Power of Love.* Boston, Mass.: Beacon Press, 1954. An analysis of moral transformation. An examination of the problems of humanity with the conclusion that creative altruism is the answer, by the sociologist founder of the Harvard Research Center in Creative Altruism.

Stoops, John, *Religious Values in Education.* Danville, Ill.: The Interstate Printers & Publishers, Inc., 1967. Unique in style and format, this analysis of religious values in education, if somewhat controversial, is thought-provoking. A book for educators interested in moral and spiritual values and their place in education.

Teilhard de Chardin, Pierre, *The Phenomenon of Man*, trans. Bernard Wall. New York: Harper & Row, Publishers, 1959. Thoughts on evolution and the development of consciousness written by a philosophically minded Jesuit archeologist. Published after his death.

Tillich, Paul, *The Courage to Be*. New Haven, Conn.: Yale University Press, 1952. A theologian and philosopher lucidly presents difficult concepts about courage and the conquest of anxiety.

Tournier, Paul, *The Meaning of Persons*. New York: Harper & Row, Publishers, 1957. The author draws on his long experience as physician and psychologist to stress the value of interpersonal relationships, covering such subjects as Who Am I? The Contradictory Being, Psychology and Spirit, Dialogue and Commitment.

Watts, Alan W., *The Book*. New York: The Macmillan Company (Collier Books), 1967. The author suggests that there is a taboo against our knowing who we are. An attack on alienation with suggestions for solving our own identity problems.

Weinberg, Harry L., *Levels of Knowing and Existence*. New York: Harper & Row, Publishers, 1959. An attempt to show that misunderstanding occurs because of certain patterns of misevaluation. Dialogue and encounter involve communication. Evaluation of ourselves as communicators and the communication process are well presented.

III. VIEWS AND REVIEWS OF SCIENCE

Bachelard, Gaston, *The Philosophy of No: A Philosophy of the New Scientific Mind*, trans. G. C. Waterston. New York: Grossman Publishers, Inc. (Orion Press), 1968. Originally published in France, 1940. Review of the major philosophies of science. Discussion of the polarities of scientific activity: empiricism and rationalism. Builds a philosophy of science which recognizes both.

Barzun, Jacques, *Science: The Glorious Entertainment*. New York: Harper & Row, Publishers, 1964. Examines the all-pervasive influence of science and its imperialistic thought. The implications of this for man's alienated condition with a plea for skepticism towards science and optimism for the capacity of man's mind.

Boulding, Kenneth E., *The Image: Knowledge in Life and Society*. Ann Arbor, Mich.: University of Michigan Press, 1961. Discusses the images that lie behind the actions of all of us. The author relates this to the growth of causes: scientific, social, psychological, crusades, etc. Aware of this in all fields, he proposes a new science, "eiconics," which could restructure our present knowledge of man.

Bronowski, Jacob, *Science and Human Values*, rev. ed. New York: Harper & Row, Publishers, 1965. These three delightful essays "The Creative Mind," "The Habit of Truth," and "The Sense of Human Dignity" are brought together under an apt title.

Conant, James, *Modern Science and Modern Man*. Garden City, N.Y.: Doubleday & Company, Inc. (Anchor Books), 1952. The ideas presented in this book have serious implications. The role of science and its exalted position in our society demand a healthy skepticism. A thought-provoking book.

Coulson, William R., and Carl R. Rogers, eds., *Man and the Science of Man*. Columbus, Ohio: Charles E. Merrill Publishing Company, 1968. The first of a series of foundational books in the human sciences. Reports a conference held at Western Behavioral Sciences Institute to help determine the direction our sciences have been and are taking us.

Farson, Richard E., ed., *Science and Human Affairs*. Palo Alto, Calif.: Science & Behavior Books, Inc., 1966. Lectures sponsored by Western Behavioral Sciences Institute cover a wide range. Associated with humanistic values.

Kaplan, Abraham, *Conduct of Inquiry*. San Francisco, Calif.: Chandler Publishing Co., 1964. An indispensable book for behavioral scientists. Major issues and common concerns of all social scientists are emphasized clearly, simply, and concisely.

Koestler, Arthur, *The Ghost in the Machine*. New York: The Macmillan Company, 1968. While the major portion of the book is involved with the evolution of man and his urge for self destruction, Koestler is well aware of the creativeness of man. He feels that the scientific approach to man through the behaviorist approach and what he terms "Ratomorphism" can only *add* to modern man's predicament. Erudite condemnation of behavioristic schools of thought.

Medawar, Peter Brian, *The Future of Man*. New York: Basic Books, Inc., Publishers, 1959. BBC Reith Lectures by the Nobel Prize winner who skillfully synthesizes genetics, demography, and sociology, stressing urgent need for a moral biological approach to man which does not jump to rash "scientific" conclusions.

Polanyi, Michael, *Personal Knowledge*. New York: Harper & Row, Publishers, 1964. A fresh humanistic view of science presented in a scholarly manner. An erudite presentation of the art of knowing, being, and commitment in attaining personal knowledge; a rejection of the ideal of scientific detachment.

Standen, Anthony, *Science Is a Sacred Cow*. New York: E. P. Dutton & Co., Inc., 1950. The debunking of science by a scientist. This informative book is highly amusing and witty.

White, Lynn R., ed., *Frontiers of Knowledge in the Study of Man*. New York: Harper & Row, Publishers, 1956. In non-technical language the editor brings together great writers to discuss new methods of research and new insights for those interested in human nature and self understanding. Presentation of a new kind of humanism.

Whitehead, Alfred North, *Science and the Modern World*. New York: The Macmillan Company, 1948. A history of the aspects of Western culture in the past three centuries and the ways in which it has been influenced by science. Last chapter cites some requisites for social progress.

Whyte, Lancelot Law, *The Next Development in Man*. New York: Mentor Books, 1962. Permanence may appear to exist. Change is not arbitrary. A continuity in the sequence of change is evident. It is called "process" and implies becoming. Man is participating and becoming the next development.

Young, J. Z., *Doubt and Certainty in Science*. New York: Oxford University Press, Inc., 1950. A study of human society as seen through the eyes of a biologist. A learned man presents to the layman his views stressing the communication difficulties involved in working toward a unification of science and its effects on the future of man and society.

INDEX